STÉPHANE MALLARMÉ

Modern Critical Views

Continued at back of book

Modern Critical Views

STÉPHANE MALLARMÉ

Edited and with an introduction by
Harold Bloom
Sterling Professor of the Humanities
Yale University

CHELSEA HOUSE PUBLISHERS ◊ 1987
New York ◊ New Haven ◊ Philadelphia

© 1987 by Chelsea House Publishers,
a division of Chelsea House Educational Communications, Inc.,
   95 Madison Avenue, New York, NY 10016
   345 Whitney Avenue, New Haven, CT 06511
   5068B West Chester Pike, Edgemont, PA 19028

Introduction © 1987 by Harold Bloom

Printed and bound in the United States of America

10   9   8   7   6   5   4   3   2   1

∞ The paper used in this publication meets the minimum
requirements of the American National Standard for
Permanence of Paper for Printed Library Materials,
Z39.48-1984.

Library of Congress Cataloging-in-Publication Data
Stéphane Mallarmé.
   (Modern critical views)
   Bibliography: p.
   Includes index.
   1. Mallarmé, Stéphane, 1842–1898—Criticism and
interpretation.   I. Bloom, Harold.   II. Series.
PQ2344.Z5S78   1987   841'.8   87–8084
ISBN 1-55546-289-8 (alk. paper)

Contents

Editor's Note

This book brings together a representative selection of the most useful modern criticism available in English on the poetry of Stéphane Mallarmé. The critical essays are reprinted here in the chronological order of their original publication. I am grateful to Karin Cope for her assistance in editing this volume.

My introduction meditates upon the relation between Mallarmé and Valéry, and attempts to locate Mallarmé in relation to parallel figures in Britain and America. The chronological sequence begins with Maurice Blanchot's characteristically problematic sketch of Mallarmé's *Hamlet*-like excursus, *Igitur*. Georges Poulet then expounds the modes of consciousness represented in the poet's "Prose pour Des Esseintes."

An almost Kabbalistic zeal is manifested by Robert Greer Cohn in his account of "Hommage (à Richard Wagner)," after which Philippe Sollers celebrates Mallarmé as high priest of Modernism, laboring to achieve "totality" through poetry.

The late Paul de Man correctively employs Mallarmé as he combats several short-sighted views of Modernity in lyric poetry. Mallarmé's prose heir (together with Lacan), Jacques Derrida, accomplishes a baroque elaboration of the master even as he rhetorically deconstructs him.

Readings in the contemporary mode are given to "Sonnet en *yx*" and "Le Nénuphar blanc" by E. S. Burt and Roger Dragonetti, respectively. Hans-Jost Frey considers Mallarmé's most famous poem, "L'Après-midi d'un faune," and identifies the Faun as "the tree that has become man's language."

In the first of her two essays in this volume, Barbara Johnson, the leading deconstructive critic of her generation, reads Mallarmé in terms supplied by the English linguistic philosopher, J. L. Austin. "Un Coup de dés" is juxtaposed with Michel Serres's speculations by Bonnie J. Isaac, after which Leo Bersani gives us a masterly overview of Mallarmé's "experience of Nothingness." Barbara Johnson concludes this volume with a brilliant and disconcerting exploration of Mallarmé's modes of subverting his precursors.

Introduction

*Like all true poets, Verlaine is a poet of death, but death for
Mallarmé means precisely the discontinuity between the personal self
and the voice that speaks in the poetry from the other bank of the
river, beyond death.*

—PAUL DE MAN

How much discontinuity can there be between a poet's personal self and the voice that goes on speaking in her poetry after she herself is dead? The question is itself figurative, since discontinuity, in this context, is professedly a trope for death, an irony or allegory rather than a synecdoche or symbol. Poet's elegies, frequently for other poets, notoriously are elegies for the later poet's own poetic self. Spenser for Sidney; Milton for the minor versifier, Edward King; Shelley for Keats; Arnold for Clough; Swinburne for Baudelaire—these follow a common pattern, in which the elegist's concern has little to do with the dead poet. Whitman lamenting Lincoln; Wallace Stevens meditating upon his friend, Henry Church; Hart Crane praising the urn of the painter, Ernest Nelson—these depart from the pattern, because of the American difference, first established by Emerson in his essays and addresses.

The grandest elegy of poet for poet in the French tradition is Hugo's farewell to Gautier, but Mallarmé is generally taken as the central elegist, because of his Homages and Tombs: for Poe, Baudelaire, Verlaine, and Wagner. One might propose Paul Valéry for the distinction, not in his verse, but in his copious prose memorializations of his crucial precursor. In his "Note and Digression" (1919) written a quarter century after his study of Leonardo, Valéry sets forth his vision of writing, with exemplary clarity:

> In the case of writing, however, the author feels himself to be at once the *source* of energy, the *engineer,* and the *restraints.* One

1

part of him is impulsion; another foresees, organizes, moderates, suppresses; a third part (logic and memory) maintains the conditions, preserves the connections, and assures some fixity to the *calculated* design. *To write* should mean to construct, as precisely and solidly as possible, a machine of language in which the released energy of the mind is used in overcoming *real* obstacles; hence the writer must be divided against himself. That is the only respect in which, strictly speaking, the whole man acts as *author*. Everything else is not *his,* but belongs to a part of him that has escaped. Between the emotion or initial intention and its natural ending, which is disorder, vagueness, and forgetting—the destiny of all thinking—it is his task to introduce obstacles created by himself, so that, being interposed, they may struggle with the purely transitory nature of psychic phenomena to win a measure of renewable action, a share of independent existence.

Is the presence of the precursor in one's own work also an obstacle created by oneself? Is the writer divided against herself in a wholly autonomous way? Valéry, beautifully consistent, persuaded himself of this, but should he persuade us? "Opposites are born from opposites," he observes in his remarkably influential "Letter about Mallarmé," where he even introduces (without developing) the evasive notions of "the influence of a mind on itself and of a work on its author." If we substitute "Valéry" for "Mallarmé," and add "Mallarmé" to "the Romantic poets and Baudelaire," then this famous paragraph of Valéry ostensibly on Mallarmé becomes a self-analysis:

> So it was that Mallarmé, developing in himself a few qualities of the Romantic poets and Baudelaire—selecting whatever they offered that was most exquisitely finished, making it his constant rule to obtain at every point the sort of results that in them were rare, exceptional, and produced as if purely by chance—little by little wrought out a highly individual *manner* from this obstinacy in choosing the best and this rigor in exclusion; and then went on to deduce from them a doctrine and problems that, in addition *to being completely novel, were prodigiously foreign to the modes of thinking and feeling known to his fathers and brothers in poetry.* For the direct desire, the instinctive or traditional (and in either case unreflecting) activity of his predecessors, he substituted an artificial conception, minutely reasoned and obtained by a certain sort of analysis.

In his Notebooks, Valéry insisted that: "I was struck by Mallarmé. I admired—from a distance. I loved him. I rethought him. I felt and developed my difference." Yet in a letter to Albert Thibaudet, Valéry wrote: "I knew Mallarmé, *after* having undergone his influence to the limit, and at the very moment when in my own mind I wanted to guillotine all literature." The statements are subtly irreconcilable, even by the subtlest of minds, Valéry's. In a further letter to Thibaudet, rather less interestingly, Valéry says: "as to Mallarmé's influence, my view briefly is that it was almost nonexistent."

Concerning Mallarmé's "Un Coup de dés," Valéry extravagantly observed: "He has undertaken finally to raise a printed page to the power of the midnight sky." Were this remarked of *Hamlet* or of *Paradise Lost,* it would be hyperbolic, but it helped set the standard for Mallarmé's critical admirers, who lead me to expect such astonishing displays of unprecedented poetic power that the actual pages of Mallarmé are liable to be somewhat disappointing. Since such luminaries as Lacan and Derrida seem to me closer to Mallarmé than they are to Nietzsche or Freud, it becomes difficult not to read Mallarmé through Hegelian lenses, or even as so many Heideggerian vistas. None of this is fair to Mallarmé, or to the American reader who is not a faithful follower of Gallic deconstruction. "Hérodiade" seems to me to find its authentic equivalents in Tennyson, Mallarmé's older contemporary, particularly in his great monologues, "Tithonus" and "Lucretius." The poetic metaphysics of solipsism, night, and death are curiously compounded by both visionaries, as they are by Walt Whitman in America. That peculiar anguish of poetic creation, more striking in Mallarmé than in Baudelaire, finds its strong analogue in the horror of self-consciousness in Tennyson's "Lucretius," and in Whitman as he ebbs with the ocean of life.

Several of the critics in *Modern Critical Views: Mallarmé* present Mallarmé as the unique poet of discontinuity, negativity, and a lyricism released both from subjectivity and from referentiality. Sometimes I reflect that what we now call Symbolist or Modernist poetry in France, is what we still call Victorian poetry in Great Britain and the work of the American Renaissance here. Much of what Leo Bersani locates in Rimbaud and Mallarmé, or Paul de Man in Mallarmé alone, is precisely akin to what perceptive readers find in Browning, Tennyson, and Whitman. They, rather than the dreadful Poe, are the original and vital continuators of Blake and Wordsworth, Shelley and Keats, even as Baudelaire, Rimbaud, and Mallarmé were the crucial continuators of Hugo and French Romanticism. The blinkers of Anglo-American literary Modernism, of the Eliot-Pound era, do not afflict our critical vision now in America, but they order these matters differently in literary France, where everything has been belated at least from Romanticism on and where they still discover *Finnegans Wake* daily.

MAURICE BLANCHOT

The Igitur *Experience*

One can sense how it was that in Mallarmé concern for the work became confused for a time with the affirmation of suicide. But one also sees how this same concern led Rilke to seek a relationship with death that would be more "exact" than that of voluntary death. These two experiences merit reflection.

Mallarmé acknowledged, in a letter to Cazalis (November 14, 1896), that *Igitur* is an undertaking in which poetry itself is at stake. "It is a tale with which I want to conquer the old monster Impotence, which is, moreover, its subject, in order to cloister myself in a great labor already planned and replanned. If it gets finished (the tale), I shall be cured." The great labor was *Hérodiade,* and also poetic work in the largest sense. *Igitur* is an attempt to make the work possible by grasping it at the point where what is present is the absence of all power, impotence. Mallarmé feels deeply here that the state of aridity which he knows so well is linked to the work's demand, and is neither simply deprivation of the work nor a psychological state peculiar to him.

"Unfortunately, by digging this thoroughly into verse, I have encountered two abysses which make me despair. One is Nothingness. . . . The other void which I have found is the one in my breast." "And now, having reached the horrible vision of a pure work, I have almost lost my reason and the meaning of the most familiar words." "Everything which, as a result, my being has suffered during this long agony is indescribable, but fortunately I

From *The Space of Literature,* translated by Ann Smock. © 1982 by the University of Nebraska Press. University of Nebraska Press, 1982.

am perfectly dead. . . . Which is to convey to you that I am now impersonal, and no longer Stéphane whom you know." When one recalls these remarks, one cannot doubt that *Igitur* was born of the obscure, essentially hazardous experience into which the craft of poetry, over the course of years, drew Mallarmé. This risk affects his normal relationship to the world, his habitual use of language; it destroys all ideal certainties, deprives the poet of the physical assurance of living. It exposes him finally to death—the death of truth, the death of his person; it yields him up to the impersonality of death.

THE EXPLORATION AND PURIFICATION OF ABSENCE

Igitur's interest does not come directly from the thought which serves as its theme, which is such that thinking would smother it, and which is similar in this respect to Hölderlin's. Hölderlin's is, however, richer, more active. He was familiar from youth with Hegel, whereas Mallarmé received only an impression of Hegelian philosophy. And yet this impression corresponds to the deep current which drew him, precisely, to the "frightful years." Everything is summed up for Mallarmé by the relationship among the words *thought, absence, language,* and *death.* The materialist profession of faith ("Yes, I know, we are but vain forms of matter"), is not Mallarmé's point of departure. Such a revelation would have obliged him to reduce thought, God, and all the other figures of the ideal to nothing. Quite obviously it is from this *nothing* that he starts. He felt its secret vitality, its force and mystery in his contemplation and accomplishment of the poetic task. His Hegelian vocabulary would merit no attention, were it not animated by an authentic experience, and this experience is that of the power of the negative.

One can say that Mallarmé saw this nothing in action; he experienced the activity of absence. In absence he grasped a presence, a strength still persisting, as if in nothingness there were a strange power of affirmation. All his remarks on language tend to acknowledge the word's ability to make things absent, to evoke them in this absence, and then to remain faithful to this value of absence, realizing it completely in a supreme and silent disappearance. In fact, the problem for Mallarmé is not to escape from the real in which he feels trapped, according to a still generally accepted interpretation of the sonnet on the swan. The true search and the drama take place in the other sphere, the one in which pure absence affirms itself and where, in so doing, it eludes itself, causing itself still to be present. It subsists as the dissimulated presence of being, and in this dissimulation it persists as chance which cannot be abolished. And yet this is where everything is at stake, for the work is possible only if absence is pure and perfect, only if, in the presence of Midnight, the dice can be thrown. There alone the work's origin speaks; there it begins, it finds there the force of the beginning.

More precisely: the greatest difficulty does not come from the pressure of beings, from what we call their reality, their persistent affirmation, whose action can never be altogether suspended. It is in unreality itself that the poet encounters the resistance of a muffled presence. It is unreality from which he cannot free himself; it is in unreality that, disengaged from beings, he meets with the mystery of "those very words: *it is.*" And this is not because in the unreal something subsists—not because the rejection of real things was insufficient and the work of negation brought to a halt too soon—but because when there is nothing, it is this nothing itself which can no longer be negated. It affirms, keeps on affirming, and it states nothingness as being, the inertia of being.

This is the situation which would form the subject of *Igitur,* were it not necessary to add that the narrative avoids this situation, seeking to surmount it by putting a term to it. These are pages in which some readers have thought they recognized the somber hues of despair. But actually they carry a youthful expression of great hope. For if *Igitur* were to be right—if death is true, if it is a genuine act, not a random occurrence but the supreme possibility, the extreme moment in which negation is founded and completed—then the negation that operates in words, and "this drop of nothingness" which is the presence of consciousness in us, the death from which we derive the power not to be which is our essence, also partake of truth. They bear witness to something definitive; they function to "set a limit upon the infinite." And so the work which is linked to the purity of negation can in its turn arise in the certainty of that distant Orient which is its origin.

THE THREE MOVEMENTS TOWARD DEATH

Igitur is thus not only an exploration but a purification of absence—it is an attempt to make absence possible and to glean possibility from it. The whole interest of this narrative lies in the way three movements are accomplished together. To a certain extent they are distinct from each other, and yet they are so closely linked that their interdependence remains hidden. All three movements are necessary to reach death; but which controls the others, which is the most important? The act by which the hero leaves the chamber, descends the staircase, drinks the poison, and enters the tomb apparently constitutes the initial decision, the "deed" which alone gives reality to absence and authenticates nothingness. But in fact this is not the case. This accomplishment is only an insignificant moment. What is done must first be dreamed, thought, grasped in advance by the mind, not in a moment of psychological contemplation, but through an actual movement—a lucid effort on the part of the mind to advance outside of itself, to see itself disappear and to appear to itself in the mirage of this disappearance, to gather itself all up into this essential death which is the life of the consciousness and, out of all the various acts of death through which we are, to form the unique act of the death to come which thought reaches at the same time that it reaches, and thereby liquidates, itself.

Here voluntary death is no longer anything but a dying in spirit, which seems to restore to the act of dying its pure, inward dignity—but not according to the ideal of Jean-Paul Richter, whose heroes, "lofty men," die in a pure desire to die, "their eyes gazing steadfastly beyond the clouds" in response to the call of a dream which disembodies and dissolves them. The idea of suicide found in *Igitur* is more akin to what Novalis means when he makes suicide "the principle of his entire philosophy." "The truly philosophical act is suicide; the real beginning of all philosophy lies in it; all the philosopher's desires tend toward it. Only this act fulfills all the conditions and bears all the marks of a trans-worldly action." Yet these last words indicate a horizon unknown to *Igitur*. Novalis, like most of the German Romantics, seeks in death a further region beyond death, something more than death, a return to the transfigured whole—in that night, for example, which is not night but the peaceful oneness of day and night. Moreover, in Novalis the movement toward death is a concentration of the will, an affirmation of its magical force, an energetic expenditure or yet again an unruly affection for the remote. But *Igitur* does not seek to surpass itself or to discover, through this voluntary move, a new point of view on the other side of life. It dies by the spirit—through the spirit's very development, through its presence to itself, to its own profound, beating heart, which is precisely absence, the intimacy of absence, night.

MIDNIGHT

Night: here is where the true profundity of *Igitur* is to be felt, and it is here that we can find the third movement, which, perhaps, commands the two others. If the narrative begins with the episode called "Midnight"—with the evocation of that pure presence where nothing but the subsistence of nothing subsists—this is certainly not in order to offer us a choice literary passage, nor is it, as some have claimed, in order to set the scene for the action: the empty chamber and its lavish furnishings enveloped, however, in shadows, the image of which is, in Mallarmé, something like the original medium of poetry. This "décor" is in reality the center of the narration whose true hero is Midnight and whose action is the ebb and flow of Midnight.

The story begins with the end, and that is what forms its troubling truth. With the very first words, the chamber is empty, as if everything were already accomplished, the poison drunk, the vial emptied, and the "lamentable personage" laid out upon his own ashes. Midnight is here; the hour when the cast dice have absolved all movement is here; night has been restored to itself, absence is complete, and silence is pure. Thus everything has come to an end. Everything the end must make manifest, all that Igitur seeks to create by means of his death—the solitude of darkness, the deep of disappearance—is given in advance, and seems the condition for this death: its anticipated appearance, its eternal image. A strange reversal. It is not the youth who, by disappearing into death, institutes disappearance and therein establishes the night. It is the absolute presence of this disappearance, its dark glistening, which alone permits him to die. It alone introduces him to his mortal decision and act. It is as though death had first to be anonymous in order to occur with certainty in someone's name, or as if, before being my death, a personal act in which my person deliberately comes to an end, death had to be the neutrality and impersonality in which nothing is accomplished, the empty omnipotence which consumes itself eternally.

We are now a long way away from that voluntary death which the final episode let us see. Drawing back from the precise action which consists in emptying the vial, we have returned to a thought, the ideal act, already impersonal, where thinking and dying explored each other in their reciprocal truth and their hidden identity. But now we find ourselves before the immense passivity which, in advance, dissolves all action, even the action by which Igitur wants to die, the momentary master of chance. It seems that three figures of death confront each other here in a motionless simultaneity. All three are necessary for death's accomplishment, and the most secret is apparently the substance of absence, the deep of the void created when one dies, the eternal outside—a space formed by my death and yet whose approach is alone what makes me die. From such a perspective the event could never happen (death could never become an event): that is what is inscribed in this prerequisite night. The situation could also be expressed as follows: in order for the hero to be able to leave the chamber and for the final chapter, "Leaving the Chamber," to be written, it is necessary that the chamber already be empty and that the word to be written have returned forever into silence. And this is not a difficulty in logic. This contradiction expresses everything that makes both death and the work difficult. One and the other are somehow unapproachable, as Mallarmé said in notes that seem, precisely, to concern *Igitur:* "The Drama is only insoluble because unapproachable." And he comments further in the same passage: "The Drama is caused by the Mystery of what follows—Identity (Idea) Self—of the Theater and the Hero through the Hymn. *Operation.*—the Hero disengages—the (maternal) hymn which creates him, and he restores himself to the Theater which it was—of the Mystery where this hymn was hidden." If the "Theater" here means Midnight's space, a moment which is a place, then theater and hero are indeed identical, through the hymn which is death become word. How can Igitur "disengage" this death by making it become song and hymn, and thereby restore himself to the theater, to the pure subsistence of Midnight where death is hidden? That is the "operation." It is the end which can only be a return to the beginning, as the last words of the narrative say: "Nothingness having departed, there remains the Castle of purity," that empty chamber in which everything persists.

THE "ACT OF NIGHT"

The way Mallarmé nevertheless tries to approach the drama, in order to find a solution to it, is very revealing. Among night, the hero's thoughts, and his real acts, or, in other words, among absence, the thought of this absence, and the act by which it is realized, an exchange is established, a reciprocity of movements. First we see that this Midnight, eternal beginning and eternal end, is not so immobile as one might think. "Certainly a presence of Midnight subsists." But this subsisting presence is not a presence. This substantial present is the negation of the present. It is a vanished present. And Midnight, where first "the absolute presence of things" (their unreal essence) gathered itself together, becomes "the pure dream of a Midnight vanished into itself": it is no longer a present, but the past, symbolized, as is the end of history in Hegel, by a book lying open upon the table, "page and usual décor of Night." Night is the book: the silence and inaction of a book when, after everything has been proffered, everything returns into the silence that alone speaks—that speaks from the depths of the past and is at the same time the whole future of the word. For present Midnight, that hour at which the present lacks absolutely, is also the hour in which the past touches and, *without the intervention of any timely act whatever,* immediately attains the future at its most extreme. And such, we have seen, is the very instant of death, which is never present, which is the celebration of the absolute future, the instant at which one might say that, in a time without present, what has been will be. This is announced to us in two famous sentences of *Igitur:* "I *was* the hour which *is to* make me pure"; and, more exactly, in Midnight's farewell to night—a farewell which can never end because it never takes place now, because it is present only in night's eternal absence: "Adieu, night, that I *was,* your own tomb, but which, surviving shade, *will* change into Eternity."

However, this structure of Night has already given us back a movement: its immobility is constituted by this call of the past to the future, the muffled scansion by which what has been affirms its identity with what will be beyond the wrecked and sunken present, the abyss of the present. With this "double beat," the night stirs, it acts, it becomes an act, and this act opens the gleaming doors of the tomb, creating the solution which makes the "exit from the chamber" possible. ("The hour formulates itself in this echo, at the threshold of the open doors by its *act* of night.") Here Mallarmé discovers the motionless sliding which causes things to move forward at the heart of their eternal annulment. There is an imperceptible exchange among the inner oscillation of the night, the pulse of the clock, the back and forth of the doors of the open tomb, the back and forth of consciousness which returns to and goes out from itself, which divides and escapes from itself, wandering distantly from itself with a rustling of nocturnal wings, a phantom already confused with the ghosts of those who have already died. This "rhythm," in all these forms, is the movement of a disappearance, the movement of return to the heart of disappearance—a "faltering beat," however, which bit by bit affirms itself, takes on body, and finally becomes the living heart of Igitur, that heart whose too lucid certainty then "troubles" him and summons him to the real act of death. Thus we have come from the most interior to the most exterior. Indefinite absence, immutable and sterile, has imperceptibly transformed itself. It has taken on the look and the form of this youth, and having become real in him, it finds in this reality the means of realizing the decision that annihilates him. This night, which is Igitur's intimacy, the pulsating death which is the heart of each of us, must become life itself, the sure heart of life, so that death may ensue, so that death may for an instant let itself be grasped, identified—in order that death might become the death of an identity which has decided it and willed it.

The earlier versions of Mallarmé's narrative show that in the death and the suicide of Igitur he initially saw the death and the purification of night. In these pages (in particular in scholium d), it is no longer either Igitur or his consciousness that acts and keeps watch, but night itself, and all the events are lived by the night. The heart which, in the definitive text, Igitur recognizes as his own—"I hear the pulsating of my own heart. I do not like this

noise: this perfection of my certitude troubles me; everything is too clear"—
this heart, then, is, in the earlier versions, the night's heart: "Everything was
perfect; night was pure Night, and it heard its own heart beat. Still, this
heart troubled it, gave it the disquietude of too much certainty, of a proof
too self-confident. Night wanted in its turn to plunge back into the darkness
of its unique tomb and to abjure the idea of its form." The night is Igitur,
and Igitur is that portion of night which the night must "reduce to the state
of darkness" in order to become again the liberty of night.

THE IGITUR CATASTROPHE

It is significant that, in the most recent version, Mallarmé modified the
whole perspective of the work by making it Igitur's monologue. Although in
this prolongation of Hamlet's soliloquy there is no very ringing affirmation
of the first person, that wan "I" which from moment to moment presents
itself behind the text and supports its diction is clearly perceptible. In this
way, everything changes. On account of this voice which speaks, it is no
longer night that speaks, but a voice that is still very personal, no matter
how transparent it makes itself; and where we thought we were in the
presence of the secret of Midnight, the pure destiny of absence, we now have
only the speaking presence, the rarefied but certain evidence of a consciousness which, in the night which has become its mirror, still contemplates only
itself. That is remarkable. It is as though Mallarmé had drawn back before
what he will call, in "Un Coup de dés," "the identical neutrality of the
abyss." He seemed to do justice to the night, but it is to consciousness that
he delegates all rights. Yes it is as though he had feared to see everything
dissipate, "waver, subside, madness," if he did not introduce, surreptitiously,
a living mind which, from behind, could still sustain the absolute nullity that
he claimed to evoke. Whoever wishes to speak of a "catastrophe" in *Igitur*
might well find it here. Igitur does not leave the chamber: the empty chamber is simply he—he who merely goes on speaking of the empty chamber
and who, to make it absent, has only his word, founded by no more original
absence. And if, in order to accede sovereignly to death, it is truly necessary
that he expose himself to the presence of sovereign death—that pure medium of a Midnight which "crosses him out" and obliterates him—this
confrontation, this decisive test is missed, for it takes place under the pro-
tection of consciousness, with its guarantee, and without consciousness's
running any risk.

Finally there remains only the act in the obscurity of its resolve: the vial
that is emptied, the drop of nothingness that is drunk. Granted, this act is

imbued with consciousness, but its having been decided upon does not suffice to make it decisive; it bears in itself the cloudiness of the decision. Igitur ends his monologue rather feebly with these words, "The hour has struck for me to depart," in which we see that everything remains to be done. He has not taken so much as one step toward the "therefore" which his name represents—that conclusion of himself which he wants to draw from himself, believing that solely by virtue of understanding it, knowing it in its quality as chance, he can rise to the level of necessity and annul his end as chance by adjusting himself precisely to that nullity. But how could Igitur know chance? Chance is the night he has avoided, in which he has contemplated only proof of himself and his constant certitude. Chance is death, and the dice according to which one dies are cast by chance; they signify only the utterly hazardous movement which reintroduces us within chance. Is it at Midnight that "the dice must be cast"? But Midnight is precisely the hour that does not strike until after the dice are thrown, the hour which has never yet come, which never comes, the pure, ungraspable future, the hour eternally past. Nietzsche had already come up against the same contradiction when he said, "Die at the right time." That right moment which alone will balance our life by placing opposite it on the scales a sovereignly balanced death can be grasped only as the unknowable secret: only as that which could never be elucidated unless, already dead, we could look at ourselves from a point from which it would be granted us to embrace as a whole both our life and our death—the point which is perhaps the truth of the night from which Igitur would like, precisely, to take his leave, in order to render his leave-taking possible and correct, but which he reduces to the poverty of a reflection. "Die at the right time." But death's rightful quality is impropriety, inaccuracy—the fact that it comes either too soon or too late, prematurely and as if after the fact, never coming until after its arrival. It is the abyss of present time, the reign of a time without a present, without that exactly positioned point which is the unstable balance of the instant whereby everything finds its level upon a single plane.

"UN COUP DE DÉS"

Is "Un Coup de dés" the recognition of such a failure? Is it the renunciation of the wish—to master the measurelessness of chance through a sovereignly measured death? Perhaps. But this cannot be said with certainty. Rather, it is *Igitur,* a work not simply unfinished but left dangling, that announces this failure—announces it by being thus forsaken. And thereby it recovers its meaning. It escapes the naivete of a successful undertaking to become the force and the obsession of the interminable. For thirty years *Igitur* accompanied Mallarmé, just as all his life the hope of the "great Work" kept its vigil by his side. He evoked this Work mysteriously before his friends, and he eventually made its realization credible even in his own eyes and even, for a time, in the eyes of the man who had the least confidence in the impossible, Valéry—Valéry who, startled by his own credence, never recovered from this hurt, so to speak, but hid it beneath the demands of a contrary commitment.

"Un Coup de dés" is not *Igitur,* although it resurrects almost all of *Igitur*'s elements. It is not *Igitur* reversed, the challenge abandoned, the dream defeated, hope changed to resignation. Such comparisons would be worthless. "Un Coup de dés" does not answer *Igitur* as one sentence answers another, as a solution answers a problem. That reverberating proclamation itself—A THROW OF THE DICE NEVER WILL ABOLISH CHANCE—the force of its affirmation, the peremptory brilliance of its certitude, which makes it an authoritative presence holding the whole work together physically—this lightning which seems to fall upon the mad faith of *Igitur* in order to destroy and consume it, does not contradict *Igitur,* but on the contrary gives it its last chance, which is not to annul chance, even by an act of mortal negation, but to abandon itself entirely to chance, to consecrate chance by entering without reserve into its intimacy, with the abandon of impotence, "without the ship that is vain no matter where." In an artist so fascinated by the desire for mastery, nothing is more impressive than that final phase in which the work shines suddenly above him, no longer necessary but as a "perhaps" of pure chance, in the uncertainty of "the exception," not necessary but the absolute unnecessary, a constellation of doubt which only shines in the forgotten sky of perdition. The night of *Igitur* has become the sea, "the gaping deep," "the identical neutrality of the abyss," "a whirlpool of hilarity and horror." But Igitur was still searching only for himself in the night, and he wanted to die in the heart of his thought. To make impotence a power—these were the stakes; this has been conveyed to us. In "Un Coup de dés," the youth, who has matured, however, who is now "the Master," the man of sovereign mastery, does perhaps hold the successful throw of the dice in his hand, "the unique Number which does not want to be another"; but he does not take his unique chance to master chance any more than a man who always holds in his hand the supreme power, the power to die, can exercise that power. He dies outside this power, "cadaver pulled away by the arm from the secret he holds." This massive image rejects the challenge of voluntary death, where the hand holds the secret by which we are cast out of the secret. And this chance which is not taken, which remains idle, is not even a sign of wisdom, the fruit of a carefully considered and resolute abstention. It is itself something random, linked to the happenstance of old age and its incapacities, as if impotence had to appear to us in its most devastated form, where it is nothing but misery and abandon, the ludicrous future of an extremely old man whose death is only useless inertia. "A shipwreck that." But what happens in this shipwreck? Can the supreme conjunction, the game which in the fact of dying is played not against or with chance, but in its intimacy, in that region where nothing can be grasped—can this relation to impossibility still prolong itself? Can it give rise to an "as if" with which the dizziness of the work would be suggested—a delirium contained by "a small rigorous reason," a sort of "worried" "laughter," "mute" and "expiatory"? To this no answer is offered, no other certainty than the concentration of chance, its stellar glorification, its elevation to the point where its rupture "rains down absence," "some last point which sanctifies it."

"If it gets finished (the tale), I shall be cured." This hope is touching in its simplicity. But the tale was not finished. Impotence—that abandon in which the work holds us and where it requires that we descend in the concern for its approach—knows no cure. That death is incurable. The absence that Mallarmé hoped to render pure is not pure. The night is not perfect, it does not welcome, it does not open. It is not the opposite of day— silence, repose, the cessation of tasks. In the night, silence is speech, and there is no repose, for there is no position. There the incessant and the uninterrupted reign—not the certainty of death achieved, but "the eternal torments of Dying."

GEORGES POULET

Mallarmé's "Prose pour Des Esseintes"

Hyperbole! from my memory
Triumphantly unable art thou
To rise up, today a script of gramarye
In a book clothed with iron:

For I install by science
The hymn of spiritual hearts
In the work of my patience,
Atlases, herbals and rituals.

If the poem is dedicated to Des Esseintes, i.e., to the hero of Huysmans's famous novel, *A rebours* (published in 1884), it is because it is akin to the sort of poetry Des Esseintes professes to love more than any other, the poetry of low Latinity and the Middle Ages. It is a *prose,* or a sequence, in the sense of a Church prose, such as the *Salutaris Hostia* or the *Dies Iræ;* hymns sung during Mass, usually between the Epistle and the Gospel. Thus two of the main characteristics of the poem are from the very first made apparent, its memorative quality, or the solemn recalling to the mind of a great event of long ago, and, secondly, its ritualistic or even magical aspect, the part it plays in the performing of rites through which some supernatural deed is accomplished. Such is the precise purpose of Mallarmé's poem: to create something equivalent to the ancient religious hymn, to be tantamount

From *The Metamorphoses of the Circle,* translated by Carley Dawson and Elliott Coleman in collaboration with the author. ©1966 by the Johns Hopkins University Press. The Johns Hopkins University Press, 1966.

17

to what Mallarmé calls elsewhere "liturgical remembrances." Like the medieval prose, Mallarmé's poem will be an incantation directed toward a transcendence. Or, more exactly, its object will be to answer the question: Is such an incantation still possible?

> Will a rite become exteriorized through being practiced...?
> One needs, on certain evenings, to read, as I did, the exceptional
> book of Huysmans, in order to understand that the old rite must
> be adapted or transferred to some personal hobby.

Mallarmé's poem is thus an adaptation or a transference of the Christian rites to the poet's personal preoccupation. It simultaneously borrows its form from the medieval tradition, and turns its back to this tradition. Unlike the ecclesiastical hymn, which it closely imitates, it does not aim toward an already established transcendence in order to make it come down upon earth, but it raises itself toward a nonexistent transcendence, in order to make it come to existence by the very act of the poem's rising.

The poem, therefore, will be a rising, the rising of the poet's mind toward a heaven of his own. In the etymological sense of the word *hyperbole* (*uper*, beyond; *ballein*, to project), it will be a projection upward and outward. This eccentric motion of the mind will have its starting point in the hypothetical conception of some transcendence, and its terminal point in the achievement of this transcendence by the elevation and expansion of the mind. Thus, this transcendence is, at the same time, something past and something future. It is past, since history bears witness that at one time a hyperbole was raised by the faith of men; and it is future, since in a time to come the poet will again attempt to raise a hyperbole. But in the meantime the marvelous hyperbolical motion cannot yet be accomplished. The hyperbole is unable yet to raise itself. Having raised itself in the past, destined to rise again in the future, the hymn now does not raise itself, and the poem does not exist, except in the form of the sealed word and the ironclad book. When the word is sealed and the book locked, the poem cannot be sung and the song cannot rise up. It is deprived of its magical power of elation and expansion; it is inert and dead, comparable to the genie of the Arabian Nights who, bottled up in a vase, cannot free himself nor expand.

Before the rising of the hyperbole there must be the preparation of the hyperbole. Before singing the hymn, the poet must *install* the hymn. He must place it in a text, in order to start from the text. This text is no longer the old-fashioned text of religious hymns or of books of gramarye. It is its modern counterpart, the poem: "I say that between the ancient processes and the magic with which poetry persists, there is a secret likeness." The poem, then, is a work of magic, a work of patience and alchemy (the expression *work of patience* is used by the alchemists to mean the *grand oeuvre,* or the transmutation of a vile metal into gold). But before this transmutation and elevation, there must be a preparation. The text of the poem is not the hyperbole, but the place from which the hyperbole will raise itself. It is not the alchemical operation, but the gathering, the fixing and the arranging of all the elements with the help of which the operation will be performed. Like the atlas, the herbal, and the ritual, it contains all the ingredients by the composition of which the work of patience will be completed. When it is completed, there will be no need anymore for science, patience, and craft. The period of installation will be at an end. Suddenly the future will not be the future anymore, but the actual present; the poem will not be any longer a dead world; the countries of the atlas will cover the earth, the dry flowers in the herbals will bloom again, and new prayers will arise from the rituals. The hymn, then, will be not only installed, but sung. And the song will rise up and expand. It will be a hyperbole, spreading triumphantly in space.

It is to this triumphant spreading of the hymn that Mallarmé invites us. This hymn will be the hymn of the future, but it will be also in the future the equivalent of the hymn of the past. Thus, in order to imagine what it will be, it is right to let it first appear in the aspect of a vision of the past.

II

We caused our face to wander
(For I maintain that we were two)
On many charms of the landscape
O Sister, comparing thine own to them.

What we distinguish in this first unfolding of the hymn, is primal harmony. In the far away past, in a time which is likened to the time of Eden or to the Golden Age, and which will be called, further down, the summer midday, or zenith, of existence, two beings wander in a garden. They are distinct from one another, yet, in another sense, they are one. There is a talker and there is a listener, somebody who is making comparisons and somebody who is compared. Yet the one who is compared has a sister-like resemblance to the one who is making the comparisons. Both walk with the same step, cast the same glance, have the same face. The unity of the two members of the couple is still reinforced by the use of the first person of the plural, *we.* Thus, what is suggested here is the image of a single person, walking alone but with his thoughts, talking to himself and comparing what is in his mind with what exists in the outside world. The theme is the conversation one holds with oneself, with the particular metaphysical and semantic problems which are implied by such an ordinary, and yet such a complex, action. If I speak to myself, and if I also listen to myself, am I really identical to myself in these two distinct operations? Besides, granted that what I transmit to myself is a faithful image of myself, will not this transmitted image be altered in the act of transmission? This is what happens each time an old idea comes to my mind, because, between the remoteness of the idea and the actuality of my mind, there is a distance of time which may be the cause of a misunderstanding. "We shall try to discover," says Mallarmé in 1869, "what effects the words would produce in us when pronounced by the interior voice of our mind, disposed as it is by a familiarity with the writings of the past, if these effects are a long way off from the daily ones." There is in the interior dialogue the risk that he who listens may be too far away from him who speaks, and that possessed by the present sense of the word he no longer comprehends its past sense. It is as if there were two interlocutors, one who is my old self, the other who is my present self; they may not belong to the same epoch, they may converse without being contemporaries, and the result of this discrepancy is the consciousness, not of an identity, but of a difference. Such is the customary experience of all thought that would like to remain *actual*. It finds out that in order to think itself it is mysteriously obliged to lose its actuality, to withdraw itself from itself in order to realize itself in an anterior distance.

However, such is not the case in the conversation which is described in this stanza. For, precisely, this conversation is not happening now, it is simply presented as having happened, that is to say, as having taken place in the mythical past. The mythical past, the time of Eden or of the Golden Age, is the only time which was not divided, where there was no *before* and no *after*, but an eternal Now. In that time there was always a perfect coincidence between what was said and what was heard. The spoken word and the perceived word had exactly the same meaning and were not distorted by time and distance. The harmony was perfect, the certainty absolute.

This is, then, the time of unison, and this is also the place of unison. The perfect harmony which exists between the two interlocutors is constituted, not only by the fact that they live in the same time, but also by the fact that, perceiving the same objects, they move in the same place. To the temporal identity there corresponds a spatial identity. *This* is only truly equal to *that*, if *this* and *that* are both demonstratively related in the same way to a third term. Such is the mathematical proof of identity—the only truly satisfactory one. If, as it is said in this stanza, "we were two," and yet we "had only one face," we are assured of the oneness of this face only by the fact that both representations of this single entity bear the same relation to a third term. This term is *place*. In the exteriority of place the one who is talking and the one who is listening find a common relation. Comparing their own charms to the charms of the garden, they discover that these charms are the same. Therefore, they themselves are also the same. A landscape which is identical to themselves, reveals to themselves their own inner identity.

Self-consciousness, then, or the inner dialogue of the self with the self, is achieved by an identification of the self with the outside world. The world and the mind do not differ in the least, except in the fact that the former expresses the latter. Thanks to the outside reality of things, the mind can know itself. The world is a language with the aid of which the mind can speak and listen to itself, and identify itself with itself. Between inner and outer realities there can be made a comparison, which is an equation: "Man," Mallarmé says, "and his sojourn upon earth make a reciprocal exchange of proofs."

Everything, thus, is perfectly simultaneous in time and place. Every-thing, inside and outside, is immediately discovered as being the same. But this primal and essential comparison is nevertheless a motion: the discursive motion by which the mind goes from object to object, comparing their external charms with its own inner beauty. Hence, in the perfect harmony of identification, there is introduced the possibility of discord and dissen-sion. The oneness of the mind is discovered only through the multiplicity of the charms of the garden; and it can be expressed only by an equal multi-plicity of words, an enumeration.

III

> The era of authority is troubled
> When, without motive, it is said
> Of this midday that our double
> Unconsciousness investigates,
>
> That, ground of the hundred irises, its site
> —They know whether it really was—
> Bears no name that is proclaimed
> By the gold of the summer bugle.

The era of authority is troubled. Before this trouble of authority, which is also a trouble of authorship or of the relation of the poet with nature, the former lived harmoniously with the latter, enjoying a perfect understanding and rectitude of language, which were given him by the constant adequacy between his mind and all the objects of the outside world. There was no discrepancy between his thoughts, his words, and the things designated by his words. Now this era of authority, certainty, and orderliness comes abruptly to an end. Without any motive or positive advantage, carried away subconsciously or thoughtlessly by the pleasure it takes at investigating things, the mind introduces in the general harmony a grave disorder. First of all, this disorder becomes patent in the disposition of space. The unity of the garden is troubled. It becomes obscured by the very number of plants which grow in it. Each one attracts the attention of the mind, and therefore also distracts it from the whole. Each particular plant, each individual part in the totality of the garden, has to receive a distinct name, and in order to be so named, has to be separated from all the other plants and parts of the garden. So, instead of having only one garden and a single name for the whole of the garden, the mind now has an infinity of names, each of which designates a part, and none of them designates the whole. The outside world as a whole bears no name any longer. It has become anonymous, and therefore unthinkable. And what happens for the outside world, happens also for the self. Instead of enjoying the consciousness of its own identity, the mind now is aware only of the confused multiplicity of its thoughts.

Through the dangerous growth of science and language, the mind has lost touch with the simplicity of truth. It does not see the forest for the trees. It has also lost touch with itself. Within and without the mind, there is no longer any simplicity, but an endless proliferation of things and names.

To this parcelling of space there corresponds parcelling of time. Instead of keeping simultaneously under its eye all the charms of the landscape, the mind proceeds now from one to the other, in an essentially transitive manner. Moving toward new prospects, it leaves behind the old ones. These old prospects become therefore retrospects. What they fill up, bit by bit, is the past. The more rapidly the mind progresses in its investigation of things, the more quickly these things are named, catalogued and finally ranged in memory. There, they constitute an ever expanding demesne of things which are known and named. On the one hand, the mind constantly progresses, on the other hand, whatever is acquired by the means of this progress is immediately pushed into the past. Thus a growing distance appears between the actuality of the mind and the nonactuality of everything that is, or has been, thought by the mind.

IV

Yes, in an isle the air charges
With sight and not with visions,
Each flower was growing larger
Without our discussing it.
So much so, immense, that each flower
Ordinarily adorned itself
With a lucid contour, a hiatus
Which separated it from the gardens.

Suddenly, after the negation, we hear again the affirmation. After the description of obscurity and disorder, there is again a picture of certainty and harmony. But the affirmation which, with a great energy, is introduced here by the *yes* at the beginning of the sixth stanza, does not proclaim the renewal of the Golden Age. It simply reemphasizes its past existence. It cannot be denied, Mallarmé concedes, that now science and language proceed by successive visions and expressions. But it cannot be denied, either, that, once, science and language, far from proceeding successively, had the power of possessing truth instantaneously and intuitively; and that this intuition revealed the fundamental identity of the mind and the world. Today, it is true, this intuition is not possible any longer; it does not constitute any more an integrant part of the present experience. But it existed undeniably in the past, and therefore it still constitutes an integrant part of the past. The past is like an island, seen far-away in the great sea of existence, an island made of time and space, the midday of old, a place distinct and remote from the present moment, but in which it is still possible to find the perfect harmony between being and thought, and between thought and language. There, hyperbolically, everything that exists can be seen in a larger, clearer, and simpler form, without it being necessary to consider successively all its aspects or enumerate all its charms. Thus in the past, in the contemplation of the past by the means of memory, I can still rediscover and reconstitute the old harmony, I can detach myself from the actual and betake my mind into a spiritual island in which whatever is thought by me is named, and, by being named, becomes a reflection and an explanation of my own self. The past, or, at least, the ennobled and enlarged version of it which is given to me by memory, is the true and only place in which I can still find between me and nature a universal analogy. There the intelligibility of all the objects of the external world still provides me with a language by the means of which I can communicate with myself and understand myself. Therefore self-knowledge still depends on my relation with nature, but with a nature which does not belong to the present—a past nature. The language which I use in order to communicate with myself is borrowed from a world which, it is true, does not exist any longer, since it is past, but which necessarily still subsists in my mind. All around me, at an increasingly greater distance, in increasingly larger forms, there are flowers which do not grow in any garden of today. Indeed, they are separated from today and from any actual place by the hiatus of time, but they have continued to grow immensely in the immense site of my thought. These flowers are *thought* flowers, recollected flowers; they are essentially non-actual and such that they are absent from all present gardens or nosegays. But precisely because they are abstracted from the reality of today, and yet present to the mind which names them, they have become mental things, verbal entities, with the aid of which the mind can speak. Each object of this new world is susceptible to being detached and considered independently. Each thing is not a thing any more, it is not imprisoned, as things are, in the confused multiplicity of other things. It can be isolated, considered in itself, because it is not a thing, but simply the abstract notion of a thing. Thus it appears in the mind, miraculously separated from everything else, defined by a lucid contour. The universe in which I find the exact equivalent of my thought is a universe which is not different any more from my thought. It is not made up of existing objects, but of nonexistent objects, that is to say, of objects about which, when I realize that they have existed, I assume that they can exist again. They are past and future, but never present; therefore they are purely mental. Consequently the equivalence which I establish between nature and myself is not any longer an equivalence between what I think and what is existing, but an equivalence between what I think and what is no more or not yet, but, being no more or not yet, is still present in my thought. My thought is not to be identified any longer with an external world, but with a world which, having become entirely internal and ideal, is now simply the content of my mind. Everything else having been eliminated, I compare myself to my spiritual objects, i.e., to my Ideas.

V

> Glory of the long desire, Ideas,
> Everything in me was elated at seeing
> The family of the Irideae
> Rise up to this new duty.

The world in which I find the exact equivalent of my self is a world of ideas—a world made up exclusively of my ideas. In realizing this, I realize the most glorious progress of my mind. The long search, undertaken in order to find in things the exact equivalent of my thoughts, has brought me finally to the point of retaining only the reflection of these things in my mind. Born of my long desire, the ideas of things rise up to a new duty which does not consist any longer in being, but in being thought. Out of the very depth of my thoughts I see the ideas springing, surging, growing, and invading the field of my spiritual space. Their growing is my growing, their propagation is my propagation. I rise up with them; I participate in the enlarging of their forms. Everything in me is elated at seeing them multiply their stalks and occupy a space more and more vast, in which my transfigured mind progresses and expands at the same rate. I had denied nature; I had forgotten its name. I had reduced it to anonymity. Now, I find it again, idealized, identical to my rising song. "The idea grows only by means of its own negation," says Villiers de l'Isle Adam, quoting Hegel. "Is not the continuous motion in the growing of trees and blades of grass the same as the one which makes the suns projecting their rings oscillate and jump out of themselves?" By the same motion, the Mallarméan prose or hymn oscillates and jumps out of itself in the cosmos of the mind. It is as if a "metaphorical heaven were propagating itself around the thunderbolt of the verse," or indeed a "turning fire of hymns." The poem, Mallarmé says, is "the enlarging of space by vibrations up to the infinite." And elsewhere: "Around this center of myself I sit like a sacred spider connected with all the threads already issued from my mind." The mind is a web of ideas, a network of all the crossing points at which ideas are connected with other ideas and with the central point, which is myself. Thoughts and words spread outward, like "the reflection of a circular flight, high up, of jewels or souls," enveloping in its circumvoluted play of light all the mental activities of the central self.

Such is the exaltation, the ecstasy of Mallarmé's poetry. This exaltation is, at the same time, glorious and solitary, since the glory it aims at has nothing to do with external fame. It is the spectacle offered by the self to the self, when it projects itself, so to speak, circularly, at a cosmic distance, but always in itself, in such a way as to be always able to bring back to itself the reflection of its hyperbolical image: "The self, projected, absolute!" It is as if, in a room made up of mirrors, a prince would treat himself to a gala performance of which he would be at once the author, the audience, and the infinitely multiplied hero. Or as if, to use another hyperbolical image, a God, intending to create a world, would content himself with the display of all the ideas of that world, without ever passing to the act of creation.

The Mallarméan exaltation is a spectacle. It is primarily commanded by *sight*. But the universal flowering and scintillating of forms, irises, and rainbows, which is thus seen, is seen only inside the mind, and this sight is nothing but an in-sight, an introspection. Mallarmé's poetry is a mirror, the facets of which are disposed in such a way as to send back to the poet a single image—his own. Not the image, of course, of Stéphane Mallarmé in the flesh, but of the spiritual being, which, through the disappearance of all individual features, becomes the anonymous subject of an action which is an elevation and an elation. Each reader of Mallarmé's poetry, each "spiritual heart" can, indeed, repeat for his own sake the same experience and, to use the expression of Gérard de Nerval, become thus the God of the universe of his dreams; with the single reservation that, unlike Nerval's dream, the dream of Mallarmé manifests itself, not in the form of feelings, but in the form of the most severely abstracted notions. The flowers, roses or irises, the swans, the constellations, the jewels or the hair of women, which are the familiar objects of Mallarmé's world, have no more existence than the symbols of the world of geometry; that is to say, like points, triangles, circles, and spheres, they are purely fictitious. Invented by the mind, they are nothing but figments of the mind.

VI

But this sensible and tender sister
Carried her glance no farther
Than to smile and to understand her
I confine my ancient care.

Scattering in all directions its multitudinous and scintillating image, the Mallarméan mind has spread itself hyperbolically in a space of its own. This space is constantly crossed and recrossed. Not only are ideas thrown upward and outward in it, like rockets, but when they reach the outer limit of their journey, they flash back their reflection to the mind. "Through the convergence of the harmonic fragments to the center," everything flows back to its source. "I perceive myself," Mallarmé writes, "like the undulating motion of a tranquillizing opiate, the vibrating circles of which flowing in and out, constitute an infinite limit which never coincides with the stillness of the center." Thus the mind is, simultaneously, the infinite limit of the spreading thoughts and the still point from which they proceed and to which they come back. Through this constant outflowing and inflowing, space is possessed by the mind, even more so, it is literally lived in all its parts.—More than once in the poem, up to now, we have seen space described in one way or another: as the closed book, as the place of the installation of the hymn, as the garden in which the hundred irises bloom, as the isle in which the flowers grow larger. But neither the simplicity of Edenic nature, nor the plurality of the external world, nor even memory—this space which is nearly entirely ideal—constituted for Mallarmé the perfect space, i.e., the perfect site for the mind. All these symbolical places were, more or less, vitiated by a grave defect: they were all exterior to the mind. They encompassed it, yet excluded it. Existing outwardly, when the mind existed inwardly, they formed, all around it, a reality which was essentially heterogeneous to it. They allowed it to situate itself in their center, to compare itself to them, not to spread itself within them. Space and mind seemed therefore to be two mutually exclusive entities. Now, by abolishing the external universe and replacing it by a combination of pure notions, Mallarmé eliminates this classical opposition of space and mind. Space is reduced to its mental equivalent. It becomes a purely notional extension. In the same way as the poet conceives his ideas, so he conceives the space in which they gravitate. He "installs . . . a purely fictional milieu."

Space, then, is not any longer heterogeneous, not exterior to the mind. It is the field which the mind gives itself in order to proceed freely, through its own expansion, toward its glorification.

Infinitely enlarging its own sphere, the Mallarméan mind works toward its "total expansion." But this "enlargement of place through vibrations up to the infinite" cannot be achieved without a corresponding diffusion, in that place, of all the images by which the poet accomplishes this spiritual amplification. There is always in Mallarmé's poetry an eccentric motion by which things get vaster and vaster, but by which also they disappear in their own vastness. This is, for instance, what happens in the Funereal Toast in honor of Théophile Gautier:

> I want to see
> To it that he who vanished yesterday, in the ideal
> Duty which the gardens of this star exact of us,
> For the honor of the tranquil disaster
> Survives by a solemn agitation in the air
> Of words.

True, the vanishing which is alluded to here, is the vanishing through death, of the person of Théophile Gautier, and what Mallarmé wants to see survive here, are the words of the dead poet; but these words are represented as an agitation and vibration of the air, which gets more and more remote. The waves of sound which they emit, get vaster and vaster, but also fainter and fainter. Hence we understand that the tranquil disaster, which is depicted in the Funereal Toast, does not consist only of the disappearance of the central figure, but also of the disappearance of all images which represented it. Poetry, like all the projections of the mind, evaporates in the same way as the smoke of a cigarette. It disappears upward, outward, in whirls of mist:

> All the breath summed up,
> When slowly we expire it,
> In several rings of smoke
> Is abolished in other rings.

From ring to ring, from circle to circle, the breath of the mind diffuses itself in space; but, at the same time, it expires, all the circles disaggregate and vanish. Thought is like the spiral staircase of *Igitur;* it is "a dizzying winding process, indefinitely flying away." At the extreme of its movement of expansion, when the mind sees its own image infinitely and gloriously dilated. "Vibratory vanishing," it does not see anything any longer. By dilating itself everywhere, the mind has abolished itself everywhere.

This catastrophe is cosmic. It is also ridiculous. For nothing is more ridiculous than attempting to become all, and ending by being nothing. The experience of what we may call peripheral nothingness, is for Mallarmé, as for Nerval or Baudelaire, a disaster on a colossal scale, but for Mallarmé it has also its funny side, it is quite a laughable matter. The consciousness of absolute failure always marks in Mallarmé a return to common sense. The vaporous and vibratory disappearance of all the objects of his mental universe, is, after all, for Mallarmé, of slight importance, since, from the beginning, he had perfectly understood that these objects were purely fictional. Therefore why be sorry about their loss? While there is in Mallarmé a part of himself, which, through ecstasy and hyperbole, gets monstrously inflated, there is also another part, lucid, tenderly skeptical, "a sensible and tender sister" of the ecstasy, who, observing this inflation, is perfectly aware of its exaggeration and silliness. Of these two dialoguing sisters, Irony is the sensible one. She is the wise virgin. Her mission, purely negative, consists in gently, but firmly, declining to accompany her foolish sister in the reckless imaginary excursion the latter makes. Mallarmé's irony applies to the expansive force of the ideal the most potent brake, which is the consciousness of the unreality of this ideal. If there is a ridiculously swollen-headed Mallarmé who disappears in the distance, there is a quite uninflated Mallarmé who "does not carry his glance farther than to smile." Denying the truth of the hyperbole, refusing to budge and to bulge, he sits still at the center of the deflated world.

VII

Oh! may the Spirit of litigation know
In this hour when we are silent,
That the stems of multiple lilies
Were growing too much for our reason

And not as the riverbank weeps
When its monotonous play lies
In wishing for the amplitude to come
Among my young amazement

At hearing all the sky and the map
Endlessly attested on my walk
By the very wave which recedes,
That this country did not exist.

To the affirmation there has succeeded again the negation. Ecstasy has been answered by irony. In the conversation which the mind holds with itself, we can thus see an alternate motion which causes it to lean sometimes toward the *yes,* and sometimes toward the *no.* The conversation is a dispute of the self with the self, a litigation. The issue is as follows: Must we allow our thoughts and words to multiply and grow vaster, so much so that they will become a lie and lose all contact with reason; is it necessary to say that only what is, is, or must we bring ourselves back to the narrow rock of truth? Such is the Mallarméan dilemma. One alternative necessarily carries the mind toward the affirmation, the multiplication, the amplification of hyperbole; the other one brings it back to truth, constriction, negation, and therefore also to sterility, stillness, and silence. Irony is the negative act, through which, everything being reduced to nothing, it appears clearly that there is nothing more to say and that the business of the poet is to stop and be silent. All other alternatives are excluded, and especially the one which would consist in monotonously and plaintively wishing for the amplitude of the ideal to come, when it is very well known that, in spite of all the attestations of the imagination, it can never come and can never be. So the adult Mallarmé of the "Prose" specifically rejects the attitude adopted by the youthful Mallarmé of twenty years before. He does not want to maintain, with an unreachable ideal, purely negative relations, based only on one's incapacity to attain it and sing it. Mallarmé, now, says *no* to the kind of poetry which was his own at the time when he could only weep at the idea that the country of his dreams did not exist. Nay! if the country of dreams does not exist, if the poet was wrong in thinking that he could extract from his mind a universe authenticated only by his words, in this case, as Irony points out, the only solution is to keep silent, and in the absence of the dream world, to resign oneself to be, like a swan caught in the ice of a congealed pool, a motionless point all around which there is nothing but blankness and negation.

VIII

> The child abdicates her ecstasy
> And already wise in her ways
> She says the word: Anastasis!
> Born for eternal parchments,
>
> Before a sepulchre starts laughing
> Under some sky, her ancestor,
> At bearing this name: Pulcheria!
> Hidden by the too large gladiolus.

Thus ends the conversation Mallarmé holds with himself. It ends, like all conversations, in silence. Or, rather, it would so end, were it not for the fact that, just before ending their talk, the two interlocutors will utter, one a last word, the other a laugh, which is a last exclamation.

Just before this supreme moment, the difference which divides the two members of the couple, is as great as possible. One affirms the actual existence of the dream, and pretends hyperbolically to be diffused in all its vast extension. The other one, on the contrary, denies the existence of this dream, replaces expansion by a void, and substitues for the hyperbolical discourse the silence of disillusion. No doubt, it was possible to stop the conversation at this precise moment, when the contradiction is most blatant and when the antithesis denies and dissolves the thesis: "We will choose," Mallarmé writes elsewhere, "the tone of conversation as the supreme limit . . . and stopping-point of the vibrating circles of our thought." Now, the tone of conversation is the tone of irony; and, indeed, it is Irony herself which, by the means of her antithetic smile, stops here—and definitely, it seems—the expanding circles described by the mind of her foolish sister. The principle of negation, then, has won. The dialectic of poetic consciousness ends with the defeat of poetry and the triumph of irony.

Yet, at this last moment, the defeated principle, Poetry, still finds the means of throwing at her opponent a supreme argument. Irony, she says, is right. Youth is made wiser by the ways of experience. One must abdicate ecstasy, and acknowledge that the multitudinous and immense world of dreams does not exist. Everything is conceded; everything is given up and lost. Yet, abdicating her present experience, the Mallarméan child abdicates only the *presentness* of it. Like a king who renounces his throne, but who still continues to be called a king, poetry renounces her queenship, but does not forego having been a queen. This royal quality, or virtue, reigning over a spiritual kingdom, is not an existence, but an essence; not a reality, but an ideality. I cannot say that I am the God or the King of the universe of my dreams, but nothing and nobody can deny me the right of saying that I *have* been God or King of these dreams; and therefore, that I can be again, in some future time, God or King of new dreams. Only the present moment is real. Only this moment can compel me into being nothing but what I am. But if I am a prisoner of the absolute principle, according to which *only what is, is,* the validity of this principle is strictly confined to the present moment. When, on the contrary, I imagine myself in the past or in the future, I can always be ideally what I wish to be. Therefore I proclaim the *anastasis,* that is to say, the renewal of my dreams, the perpetual possibility of identifying myself anew with them, not in the present moment, which is necessarily the moment of the death of my dreams, but beyond the present moment, in a future in which the past is resurrected ideally.

Thus, beyond the negation, there comes again the affirmation. But by a processus which is closely similar to the one we find in Hegelian philosophy, the new affirmation is not a mere repetition of the first one. It has assimilated the negation and therefore changed its own character. The new affirmation implies now the renunciation of ecstasy, i.e., of the immediate expansion of the mind in its dreams. To proclaim the *anastasis* of the dreams, is not to proclaim their eternal actuality, but, on the contrary, their eternal nonactuality. The dreams can never be actualized, they can never become real, except ideally,—not in the real world, but in the poem on the eternal parchment.

The *anastasis,* then, is the affirmation of the eternal renewal of the poem in the mind and in the book.

Everything was lost, everything now seems to be regained. For the hyperbole of ecstasy there is substituted the hyperbole of true poetry, the work of wisdom and patience. Through the practice of these virtues, the poet will go back into the past and acquire there the science of rites, thanks to which, in the future, the poem again will spring to life and expand in space. Everything is regained, yet everything is lost again, since, at this very moment, the old opponent, Irony, starts laughing. She is no longer the tender sister of Poetry, but her grim ancestor. She does not smile, but utters a sarcastic laugh. For Irony is nothing ultimately but Death. Grim and senile shadow of the ghost that the child will become inevitably in time, narrow grave in which the inflated possessor of space finally will be entombed, Death throws to her enemy a last denial. True, everything is saved, since the object of the dream is outside the reach of Death. Death can only destroy the real and can never touch the ideal. But everything is also lost, everything *will be* lost, since the dreamer himself is not immortal. Death kills, not the dream, but, at least, the subject in whom the dream must be born. The dream is eternal, but the dreamer is mortal. Everything is thus lost, since the dreamer, the one upon whom everything depends, will be lost. *Pulcheria,* the name of Beauty will be engraved—but upon a grave.

This final negation is directed, not toward the existence of the dream, or of the poem, but toward the existence of the dreamer, the poet. It lays him in his sepulchre. It abolishes him. Irony, death, negation have the last word. But in the most unexpected way the argument contained in this last word can be reversed. By abolishing the poet, that is to say, the living subject in whose mind the poem must take shape, Death gives him unintentionally the last perfection he needed in order to identify himself completely with his poem. Being dead, having become a non-being, like the poem, the poet has become, like the poem again, a purely ideal entity. He is not any longer the author of the poem, but the ideal subject of an ideal object, which is the poem. The last word of Mallarmé is a word of death, but it is not a word of defeat. Taking away all actuality, first, from the poem, then, from the poet, Mallarmé places them, one after the other, in the only region where they are safe from death. This is the region, not of reality, but of virtuality. There, everything can grow freely and immensely; there, irises, lilies, gladioli, and all the rest of the family of Irideae get so much enlarged that they become celestial and produce another species of irises, the iridescent rainbow, the hyperbolical scarf of the goddess Iris. The poem is "a circular flight of images and words," an exuberant growth in an imaginary sky. And at the center of this flight there is also an imaginary being, a hero who does not exist, a mind which is a void. From the center to the periphery and from the periphery to the center, there is a constant play of words and light, but this play is only a play, nothing ever takes place there, except in a fictitious way. "Everything is magically illusion and disillusion."

ROBERT GREER COHN

"Hommage (à Richard Wagner)"

Mallarmé uses the title "Hommage" for a dead fellow artist who is not a poet, but a kissin' cousin, as it were; "Tombeau" was reserved for Poe, Baudelaire, Verlaine. The first title of this sonnet was "Hommage à Wagner," when it appeared in the January 8, 1886, number of the *Revue wagnérienne*.

As Mondor says, "Written after [the essay] 'Richard Wagner rêverie d'un poète français', 'Hommage' is somewhat a restatement of it, utilizing a vocabulary often identical; and, like the prose piece, praising the musician for having realized, or at least approached, the ideal drama of which he never ceased dreaming." Actually, Mallarmé was subtly implying in the essay that Wagner got only *half*way to the ideal summit that he, the poet, knew to exist and hoped to reach. In the poem he speaks admiringly of the recently-deceased German master's authenticity, springing from the original source of beauty and truth, and thereby shaming the cheap clutter of contemporary art. There is a wistful echo, at the end, of his desire to surpass Wagner by means of literature.

The sonnet (excessively complex and not one of his best) is constructed as follows: the first quatrain alludes to the rottenness of contemporary theater, which must fall—"the [theater] trappings that a settling of the main pillar must pull down with the lack of memory" (literally, this last means "un-originality," as well as forgetting its finest tradition). The *moire* is a sort of *housse* or cloth covering laid on the furniture in the empty theater (a *relâche*, because of the death of Wagner, or empty because of the inanity of modern dramatic works). It is also the shroud of Time which will be laid on

From *Toward the Poems of Mallarmé*. © 1965 by the Regents of the University of California. The University of California Press, 1965.

33

this decadent institution and, incidentally, the shroud of Richard Wagner, whose recent demise is being commemorated.

The second quatrain turns to an even closer Mallarméan concern, the book. This wonderful old tradition has also been perverted to vulgar uses, cheap sensationalism—*frisson familier!* So let the book—or *that* kind—be shoved into a closet.

The tercets describe Wagner's telling off, or showing up, the literary people with his splendid, fresh art. He has taken over the "stage" ("parvis né pour . . . [un] simulacre"), which Mallarmé thought ought to be occupied by a modern cult replacing outworn religions. In the last line he decorously refers to the possibilities of a poet, who may not be completely outshone.

Le silence déjà funèbre d'une moire	The silence already funereal of a moire [watered cloth]
Dispose plus qu'un pli seul sur le mobilier	Lays more than just a fold on the furniture
Que doit un tassement du principal pilier	That a subsidence of the principal pillar
Précipiter avec le manque de mémoire.	Must hurl down with the lack of memory.

Le silence déjà funèbre d'une moire: the moire is here, as we said, a cloth covering, laid over the furniture of an empty theater. The theater is empty because of the death of its master, Wagner; and it is empty in the sense that the modern theater is generally lacking in substance—"faux temple . . . Odéon . . . culte factice"; "flux de banalité charrié par les arts dans le faux semblant de civilisation" ("Wagner"); "institution [théâtrale] plutôt vacante."

silence: the hush in the now empty theater. This hush is "déjà funèbre" in the sense that it (already) prefigures another death, that of the sick art that will be swept out.

The scene is, vaguely, a temple "ton [Wagner's] Temple"—or Theater of a cult, recalling the shift from Old to New Testament upon the death of Christ: "une inquiétude du voile dans le temple avec des plis [note *pli*] significatifs et un peu sa déchirure."

The *moire* is a shroud, image of the death of Wagner and also of the traditional art he has eclipsed. It is *finis* to the useless popular sort of drama Mallarmé consistently decries in his article on the musician, as in the words "nos rêves de sites ou de paradis, qu'engouffre l'antique scène une prétention vide à les contenir" and "un théâtre, le seul qu'on peut appeler caduc."

There is in the *moire* a hint of a new text, a "New Testament" of art, laid over an old; *moire*, with its *pli*, is a common Mallarméan expression for text (*textus:* woven); the important rime *grimoire-moire* is part of the reason; another is the overtone *Moire,* the spinner and weaver of fate. Mallarmé thus uses the word for the texture of thought, in "Ouverture ancienne," where we have the image of an original beauty springing up from under a shroud, as in the "Hommage":

> Par les . . . *plis* [cf. *pli*] roidis
> Percés selon le rythme et les dentelles pures
> Du *moire* laissant par ses belles guipures
> Désespéré monter le vieil éclat voilé
>
> .   .   .   .
>
> Jettera-t-il son or par dernières splendeurs [?]

This last line is the final image of the sonnet; compare [referring to Wagner's music] "Ouïr l'indiscutable rayon . . . l'évidence sous le voile," that is to say, radiantly eloquent beneath the garb of nonverbal sounds.

The association with text is further confirmed by "Ce *pli* de sombre dentelle tissé [*textus*] par mille": see under *dentelle* of *Triptyque.*

dispose plus qu'un pli seul sur le mobilier: the "more than just a fold" means that the cloth is also a text; moreover, it is not *merely* a decorative or protective cloth, but also carries more sinister implications, those of a "funereal" cloth, dooming the cumbersome trappings—a shroud. Thus, in the "Tombeau (de Verlaine)" we have the lines "Cet immatériel deuil opprime de maints / Nubiles plis l'astre mûri des lendemains"; compare "Et nous avons laissé, tous, la foi de nos pères / Au fond des plis de leurs linceuls" (Villiers, *Santa Magdalena*); also "l'espèce de grand suaire qui couvre les choses dans leur état primordial" (*Isis*).

mobilier: the furniture in a theater, with a strong suggestion of clutter, old trappings (the very idea of "movables" supports this tone; things that are arbitrary, unnecessary), as in "on ouït craquer jusque dans sa membrure définitive la menuiserie et le cartonnage de la bête [mediocre theater]."

tassement: means "subsidence" (crumbling) as of an edifice, "ruine à demi écroulée sur un sol de foi . . . à tout jamais *tassée*"—"théâtre caduc"—brought down by decadence. A second sense is the "packing" of a stagnant substance, with the spirit gone out of it (Richard) as in *Igitur:* "se *tassera* en ténèbres."

doit: Mallarmé implies it "must" come down, it cannot survive, this corrupt modern theater.

pilier: as of a temple, or a church, is connected with this notion of outmoded cult—"un édifice voué aux fêtes, implique une vision d'avenir . . . on a repris à l'église plusieurs traits . . . cette songerie restreinte par hasard à quelques *piliers* de paroisse." Wagner, like Mallarmé, would inaugurate a brand new cult. This crisis mood, referring to the death of Christianity and of old-fashioned art, is expressed in "Tout s'interrompt, effectif, dans l'histoire . . . L'éternel, ce qui le parut, ne rajeunit, enfonce aux cavernes et se tasse [cf. *tassement,* the packed, stagnant traditional art]: ni rien dorénavant, neuf, ne naîtra que de source. / Oublions / Une magnificence se déploiera, quelconque, analogue à l'ombre de jadis." Here we have an ambivalent filial attitude of respect and burial.

précipiter: the main idea is the pulling down, the "sweeping out" of uninspired literature by music, as in "La Musique, à sa date, est venue balayer cela . . . éclat triomphal . . . splendeur définitive simple"; together with the *tassement . . . pilier* and Temple image, we have a mild suggestion of old Samson bringing down the house with his own demise; compare "quelle étrange aventure a *précipité* ainsi cette race?" (*Le Livre*).

manque de mémoire: primarily the inauthenticity of modern art, which has lost its contact with the prime sources of being (as Heidegger would say); "la peur qu'a d'elle-même . . . la métaphysique et claustrale éternité" ("Catholicisme"); "le vieux sense s'oblitéra."

The *manque de mémoire* is thus the lack of original inspiration in the contemporary public theater (contrast the golden voice from the past surging up from under the shroud of *Ouverture ancienne,* previously quoted). The dramatic opposition between a useless present state of creative mind, represented as a stagnant text, *grimoire* (with overtones of *moire,* a *textus,* woven cloth) and, on the other hand, the original spirit of beauty, is the opening situation of "Prose": "Hyperbole . . . Triomphalement ne sais-tu / Te lever" versus "mémoire . . . aujourd'hui grimoire / Dans un livre de fer vêtu." The echoes of *triomphal-trompette-trop* (hyperbole) are important in both poems.

Notre si vieil ébat triomphal du grimoire,	Our so-old triumphal struggle of the grammar book,
Hiéroglyphes dont s'exalte le millier	Hieroglyphics which delight the crowd
À propager de l'aile un frisson familier!	Propagating a familiar shiver of the wing!
Enfouissez-le-moi plutôt dans une armoire.	Shove it for me rather in a closet.

grimoire: is the old tradition of books, admired (*triomphal*), but outmoded, just as Mallarmé both admired the crowd which reads the books— "la foule . . . où inclus le génie," and scorned it: "le chiffre brutal universel." The *grimoire* of *Igitur* is similarly respected and *vieux jeu.*

hiéroglyphes: a vaguely perjorative use, as in his translation of Whistler, or as in "Plus l'art voudra être clair, plus il se dégradera et remontera vers l'hiéroglyphe enfantin" (Baudelaire, *L'Art romantique*). Mallarmé was somewhat condescending also in his reference to the "hiéroglyphes inviolés des rouleaux de papyrus." The quasi-scientific "heavy" word is naturally unprepossessing and odd to a poetic mind.

millier: is, in its primary sense here, not just the mass but the restricted group of a reading public, as in "Millier . . . en auditoires . . . le chef d'oeuvre convoque"; compare "les mille têtes [d'un public]" and "sous le vrai jour des *mille* imaginations latentes . . . elle [la danseuse] te livre à travers le voile dernier qui toujours reste, la nudité de tes concepts." Secondly, the line may refer to the similarly limited mass of signs in a traditional book, as in *Igitur,* or *Les Mots anglais:* "les *milliers* de mots d'une langue sont apparentés *entre eux.*"

aile: is any spiritual impulse for Mallarmé. Here it is obviously *too* kinetic, the emotional response of the mass, or thrill ("frisson familier") as in "banal coup d'aile d'un enthousiasme humain," or "le trop d'aile."

frisson familier: this is linked with the *millier* and refers to popular art, as in "aux jeux antiques [grecques] il convenait d'envelopper les gradins de légende, dont le *frisson* restât, certes, aux robes spectatrices . . . la terreur en ce *pli.*"

Du souriant fracas originel haï	From the smiling original din [of clarities now usually] hated
Entre elles de clartés maîtresses a jailli	Among them of supreme clarities [the god] has surged up
Jusque vers un parvis né pour leur simulacre,	To a parvis made for their [clarities'] representation,
Trompettes tout haut d'or pâmé sur les vélins,	[The god has surged up as] Trumpets aloud of gold fainted on the vellums,
Le dieu Richard Wagner irradiant un sacre	The god Richard Wagner radiating a sacrament
Mal tu par l'encre même en sanglots sibyllins.	Ill hushed by ink itself in sybilline sobs.

The syntax is: From the smiling original din (pure Beauty, now hated by false artists) of supreme clarities, among them, has surged up their god—up to the parvis made for their representation—the god Richard Wagner, irradiating a blessing—he being golden trumpets aloud (and not) fainting on vellum paper (unlike literary art which is silent); (but this beauty is) not really silent even in ink, in (subtle) sybilline sobs.

The main idea is found in "La Musique et les lettres": "de l'orchestre

... tout à coup l'éruptif multiple [cf. *entre elles*] sursautement de la *clarté*, comme les proches *irradiations* d'un lever de jour; vain si le langage (*encre*) ... n'y confère un sens." The partiality to language is not so strongly put in the sonnet, but is there, just the same; compare "C'est la même chose que l'orchestre, sauf que littérairement ou silencieusement ... musique ... plus divine que dans l'expression publique ou symphonique" (Letter to Gosse). The Wagner essay hints at the same distinction.

The original source of light and beautiful sound ("music" in the broad sense Mallarmé favored: harmony) erupts in Wagner's art which, like the pure source, is now hated by false artists and their followers. His music-drama occupies the stage—the *parvis* is the area in front of a church where Western theater began; and the implication is that both the Church and the traditional theater are now outmoded; as Mallarmé said in "Catholicisme": "Oublions." The radiation of the golden sound, with the awe-inspiring din of Wagnerian brass, echoes the serious original pain underlying life; but the music "tames" it, as Mallarmé describes the process in "De Même," see below. This is the play of meaning between *souriant* and *fracas*. The actual quality of Wagner is rendered in this mixture of golden blare ... "l'or de leurs trompettes"—or din, and fainting (*pâmé*), as in the various sweetly swooning or dying falls so typical of the *Meistersinger* prelude, *Tristan*, *Parsifal*. The gold fainted on the vellums is a modulation from this mood to the literature that must, as Mallarmé said—"vain si le langage n'y confère un sens"—have the last word. The last line modestly avers that "this authentic beauty is not badly expressed even in ink," meaning, of course, in his own but partly also in the art to come, for which, as he said to Vielé-Griffin ("Dialogue") and Verlaine ("Autobiographie") he was merely preparing the way.

souriant fracas originel: this is like the explosion at the origin of the cosmos, which is implied on the first page of "Un Coup de dés" (as it is in "Eureka") or "on peut du reste commencer d'un éclat triomphal trop brusque pour durer ... Ce procédé ... notable dans les symphonies, qui le trouvèrent au répertoire de la nature et du ciel," that is, the original burst of light (from a cosmic explosion) repeated in each daybreak or in glorious art.

souriant: implies the taming of the original fear (the birth trauma thunder of air on the freshly exposed ear) through the symmetries, the measured rhythms, hence the control, of art. This is, by now, a well-established psychological truth, which Mallarmé formulated in "l'orgue ... exprime le dehors, un balbutiement de ténèbres énorme, ou leur exclusion de refuge, avant se s'y déverser, extasiées et pacifiées ... causant aux hôtes une plénitude de fierté et ce sécurité." Compare the *sourire* of "Prose."

originel: "[Wagner] considère le secret, représenté, des origines"; note the *or*, the *o* as womb-source, the bright *igi* springing therefrom, as in *Igitur.*

haï: the authentic source is now "hated," ignored by false artists; the word, incidentally, adds some flavor to the *fracas* of Wagner's music, just as in the *Faune* it contributes to the feeling of deep shadow: "massif [ensoleillé] haï par l'ombrage."

entre elles: amid the clarities springs up their god, Wagner; the syntax is: "From the smiling din . . . of supreme clarities, amid them, has sprung up their ("de clartés maîtresses . . . Le dieu") god, Richard Wagner." Also the formula suggests recreated Unity, or harmony, as in "Mots . . . apparentés *entre eux"*; *elles* has a suggestion of *ailes,* the rising "wings" of song, see under *irradier* below.

maîtresses: the light is "masterly" in the sense of cosmic truth. Also, Wagner is called "le Maître."

parvis: "dans ton Temple, à mi-côte de la montagne sainte, dont le lever, de vérités, le plus compréhensif encore, trompette la coupole et invite, à perte de vue du *parvis,* les gazons que le pas de tes élus foule, un repos." The ritual quality of the Wagnerian cult is joined with Mallarmé's meditations on the now-outmoded Church (in "Catholicisme," "De Même," etc.) whose *parvis* would give way to a less sectarian, less vulgarly legendary stage, or a modern cult of his own devising.

simulacre: basically, this refers merely to the "representation," that art is, of the original verities—"Livres, théâtres, et simulacres obtenus avec la couleur ou les marbres: l'Art"; "un simulacre approprié au besoin immédiat, ou l'art officiel qu'on peut aussi appeler vulgaire"; a similar neutral (perhaps slightly condescending) use is found in the Wagner essay: "votre [the public's] raison aux prises avec un simulacre [representation]."

trompettes: like the "trompettes d'or de l'Été" ("Prose"), they combine the golden blare of music with the original source, the sun.

tout haut . . . pâmé: "ces pâmoisons, ou l'âme tout haut" (referring to music). Baudelaire's article on Wagner had spoken of "une lumière intense qui réjouit les yeux et l'âme jusqu'à la pâmoison" (*L'Art romantique*).

The modulation to literary expression, which is silent, is implied in this *pâmé* along with *tu* (hushed). Mallarmé discreetly implies that the expression is all the more (subtly) powerful for that; compare his *"Musicienne du silence"* ("Sainte") or Keats's "unheard music." Another meaning is that words are silenced, "faint"; they are humbled by Wagner's music. Still a further possibility is an allusion to written music, which Mallarmé had early admired for being closed to a profane public: "Ouvrons . . . Wagner . . . nous sommes pris d'un religieux étonnement à la vue de ces processions macabres de signes sévères, chastes, inconnus." Something of the "fainting" modesty (*chastes*) of these figures may be left in the sonnet; compare:

> Magnificat ruisselant
> Jadis selon vêpre et complie:
> (*Sainte*)

Le dieu: "l'évidence du dieu" ("Wagner").

irradiant: "irradiant, par un jeu direct, du principe" ("Wagner"); "prompte irradier ainsi qu'aile l'esprit" ("Remémoration"); compare *entre elles* above.

sacre: In "Le Pitre châtié" the word means "true art"; compare, in "Un Coup de dés," "dernier point qui sacre"; it indicates the metaphysical, quasi-religious value of artistic authenticity.

mal tu: a double negative, implying "not badly expressed"; also, the blackness of ink is in the *mal,* like the original sin implied in the word *doute* ("mon doute ... amas de nuit ancienne," "Faune"; "doute ... l'encre apparentée à la nuit"); *mal* is used in this way on page 3 of "Un Coup de dés."

tu: "La musique, proprement dite, que nous devons piller, démarquer, si le nôtre propre, *tue,* est insuffisante, suggère ce tel poème [the Great Work]" ("Propos"); compare "singulier défi qu'aux poètes dont il usurpe le devoir ... inflige Richard Wagner."

The sense is mainly the quiet "music" of (Mallarmé's) verse as opposed to the *tout haut* "musique proprement dite" of Wagner, admired, but, after all, a bit vulgar, for "Tout se retrempe au ruisseau primitif: pas jusqu'à la source." The subtlety of letters is further implied in the mysterious *sybillins.*

sanglots sybillins: literally, a rapturous but subtle artistic expression. The two words are central to Mallarmé and join in the interesting network of *blancheur sybilline* ("Don du poème"), referring to milk; *blancs sanglots* ("Apparition") referring to music and white flower cups. Thus musical sobs, like the throaty white flower calyxes, are linked with the infantile gulping of milk, the "sybilline whiteness" of which flows from the woman in "Don du poème" or from the "sybilline" nurse in "Hérodiade" ("Scène": "ton lait bu jadis"). The *gl* is sobbing exultation, as in the *gloire du long désir* of "Prose"; "G ... une aspiration simple ... le désir, comme satisfait par *l,* exprime avec la dite liquide, joie, lumière, etc." Note all the *i*'s, which express a brightness and a springing-forth, as in the *jailli,* above.

PHILIPPE SOLLERS

Literature and Totality

He can advance because he goes in mystery.
—IGITUR

THE RUPTURE

If we inquire into the history of literature over the last one hundred years, what strikes us first is the complexity and ambiguity of that adventure, qualities most evident in the fact that a new literary space, a profoundly modified understanding and communication, is combined with a reflexivity (réflexion) within certain texts that renders them somehow indefinitely open in and of themselves. How can we define this situation? As the development of a "new rhetoric"? Or, if rhetoric implies a bimillenary, Greco-Latin culture—a shared, juridical, proprietary speech—as the appareance of something radically other, something that would be linked to an increasingly urgent meditation on *writing* that a philosopher like Jacques Derrida, in a recent and important text, proposes to call *grammatology*? In any case, it would seem that the birth of the concept of *literature* as we know it (which may be precisely situated in the second half of the nineteenth century, at the turning point of the romantic movement, and by names such as Flaubert, Poe, Baudelaire) remains largely inexplicable for us today. In a constellation of names that includes Lautréamont, Rimbaud, Raymond Roussel, Proust, Joyce, Kafka, surrealism and everything related to it, Mallarmé occupies a key position, seemingly equidistant from all the rest. Nor is this constellation so incoherent as it might initially seem: it unfolds against a philosophical and aesthetic background overthrown by Marx, Kierkegaard, Nietzsche, and Freud (and later linguistics); by Manet,

From *Writing and the Experience of Limits*, edited by David Hayman, translated by Philip Barnard with David Hayman. © 1983 by Columbia University Press.

Cézanne, Wagner, Debussy—a background itself referring to an unprecedented scientific, economic, and technical mutation. Mallarmé occupies a
particularly illuminating position for us, because we believe his experience
of language and of literature, of their mutual questioning, as well as his
exposition of this experience, to be the most *explicit* one this movement
produced. We will try here, as Roland Barthes has put it, to give the verb *to
write* its intransitive function, bringing an absolutely literal sense to the act
of reading; in sum, through a series of practical and theoretical gestures, to
define a coherent myth that would correspond to the reality of our situation
today.

The experience of Mallarmé, at once similar to and the opposite of
Dante's ("Destruction was my Beatrice," he writes in one of the letters),
may be briefly defined as a creative (*productrice*) and critical activity bearing
on the symbolism of the book (of the end of the book and its absence) and
of writing: with Mallarmé, this long-eclipsed symbolism seems to reemerge
in a new and reversed form. This does not mean that the term "symbolist,"
a term generally reserved for a category of minor French poets, would be in
any way appropriate here. "Symbolist" has taken on a pejorative meaning,
being a matter of literature, and, not unjustly, immediately evoking the
literary in the worst sense of the word: an obsolete, constricting, idealizing
element, an aesthetic decadentism, in short precisely what some, by a sort of
willful misunderstanding, still attempt to impose on Mallarmé by isolating
fragments of his poems in which these shortcomings may be found. Clearly,
this attitude is not without a certain amount of bad faith, a bad faith openly
shared, moreover, by those who insist on reducing Mallarmé's position to
the "poetic," making him a poet—tormented no doubt, but a poet nonetheless. But Mallarmé does not seen reducible to the type of culture that still
flourishes in our society and benefits from outdated classifications. Quite the
contrary, he is for us one of the experimenters in "this impetuous, insistent
literature that no longer tolerates distinctions between genres and seeks to
burst their limits" (Maurice Blanchot, *Le Livre à Venir*), an insistence whose
significance and goal, whose enigmatic means and end we must attempt to
understand; a bursting and overflow that speak to us, provided we give up
trying to fix them in a mode of thinking that their very appearance transformed and denied. There, where some would see a "failure," an end,
something exhausted, precious, and crepuscular, we sense a recommence-
ment, a summons, something inflexible, the unknown, risk. Today, the
"Mallarmé question" designates both a past and a future, or rather this
poiint in time where the past-future distinction dissolves, where the past
seems accessible from every direction and the future appears to flow back

toward us; this historical turning point that presents itself as the end of history; this *beginning of the return* whose unforeseeable effects, whose organic animation, regrouping and redistribution of final and fundamental elements we are only beginning to decipher: as if a bottom had been touched and a limit attained which would confront us with an absence of time, an ungraspable space, an endless but *finite* totality, another logic, another function of the perhaps still empty pronoun we have just employed: we.

Significantly, Mallarmé initially presents himself as consciously continuing the work of Poe and Baudelaire, from whom he borrows a still classical letter and an already revolutionary spirit. But very soon everything changes. During the well-known crisis of 1866–70, he condemns his early, Baudelairean poems and states one of the essential postulates of his thought: the necessary impersonality of the author. In writing "Hérodiade," in "hollowing out verse," he has, he says, encountered nothingness and death. An event whose import is stranger than one might be led to believe. For this nothingness, this death (this absurdity and this madness) constitute the kernel of the most difficult of his writings: *Igitur. Igitur*, meaning *therefore* in Latin, is thus substituted for another *therefore*, that of Descartes's *cogito* (Descartes who, along with Shakespeare, is Mallarmé's continual reference). With Mallarmé, the "I think, therefore I am" becomes, in a manner of speaking: "I write, therefore I think of the question 'who am I?' " Or: *"who is this therefore in the phrase 'I think, therefore I am'?"* This therefore, this name, this *Igitur*, will function as language returned to its ultimate role, to its own resumé; a locus of negation and absence, but also of self-consciousness in death where one becomes "absolved from movement," locus of an impersonality seized from the "race" (i.e., from history and the individual's biological ancestry)—an experience that will also entail a grave and unsuspected risk (Mallarmé will speak of "very disquieting symptoms brought on by the mere act of writing"). From this point on, an indissociable theory and practice of literary totality will be elaborated through him, a totality that will be the only possible totality of *meaning:* "this subject where everything is interconnected, literary art." "Yes, that literature exists and, if one likes, alone, to the exclusion of everything." "Everything, in the world, exists to end in a book." How should we understand this *everything* (and the exception it provides for)?

Literature, as Mallarmé discovers, is a great deal more than literature (he will go so far as to speak of theology). Or rather, it would seem that the violent crisis in which literature dissimulates and reveals itself, disappears and is defined, confronts us with the indefinite question of meaning itself. Claudel saw Mallarmé superficially as the first writer to have placed himself before the exterior as before a *text* (and not a spectacle) and to have asked himself: "What does it mean?" But that is not the question: it does not "mean," it *writes itself* (*ça s'écrit*). This distinction is decisive, in that it questions not only the habitual order of literature, the rhetoric already shaken by romanticism (and the various types of utterances it implies, from narrative to eloquence), but also thought itself (since "to think is to write without accessories") and simultaneously the *economy* of this thought in the world, the economy of the world *along with* thought and, consequently, social organization. In other words, Mallarmé posits, through writing, a principle of interpretation which is both singular and universal—*a meaning to be made*—and his writing, in order to designate this coincidence between production and interpretation, will be forced to undergo a transmutation that situates it in a clear position of rupture vis-à-vis the discourse of the preceding era. This era could be summed up in a single name: Hugo. Hugo had "reduced" all *prose* (philosophy, eloquence, history) to *verse* and, "as he was verse personally, he practically confiscated from him who thinks, discourses, or relates, the right to express himself (s'énoncer)." Thus Hugo made it clear that the unconscious phenomenon: *verse* (what Mallarmé refers to as the *perfect line, general sign, total word*—thus the exemplary sentence) is the symptom of the fact: literature. "The form referred to as verse is simply itself literature; verse there is as soon as diction is accentuated, rhythm as soon as is style." After Hugo, verse breaks with itself: "All of language, adjusted to metrics, recovering its vital divisions there, escapes itself, according to a free disjunction possessing a thousand discrete elements; it is, I insist, not dissimilar from the multiple cries of an orchestration, which remains verbal." In sum, under the sign of his individuality, Hugo drew all literary forms together in verse, and effectively brought about the disappearance of orthodoxy and community of signification. From this point on, given the break in verse, each individual is obliged to seek and elaborate himself within his own language: "Anyone, with his individual play (jeu) and hearing is able to construct himself an instrument as soon as he breathes, brushes, or strikes it artfully (avec science): to make his own use of it and also to dedicate it to language." "Every individual produces a prosody, new, attuned to his own breath." "For me, a true condition or possibility, not only of expressing oneself, but of modulating oneself at will, arises late."

A major revolution, then, and one that confronts each of us with our responsibility toward a practice that must, no longer metaphorically (*belles lettres* were hiding literature, rhetoric was hiding writing) but literally, "recreate everything":

Sait-on ce que c'est qu'écrire? Une ancienne et très vague mais jalouse pratique, dont gît le sense au mystère du coeur.

Qui l'accomplit, intégralement, se retranche.

Autant, par ouï-dire, que rien existe et soi, spécialement, au reflet de la divinité éparse: c'est, ce jeu insensé d'écrire, s'arroger, en vertu d'un doute—la goutte d'encre apparentée à la nuit sublime—quelque devoir de tout recréer, avec des réminiscences, pour avérer qu'on est bien là où l'on doit être (parce que, permettez-moi d'exprimer cette appréhension, demeure une incertitude). Un à un, chacun de nos orgueils, les susciter, dans leur antériorité et voir. Autrement, si ce n'était cela, une sommation au monde qu'il égale sa hantise à de riches postulats chiffrés, en tant que sa loi, sur le papier blême de tant d'audace—je crois, vraiment, qu'il y aurait duperie, à presque le suicide.

(Do we know what it is to write? An ancient and extremely vague but jealous practice, whose meaning lies in the mystery of the heart.

He who achieves it, integrally, is strengthened.

So much so, it is said, that nothing exists and (the) self, especially, in the reflection of scattered divinity: it is, this mad play of writing, to arrogate to oneself, in pursuance of a doubt—the drop of ink related to the sublime night—some task of recreating everything, with reminiscences, so as to confirm that one is indeed there where one ought to be [because, permit me this apprehension, an uncertainty remains]. One by one, each of our prides, to rouse them, in their anteriority, and to see. Otherwise, were it not this, notice served on the world to make its obsession equivalent to rich numbered postulates, as its legislation, on the paper pale of such audacity—I believe, truly, that there would be dupery, almost to the point of suicide.)

Dupery, suicide: we can see that for Mallarmé the literary engagement is absolutely earnest. He is supposed to have said: "I believe that the world will be saved by a better literature." If authentic, this statement is in no sense a witticism. As for suicide, he rejected it ("Victoriously fled the grand suicide") precisely because of the dupery it illustrates: genuine suicide can only be literary. He implies the *sacrifice* of he who writes, a sacrifice "in relation to personality" and unique in its kind. In truth, there is no subject in itself (and thus it cannot be suppressed by killing it) since the subject is the *consequence* of its language. This language must therefore be pushed to its limits in order to know what is at stake, *who* is at stake in us. A most difficult enterprise, given the extent of the unconsciousness we immediately discover buried deep within us.

SCIENCE

First of all, we must face the multiplicity of languages:

> Les langues imparfaites en cela que plusieurs, manque la suprême: penser étant écrire sans accessoires, ni chuchotement mais tacite encore l'immortelle parole, la diversité, sur terre, des idiomes empêche personne de proférer les mots qui, sinon se trouveraient, par une frappe unique, elle-même matériellement la vérité. . . .— *Seulement, sachons, n'existerait pas le vers:* lui, philosophique-ment rémunère le défaut des langues, complément supérieur.

> (Languages imperfect being several, in the absence of the su-preme one: to think being to write without accessories, not whis-per but still tacit immortal word, diversity, on earth, of individual languages prevents anyone from pronouncing words that would find themselves, by a single stroke, truth itself materialized. . . .— *Except,* let us realize, *verse would not exist:* this, philosophi-cally, pays us back for the failure of languages, a superior com-plement.)

We may then translate, since verse is "literature," it is "literature" that, philosophically, makes up for the shortcomings of languages (and not phi-losophy that would be able to do it by means of literature). This is the "purer sense given to the words of the tribe" insofar as these words correct one another through the death—the negativity—that speaks there and leads us toward a sense of a single language. But by the same token, this process also opens onto *science.* Mallarmé is foretelling here, quite precisely, the science that literature can be and whose image, as science, is none other than linguistics, whose historical development is based in a sort of "return" of the Middle Ages. "The Middle Ages, for all time, remains the incubation as well as the beginning of the world, modern." Literature and science are henceforth in close communication for Mallarmé (the second now having *to pass* into the first, permitting an originary rediscovery). Philology ("yester-day's science") finds in Mallarmé an attentive observer:

Si la vie s'alimente de son propre passé, ou d'une mort continuelle, la Science retrouvera ce fait dans le langage: lequel, distinguant l'homme du reste des choses, imitera encore celui-ci en tant que factice dans l'essence non moins que naturel: réfléchi, que fatal; volontaire, qu'aveugle.

(If life nourishes itself on its own past, or on a continual death, Science will rediscover this fact in language: which, distinguishing man from the remainder of things, will still imitate him, insofar as he is no less factitious than natural in essence; thoughtful than inevitable; willful than blind.)

(We may observe, in passing, the remarkable precision here of the distinction between nature and culture, between conscious and unconscious, or rather the announcement that this distinction is only one historical moment whose oppositions will be resolved by the dialectic of language.)

La Science ayant dans le Langage trouvé une confirmation d'elle-même, doit maintenant devenir une CONFIRMATION du Langage.

La Science n'est donc pas autre chose que la Grammaire, historique et comparée, afin de devenir général, et la Rhétorique.

(Science, having found in Language a confirmation of itself, must now become a CONFIRMATION of Language.)

(Science is thus nothing other than Grammar, historical and comparative, in order to become general, and Rhetoric.)

Mallarmé sees grammar, moreover, as a "latent and particular philosophy, as well as the armature of language." He further carefully distinguishes *speech* from *writing*, *verbal* value from *hieroglyphic* value, and develops his thinking around an autonomous manifestation of writing that, by providing a basis for diction, music, and dance, leads us to the most essential of his contributions: the great statements on the *Book* and the *Theater*. Whence the necessity of distinguishing between two states of speech: the one immediate and raw (associated with monetary circulation: "speaking only relates to things commercially"), also functioning as *universal reportage*, the press, the era's system of informational exchange; the other declared essential— and here we find literature as a generative writing recovered from mechan-

ical and unconscious writing, from vain and self-interested speech. This
distinction leads Mallarmé to a startling proposition, a statement that accurately describes our situation today: "Everything is summed up in aesthetics and political economy." Aesthetics is a phenomenon of linguistic
economy, and thought itself is comprehensible only in economical terms
("mental commodities"). Political economy may thus be understood in light
of language, and we will see how Mallarmé's reflections on the notions of
theater, festival, and fiction are altogether precise in this regard, denouncing
the poverty of a certain variety of economy that remains incapable of or-
ganizing its own play and expenditure.

Before we get to the book and theater, however, we must proceed to a
critique of literature, and above all of its pretensions and claims to realism
and expressivity. The fundamental aesthetic error—the political-economic
error—consists in believing that language is a simple instrument of representation. To naive expression that would, for example, introduce the forest
as forest into its description, Mallarmé opposes *suggestion,* or in other
words a writing that will situate itself on the same side as the world, insofar
as the world is a writing that only a writing is able to bring to light and carry
forward:

> La Nature a lieu, on n'y ajoutera pas; que des cités, les voies
> ferrées et plusieurs inventions formant notre matériel.
> Tout l'acte disponible, à jamais et seulement, reste de saisir les
> rapports, entre temps, rares ou multipliés; d'après quelque état
> intérieur et que l'on veuille à son gré étendre, simplifier le monde.
> A l'égal de créer: la notion d'un objet, échappant, qui fait
> défaut.
> Semblable occupation suffit, comparer les aspects et leur
> nombre tel qu'il frôle notre négligence: y éveillant, pour décor,
> l'ambiguïté de quelques figures belles, aux intersections. La totale
> arabesque, qui les relie, a de vertigineuses sautes en un effroi que
> reconnue; et d'anxieux accords. Avertissant par tel écart, au lieu
> de déconcerter, ou que sa similitude avec elle-même, la soustraie
> en la confondant. Chiffration mélodique tue, de ces motifs qui
> composent une logique, avec nos fibres.

> (Nature takes place, one will not augment it, except for the cities,
> railroads, and several inventions forming our material.
> The whole available act, forever and only, remains to seize
> relations, between times, scarce or multiple according to some

interior state and, willfully, whimsically, extend, simplify the world.

Equal to creating: the notion of an object, escaping, that fails to appear.

A like occupation suffices [us], to compare aspects and their number such that it brushes against our negligence: arousing there, for decor, the ambiguity of a few fine shapes, at the intersections. The total arabesque, that binds them, makes vertiginous leaps in a barely recognized fright; and anxious resolutions. Alerting by such variation, rather than disconcerting, to its similarity with itself, withdraws it while confounding it. Melodic ciphering kills [or: silenced, *tue*], with these motifs that constitute a logic, with our fibers.)

For Mallarmé, who appears to be the first to have undertaken this radiography of the text of phenomena, a landscape, for example, becomes a "rural page," where even if writing is limited to a few mental abbreviations, he can assert that "nothing violates the figures of the valley, the meadow, the tree." The complete text will thus appear as a space twice removed, or as the mirroring of an ideogrammatic and a phonetic writing. Given the profoundly negative function of language—which never names particular things, but rather the absence of that which is named—the *mise en scène* we find here comprises an opening, a renewed virtuality and a paradoxical confirmation of the concrete by means of its evocation (thus we pass from a dual dimension—one thing is equivalent to another, one thing represents another, the sign combines a signifier and a signified—to a *volume of meaning*, a trinitary system that overturns and transforms [qui révolutionne] the totality of signs):

> Au contraire d'une fonction de numéraire facile et représentatif, comme le traite d'abord le foule, le dire, avant tout, rêve et chant, retrouve chez le Poëte, par nécessité constitutive d'un art consacré aux fictions, sa virtualité.
>
> Le vers qui de plusieurs vocables refait un mot total, neuf, étranger à la langue et comme incantatoire, achève cet isolement de la parole: niant, d'un trait souverain, le hasard demeuré aux termes malgré l'artifice de leur retrempe alternée en le sens et la sonorité, et vous cause cette surprise de n'avoir ouï jamais tel fragment ordinaire d'élocution, en même temps que la réminiscence de l'objet nommé baigne dans une neuve atmosphère.

(As opposed to a facile and representative numerical function, such as it first receives from the crowd, speaking, above all, dreams and sings, rediscovers in the Poet, by the constitutive necessity of an art devoted to fictions, its virtuality.

Verse that from several vocables remakes a new, total word, foreign to language and as if incantatory, achieves this isolation of speech: denying, with a sovereign stroke, the chance that adheres to terms despite the artifice of redipping them alternately in meaning and sound, and gives you this surprise at never having heard this particular ordinary fragment of elocution, while the reminiscence of the named object bathes in a new atmosphere.)

In such an economy, silence becomes one element of language among others, since we must constantly "deny the unutterable (indicible) that lies." Here again, the error stems from the fact that we instinctively believe in the unutterable, in the inexpressible—and it is precisely to the degree that we do so that we become convinced we must *express* ourselves. Silence, in writing, is clearly the white, the blank, or in other words a "distance copied mentally," the internal and intelligible slope of music, itself "the sum of relations existing in all things":

> qu'une moyenne étendue de mots, sous la compréhension du regard, se range en traits définitifs, avec quoi le silence.

> (let a medium stretch of words, beneath the comprehension of the gaze, be organized in definite traits, with which silence.)

Mallarmé formulates a particular technique whose "guarantee" will be *syntax*, a technique intended to short-circuit the wastage of meaning that surrounds us. It becomes necessary to intervene continually in this play, to act upon it so as not to be acted upon. To this end, the scriptor distinguishes himself from the speaker's *bavardage* by means of a reversal that consists in *not expressing*, or in other words making his discourse objective, by means of a sort of ritual (and at this point we abandon our fascination with "truth"):

> Le sot bavarde sans rien dire, et errer de même à l'exclusion d'un goût notoire pour la prolixité et précisément afin de ne pas exprimer quelque chose, représente un cas spécial qui aura été le mien.

(A fool prattles without saying a thing, and likewise to talk on and on, except for a marked taste for prolixity precisely in order to express nothing at all, represents a special instance that will have been my own.)

To unmask the truth-falsity duality that governs the expressive economy, we must reach that point where what counts is no longer *me*, but rather my language:

> Je réclame la restitution, au silence impartial, pour que l'esprit essaie à se rapatrier, de tout—chocs, glissements, les trajectoires illimitées et sûres, tel état opulent aussitôt évasif, une inaptitude délicieuse à finir, ce raccourci, ce trait—l'appareil; moins le tumulte des sonorités, transfusibles, encore, en du songe.

> (I demand a return to impartial silence, so that the mind may attempt its reconciliation, of the whole—shocks, shifts, limitless and dependable trajectories, a certain opulent immediately evasive condition, a marvelous inaptitude for finishing, this abridgement, this line—apparatus; minus the tumult of sounds, yet transfusible into dream.)

We arrive, then, at the consciousness of writing, at this "reciprocal contamination of the work and the means," where that which speaks is writing itself:

> Ecrire—
> L'encrier, cristal comme une conscience, avec sa goutte, au fond, de ténèbres relative à ce que quelque chose soit: puis, écarte la lampe.
> Tu remarquas on n'écrit pas, lumineusement, sur champ obscur, l'alphabet des astres, seul, ainsi s'indique, ébauché ou interrompu; l'homme poursuit noir sur blanc.
> Ce pli de sombre dentelle, qui retient l'infini, tissé par mille, chacun selon le fil ou prolongement ignoré son secret, assemble des entrelacs distants où dort un luxe à inventorier, stryge, noeud, feuillages et présenter.
> Avec le rien de mystère, indispensable, qui demeure, exprimé, quelque peu.

> (To write—
> The inkwell, clear as a consciousness, with its drop, at the

bottom, of shadows related to the fact that something is: then, remove the lamp.

You noticed, one does not write, luminously, on a dark field, the alphabet of the stars, alone, thus indicates itself, sketched or interrupted; man pursues black on white.

This fold of somber lace, that curbs the infinite, woven by a thousand, each according to the thread or unknown extension his secret, assembles distant interweavings where sleeps a luxury to inventory, vampire, knot, leafage, and to present.

With the nothing of mystery, indispensable, that remains, expressed, somewhat.)

This is what Mallarmé refers to as *restricted action*, which for him is the only action based in reality; all others collide with the absence of a genuine *Present* (the present is the illusion of whoever lives within the field of truth), an absence that makes suicide and abstention impossible, since we can never declare ourselves to be our own contemporaries. An action that, on the contrary, deliberately and lucidly addresses itself to the future by means of a radical operation.

ECONOMY

At the same time, the author's necessary disappearance in writing, which after all has produced him, takes place in anticipation of a *reading* which is no ordinary one. Reading, for Mallarmé, is a *practice*, a *desperate practice*. First of all, rather than abandoning himself to representations, the reader must have direct access to the language of the text (and not to its images, its "characters"), he must understand that *what he reads is himself*. The crowd is manipulated by its unconscious—and this is why, in one sense, the crowd is musical. But within this crowd (and made possible only by it), the individual who reads communicates with his own language, rediscovered in what he reads. "Myth, the eternal: communion through the book. To each a total part." "A solitary tacit concert is given, through reading, to the mind." In sum, the book is the locus of a double movement: on the one hand, a suppression of the author (Mallarmé frequently compares the book to a *tomb*), who abandons speech for writing and thereby lends himself to the transformation of time into space:

L'oeuvre pure implique la disparition élocutoire du poëte, qui cède l'initiative aux mots, par le heurt de leur inégalité mobilisés,

(The pure work implies the elocutionary disappearance of the poet, who surrenders the initiative to words mobilized by the clash of their inequality.)

and on the other, the development of the reader that confirms the victory thus obtained over chance and silence:

Et, quand s'aligna, dans une brisure, la moindre, disséminée, le hasard vaincu mot par mot, indéfectiblement le blanc revient, tout à l'heure gratuit, certain maintenant, pour conclure que rien au-delà et authentiquer le silence.

(Then, when aligned, in the smallest, scattered breaks [on the page], chance has been vanquished word by word, the blank unfailingly returns, recently gratuitous, now in certainty, to show that nothing lies beyond and to authenticate silence.)

The reader's confirmation and recognition of himself, however, collides here not only with the conditioning he undergoes socially, a conditioning in which "the horizon and spectacle are reduced to a middling gust of banality" by current habits of consumption, but also with his unconscious, which, by a sort of inevitable transfer, causes the text he has only just seized from the unconscious to seem obscure, unreadable. Rather than coming to terms with his own unintelligibility vis-à-vis himself, he accuses the text of hermeticism—without realizing that, as always, he thus does no more than to speak of himself and the criteria that have been imposed on him. Mallarmé writes: "There is surely something of the occult within us all; I certainly believe in something abstruse, a closed and hidden signifier (signifiant fermé et caché), that resides in the ordinary, for no sooner does the mob pick up some trace of it (sitôt cette masse jetée vers quelque trace) than it becomes a reality, existing, for example, on a sheet of paper, in a piece of writing—although not in itself—(in) that which is obscure: the mob becomes agitated, a hurricane anxious to attribute its darkness to whatever it can, profusely, flagrantly." "Faced with aggression," he adds, "I prefer to reply that some contemporaries do not know how to read." Perhaps we can see these remarks in a fresh light through a consideration of the basic postulates of psychoanalysis, particularly the more recent one, that the unconscious is structured like a language. This *closed and hidden signifier* that Mallarmé judges to be in each person has now, so to speak, been *proven* scientifically. To such an extent that the seemingly unproblematic question of *knowing how to read* may be posed with all its virulence. Mallarmé's writing, with its abridged and multiple space, its twists, its latent relations, its internal and visible intersections, confronts us with a question for which we generally have no more than a ready-made answer, our language being in general a ready-made and received one: we fail to realize that to think is to write, that to read is to read what we are—and thus the play of language escapes us, we continually misunderstand the nature of literature insofar as we disregard the impersonality of its play:

> Impersonnifié, le volume autant qu'on s'en sépare comme auteur, ne réclame approche de lecteur. Tel, sache, entre les accessoires humains, il a lieu tout seul: fait, étant. Le sens enseveli se meut et dispose, en choeur, des feuillets.

> (Impersonalized, the volume, inasmuch as one is separated from it as author, requires no reader's proximity. As such, know, among human accessories, it takes place alone: made, being. The buried meaning stirs and arranges, in concert, the leaves.)

The book as "spiritual instrument," the book that would correspond to this necessity of the book, to its meaning, would be written by means of *transposition* and *structure* (Mallarmé's terms). We have already seen the necessity of transposition (the impossibility of "realism"); as to structure, Mallarmé remarks that "ordering (ordonnance) is necessary in order to omit the author." It is necessary, then, that the line's location in the (theatrical) play, as well as the play's in the volume, be meditated—in order to go beyond the volume, toward a new space (an intertextual space) where books would read, clarify, and write one another, where books would ultimately be replaced by a real text that would be the permanent interpretation of the world, "the orphic interpretation of the earth," the ongoing letter of meaning (la lettre courant du sens) at last formulated and brought into play. "All books fuse together a few esteemed old saws." The book that would truly be *the Book* (that which delivers and delimits everything [qui nous livre le tout] "is written in nature in such a manner as to allow only those intent upon seeing nothing to shut their eyes"; "it has been attempted, unawares, by anyone who has written." This book must consequently be *feasible;* and the object of literature, the completion of its history, will be nothing other than its culmination: "nothing that is not asserted (proféré) will endure." If Hegel saw the end of History in the form of a closed book, Mallarmé, for his part, opens, disperses and *overturns* it (le retourne), situating it within the space where we undertake to live, to write and read ourselves, and to die.

Mallarmé knows he will not be able to accomplish *the Book:* but in any case, he assigns the *impossible* to all subsequent literature as goal. Furthermore, he attempts to make its fragments conspicuous, to give instructions for its composition, to ensure that our thought moves irrevocably towards it:

> Le livre, expansion totale de la lettre, doit d'elle tirer, directement, une mobilité et spacieux, par correspondances, instituer un jeu, on ne sait, qui confirme la fiction.
>
> —Les mots, d'eux-mêmes, s'exaltent à mainte facette reconnue la plus rare ou valant pour l'esprit, centre de suspens vibratoire; qui les perçoit indépendamment de la suite ordinaire, projetés, en parois de grotte, tant que dure leur mobilité ou principe, étant ce qui ne se dit pas du discours: prompts tous, avant extinction, à une réciprocité de feux distante ou présentée de biais comme contingence.

> (The book, total expansion of the letter, must draw from it, directly, a mobility and, being spacious, through correspondences, institute a game, who can say, that confirms the fiction.
>
> On their own, words rise up and reveal many a facet recognized as the most rare or precious for the mind, center of vibratory suspension; which perceives them separated from their ordinary sequence, projected as on grotto walls, so long as that mobility which is their principle endures, being that part of discourse which remains unspoken: all quick, before dying away, to an exchange of fires that is distant, or obliquely presented as contingency.)

One of these fragments (the deferred return of *Igitur*) will be "Un Coup de dés," in which writing orchestrates its new powers (no longer the transcription of a meaning, but the virtually spontaneous upheaval of the written surface; no longer the recording and comprehension of a previous word, but an active inscription in the process of forging its own course; no longer the truth or secret of one person alone, the usual humanist reference, but nonpersonal literality in a world based on a dice throw):

> Tout se passe, par raccourci, en hypothèse; on évite le récit. Ajouter que de cet emploi à nu de la pensée avec retraits,

prolongements, fuites, ou son dessin même, résulte, pour qui
veut lire à haute voix, une partition.

(Everything takes place, through foreshortening, as hypothesis;
narrative is avoided. Add that this naked use of thought with
recesses, extensions, leakages, or its very arrangement, produces,
for whoever would read aloud, a musical score.)

This new semantic space (espace significatif) is presented vertically, *upright*
(debout); as if the uniform surface of discourse had been straightened out
and torn, as if the coffin of rhetorical speech had been forced open, as if
language were undergoing a rape whose mark was a deep—written—rupture of the sentence. "Un Coup de dés" is a single sentence: "Un coup de dés
jamais n'abolira le hasard (A toss of the dice will never abolish chance)."
Subjected to an atomic disintegration and dissemination, to an incessant
effervescence, the sentence, which we have previously experienced only as
surface, is thus presented as the most complex of organisms, as the sum-
mation of all complexity (*as a name*)—the figure and limit of the world's
henceforth manifest imbrication, of chance, play, and the thinking in which
"man" produces himself—whereas the surface of discourse, ultimately, can
refer only to an unresolvable man-world duality. Within this space, no
longer unified and horizontal, but vertically divisible—which a priori presupposes a new physics, a new topology—what emerges is no longer the
usual situation, in which one person addresses another, but rather a double
structure based in the text. Scriptor and reader are situated on the same side
of the fictive screen; their operations become simultaneous and complemen-
tary. The same and the other speak themselves together (se disent ensemble); when the same speaks, the other falls silent—but this silence remains
an active and accentuated speech. The fiction is *confirmed,* or in other
words continually written and played out at its source. The book is nothing
other than the transition between the world and the theater, the world-as-
text's theatrical appearance, the "naked use of thought," the *operation:* not
simply one work (oeuvre) among others, but the dramatization (mise en
oeuvre) of everything that exists.

MYTH

The fundamental problem is therefore the theater, the three-dimensional
book. But Mallarmé's texts have functioned in this manner since *Igitur:*
"This tale addresses itself to the reader's intelligence, which itself stages the
play." For Mallarmé, meditation on the book—since it concerns the unveil-

ing of totality as writing and as meaning—cannot be separated from all other concrete problems. The book is not made simply to be read and closed again, but to be utilized (opéré) and consumed, so that it can *take place* in *reality* which, in its absence, remains an inorganic fiction. *Fiction*, for Mallarmé, is a central term. To define a "domain of fiction," a "perfect comprehensive term" (i.e., one that would comprehend all human activities), he proposes, for example, the relation:

thus indicating that the circulation of money providing the conditions for technology corresponds to the circulation of language that determines the forms and development of (innervant) "art" (music, dance, theater). The totality of these operations, unveiling and echoing one another even at the level of the *letter* that rules them all, is referred to as *fiction*, and the book—interpreted, completed, put into practice—is what gives this fiction *meaning*, in other words, reality. We thus move into a new mode of understanding: phenomena are returned to their figures (chiffres) and to the cycles that clarify their reciprocity. Mallarmé sees clearly that the decadence of religion is linked to the fact that *expenditure* is no longer conceivable within our society. The *mass*, for example, interests him as a technique of gratuity, a symbolic ritual that could serve a particular function: "it could not be that in a religion, even in its subsequent abandonment, the race has not placed its unknown intimate secret. The time has come, with the necessary detachment, to undertake its excavation." Writing will therefore operate on the level of *myths*—and the theater can become the mode for this setting down and fixing of myths seized from the unconscious of an obscurantist society dominated by money. Mallarmé is fully aware of the obstacles: the theater is in an unprecedented state of debasement and servility—and the foundation of the modern popular Poem, "which will be marveled at by a suddenly invented reading majority," is not yet possible. Nothing but limited works, narrow mythologies, and "representations" are being put forward; we are incapable of seeing things "themselves," or in other words of seeing "the play written in the folio of the sky and mimed by Man with the gestures of his passions." The theater, which for Mallarmé is of a "superior essence," is the "moment when the horizon shines within humanity, the opening of the chimera's maw that has been misunderstood and carefully frustrated by the social order." Taking up Gautier's ironic comment that "We should have nothing but vaudeville—they'd make some changes from time to time," Mallarmé adds, more seriously: "Replace Vaudeville by Mystery, a multiple tetralogy deploying itself in parallel to a newly begun cycle of years and insist that its text be as inviolable as the Law: there you have it, almost!"

What is called for is a theater based on the Book and in which the "mental milieu equalizing stage and audience" can appear. In truth, says Mallarmé, "the mental situation is much like the meanders of a drama"; the theater consists in making this process, hidden by time, manifest in simultaneous, spatial terms: "a dramatic work shows the successive development of the action's externalizations, without any one moment achieving reality, and without anything, in the last analysis, ever happening." The Theater would be the reading of the Book, its writing operating "within the labyrinth of anguish art elaborates (que mène l'art)." The most precise theatrical approximation to this myth is Hamlet, who, "reading from the book of himself," "externalizes, on the boards, the personage of an intimate and secret tragedy," "the latent lord who cannot become"—for "there is no other subject, you may be sure: the antagonism between man's dream and the fatalities bestowed upon his existence by misfortune."

The *stage* which is "our only magnificence"—the only place where the Book's envisioned totality may appear to us—is in some sense the painting of the text, where "everything moves according to a symbolic reciprocity between types or in relation to a single figure." "Mime, thinker, the tragedian interprets as a plastic and mental sovereign of art." The world becomes intelligible, then, as a writing at the intersection of the Theater and the Book—and this intersection is the Dance: the dancer has only to trace out her corporeal writing in order for the entire company, assembled around the *star,* to mime the writing of the constellations, the inverse of that which traces itself on paper. *Choreography* reveals the role of figures which themselves supply the key to *characters* or human types. The story is a drama, and ballet an emblematics, a hieroglyphic grouping; the whole constitutes a milieu of fiction in which reading becomes a "notation of sentiments in unspoken sentences." The dancer "delivers (livre), through the final veil which always remains, the nudity of concepts and silently writes [the] vision, like a Sign, which she is." It is important to note that Mallarmé points out here, in passing, the kinship between this writing and that of the *Dream.*

Through reading we may perform any play for ourselves, "inwardly." If we want to become aware of the writing that this reading is, however, we must appear on the stage (experience life). This is the point at which the latent drama is manifested by a tearing that affirms "the irreducibility of our instincts." So we come to "a musical celebration and also a figuration of life, confiding its mystery to language alone and to mimetic evolution (l'évolution mimique)."

Thus Mallarmé posits the existence of a "theater proper to the spirit," by virture of which the poet "awakens, by means of the written, the master of revels in each of us." WE MUST THEREFORE REALIZE THE POSSIBILITY OF THE TEXT AS THEATER ALONG WITH THAT OF THE THEATER AND OF LIFE AS TEXT if we want to take our place within the writing that defines us: "knowing that in the spirit of anyone who has dreamed all of humanity in himself (a rêvé les humains jusqu'à soi) nothing exists but an exact amount of the pure rhythmic motifs of being, which are its recognizable signs; my pleasure is to decipher them everywhere."

The language that rediscovers the totality of fiction is consequently the "foundation" of all possible art:

> Aux convergences des autres arts située, issue d'eux et les gouvernant, la Fiction ou Poésie.

> (At the convergence of the other arts, emerging from and governing them, is Fiction or Poetry.)

This fundamental fiction reveals its own status as an orchestration of myths; for it is directly linked to the functioning of that thinking which dissolves myths in order to *remake* them. We may thus imagine a global, theatrical, theoretical, practical, and mental activity devoted to "the expansion of symbols or their preparation," an activity based not upon fable or legend (which, for Mallarmé, is Wagner's error), not in this or that particular myth, but on the unveiling of Myths and their unification:

> Le Théâtre les appelle, non: pas de fixes, ni de séculaires et de notoires, mais un, dégagé de personnalité, car il compose notre aspect multiple.

> (The Theater summons them [myths], no: not established, or secular and well-known, but one, removed from personality, since it composes our multiple aspect.)

Concerning this condition, Mallarmé may still write that "Man and his authentic stay on earth, exchange a reciprocity of proofs."

"THE INTERREGNUM"

We must now specify the precise role of one who in writing, in accepting death through literature, is more or less compromised within his society. This existence is initially experienced as an inconvenience: "Literary existence, except for one, [the] true, which is spent in arousing presence, within harmonies and significations, occurs, with the world, only as inconvenience." And further: "Literature, which has this in common with hunger, consists in suppressing the Gentleman who remains in the writing of it. What function can he have, in an everyday sense, in the eyes of those around him?"

The writer or, more precisely, the scriptor, whatever he may do, is therefore entirely cut off insofar as his work is directed at the unconscious functioning of language, insofar as this work constitutes a continually renewed and mute solitude which Mallarmé describes as "the derogation of destiny, at least, socially." Nevertheless, the consequences of this retreat are paradoxical: if he forbids himself all links and all ownership, if he forces himself to "satisfy some singular instinct, to possess nothing and simply to pass by," if he thus defines someone desiring to be nothing and to have nothing in particular, someone "infinitely alone on the earth"—he also discovers an unforeseen coincidence with the most alienated individual, the proletarian. It is of him that Mallarmé is thinking, as he writes: "How sad that for these my production remains, especially, like clouds at dusk, vain." "The constellations," he writes, "are beginning to glimmer: how I would like, in the darkness that steals over the blind herd, for some points of light, such as [were] thought just now, to become visible, despite these sealed eyes that do not pick them out—to establish this, to give it precision, to give it voice (pour le fait, pour l'exactitude, pour qu'il soit dit)."

To establish this, to give it precision, to give it voice: the life of whoever writes is an "interregnum," and the seemingly useless work or play he pursues is linked to that future we know to be the locus of all symbolic work. Literature belongs to the future, and the future, as Mallarmé writes, "is never anything but the flash of what must have been produced previously or near the beginning." By virtue of a strange circularity, the man who *is* nothing and the one who *has* nothing are thus profoundly joined, vis-à-vis those who possess and consequently believe themselves to be something. Mallarmé's thought, then, is neither betrayed nor distorted if we affirm that his work was ultimately directed toward a single thought, a thought we might refer to, moreover, as the *formal thought*: that of revolution, in its most literal sense.

PAUL DE MAN

Lyric and Modernity

My essay title and procedure call for some preliminary clarification before I get involved in the technicalities of detailed exegesis. I am not concerned, in this paper, with a descriptive characterization of contemporary
poetry but with the problem of literary modernity in general. The term
"modernity" is not used in a simple chronological sense as an approximate
synonym for "recent" or "contemporary" with a positive or negative value-
emphasis added. It designates more generally the problematical possibility
of all literature's existing in the present, of being considered, or read, from
a point of view that claims to share with it its own sense of a temporal
present. In theory, the question of modernity could therefore be asked of
any literature at any time, contemporaneous or not. In practice, however,
the question has to be put somewhat more pragmatically from a point of
view that postulates a roughly contemporaneous perspective and that favors
recent over older literature. This necessity is inherent in the ambivalent
status of the term "modernity," which is itself partly pragmatic and descriptive, partly conceptual and normative. In the common usage of the
word the pragmatic implications usually overshadow theoretical possibilities that remain unexplored. My emphasis tries to restore this balance to
some degree: hence the stress on literary categories and dimensions that
exist independently of historical contingencies, the main concession being
that the examples are chosen from so-called modern literature and criticism.
The conclusions, however, could, with some minor modifications, be trans-

From *Blindness and Insight: Essays in the Rhetoric of Contemporary Criticism*.
©1971, 1983 by Paul de Man. Oxford University Press, 1983.

ferred to other historical periods and be applicable whenever or wherever literature as such occurs.

What is thus assumed to be possible in time—and it is a mere assumption, since the compromise or theorizing about examples chosen on pragmatic grounds does in fact beg the question and postpones the issue—can much more easily be justified in geographical, spatial terms. My examples are taken primarily from French and German literature. The polemical aspects of the argument are directed against a trend prevalent among a relatively small group of German scholars, a group that is representative but by no means predominant in Continental criticism. But it should not be difficult to find equivalent texts and critical attitudes in English or American literature; the indirect route by way of France and Germany should allow for a clearer view of the local scene, once the necessary transitions have been made. The natural expansion of the essay would lie in this direction.

With modernity thus conceived of as a general and theoretical rather than as a historical theme, it is not a priori certain that it should be treated differently when discussing lyric poetry than it should, for example, when discussing narrative prose or the drama. Can the factual distinction between prose, poetry, and the drama relevantly be extended to modernity, a notion that is not inherently bound to any particular genre? Can we find out something about the nature of modernity by relating it to lyric poetry that we could not find out in dealing with novels or plays? Here again, the point of departure has to be chosen for reasons of expediency rather than for theoretical reasons, in the hope that the expediency may eventually receive theoretical confirmation. It is an established fact that, in contemporary criticism, the question of modernity is asked in a somewhat different manner with regard to lyric poetry than with regard to prose. Genre concepts seem somehow to be sensitive to the idea of modernity, thus suggesting a possible differentiation between them in terms of their temporal structures—since modernity is, in essence, a temporal notion. Yet the link between modernity and the basic genres is far from clear. On the one hand, lyric poetry is often seen not as an evolved but as an early and spontaneous form of language, in open contrast to more self-conscious and reflective forms of literary discourse in prose. In eighteenth-century speculations about the origins of language, the assertion that the archaic language is that of poetry, the contemporary or modern language that of prose is a commonplace. Vico, Rousseau, and Herder, to mention only the most famous names, all assert the priority of poetry over prose, often with a value-emphasis that seems to interpret the loss of spontaneity as a decline—although this particular aspect of eighteenth-century primitivism is in fact a great deal less single-minded and uniform in the authors themselves than in their later interpreters. Be this as it may, it remains that, regardless of value judgments, the definition of poetry as the first language gives it an archaic, ancient quality that is the opposite of modern, whereas the deliberate, cold, and rational character of discursive prose, which can only imitate or represent the original impulse if it does not ignore it altogether, would be the true language of modernity. The same assumption appears during the eighteenth century, with "music" substituting for "poetry" and opposed to language or literature as an equivalent of prose. This becomes, as is well known, a commonplace of post-Symbolist aesthetics, still present in writers such as Valéry or Proust, though here perhaps in an ironic context that has not always been recognized as such. Music is seen, as Proust puts it, as a unified, preanalytical "communication of the soul," a "possibility that remained without sequel [because] mankind chose other ways, those of spoken and written language" [*Remembrance of Things Past* "The Captive"]. In this nostalgic primitivism—which Proust is demystifying rather than sharing— the music of poetry and the rationality of prose are opposed as ancient is opposed to modern. Within this perspective, it would be an absurdity to speak of the modernity of lyric poetry, since the lyric is precisely the antithesis of modernity.

Yet, in our own twentieth century, the social projection of modernity known as the avant-garde consisted predominantly of poets rather than of prose writers. The most aggressively modern literary movements of the century, surrealism and expressionism, in no way value prose over poetry, the dramatic or the narrative over the lyric. In the recent past, this trend may have changed. One speaks readily, in contemporary French literature, of a *nouveau roman,* but not of a *nouvelle poésie.* French structuralist "new criticism" is much more concerned with narrative prose than with poetry and sometimes rationalizes this preference into an overtly anti-poetic aesthetics. But this is in part a local phenomenon, a reaction against a traditional bias in French criticism in favor of poetry, perhaps also an innocent rejoicing like that of a child that has been given a new toy. The discovery that there are critical devices suitable for the analysis of prose is by no means such a sensational novelty for English and American critics, in whom these new French studies of narrative modes may awaken a more sedate feeling of déjà vu. In Germany, however, among critics that are by no means adverse or ideologically opposed to the contemporary French schools, lyric poetry remains the preferred topic of investigation for a definition of modernity. The editors of a recent symposium on the subject "The Lyric as Paradigm of Modernity" assert as a matter of course that "the lyric was

chosen as paradigmatic for the evolution toward modern literature, because
the breakdown of literary forms occurred earlier and can be better documented in this genre than in any other" (*Immanente Ästhetik, Ästhetische
Reflexion: Lyrik als Paradigma der Moderne*, W. Iser, ed.). Here then, far
from being judged absurd, the question of modernity in the lyric is considered as the best means of access to a discussion of literary modernity in
general. In purely historical terms, this position is certainly sensible: it would
be impossible to speak relevantly about modern literature without giving a
prominent place to lyric poetry; some of the most suggestive theoretical
writing on modernity is to be found in essays dealing with poetry. Nevertheless, the tension that develops between poetry and prose when they are
considered within the perspective of modernity is far from meaningless; the
question is complex enough to have to be postponed until well beyond the
point we can hope to reach in this essay.

When Yeats, in 1936, had to write the introduction to his anthology of
modern English poetry, in a text that otherwise shows more traces of fatigue
than of inspiration, he largely used the opportunity to set himself apart from
Eliot and Pound as more modern than they, using Walter James Turner and
Dorothy Wellesley as props to represent a truly modern tendency of which
he considered himself to be the main representative. That he also had the
courage of his convictions is made clear by the fact that he allotted to
himself, in the body of the anthology, twice as much space as to anyone
else—with the sole exception of Oliver St. John Gogarty, hardly a dangerous rival. The theoretical justification given for this claim is slight but, in the
light of later developments, quite astute. The opposition between "good"
and modern poetry—his own—and not so good and not so modern poetry—mainly Eliot's and Pound's—is made in terms of a contrast between
poetry of representation and a poetry that would no longer be mimetic. The
mimetic poetry has for its emblem the mirror, somewhat incongruously
associated with Stendhal, though it is revealing that the reference is to a
writer of prose and that the prosaic element in Eliot's precision and in
Pound's chaos is under attack. This is a poetry depending on an outside
world, regardless of whether this world is seen in neat, objective contours or
as shapeless flux. Much less easy to characterize is the other kind of poetry,
said to be of the "private soul . . . always behind our knowledge, though
always hidden . . . the sole source of pain, stupefaction, evil" (*Oxford Book
of Modern Verse, 1892–1935*, W. B. Yeats, ed.). Its emblem, as we all know
from M. H. Abrams, if not necessarily from Yeats, is the lamp, though here
Abrams's stroke of genius in singling out this emblematic pair for the title
of his book on Romantic literary theory is perhaps slightly misleading, not

in terms of the poetics of Romanticism but with regard to Yeats's own meaning. In Abrams's book, the lamp becomes the symbol of the constitutive, autonomous self, the creative subjectivity that certainly looms large in Romantic theory, as an analogous microcosm of the world of nature. The light of that lamp is the self-knowledge of a consciousness, an internalized metaphor of daylight vision; mirror and lamp are both symbols of light, whatever their further differences and oppositions may be. But Yeats's lamp is not that of the self, but of what he calls the "soul," and self and soul, as we know from his poetry, are antithetical. Soul does not, at any rate, belong to the realm of natural or artificial (i.e., represented or imitated) light, but to that of sleep and darkness. It does not dwell in real or copied nature, but rather in the kind of wisdom that lies hidden away in books. To the extent that it is private and inward, the soul resembles the self, and only by ways of the self (and not by ways of nature) can one find access to it. But one has to move through the self and beyond the self; truly modern poetry is a poetry that has become aware of the incessant conflict that opposes a self, still engaged in the daylight world of reality, of representation, and of life, to what Yeats calls the soul. Translated into terms of poetic diction, this implies that modern poetry uses an imagery that is both symbol and allegory, that represents objects in nature but is actually taken from purely literary sources. The tension between these two modes of language also puts in question the autonomy of the self. Modern poetry is described by Yeats as the conscious expression of a conflict within the function of language as representation and within the conception of language as the act of an autonomous self.

Some literary historians, who necessarily approached the problem of modern poetry in a less personal way, have written about modern lyric poetry in strikingly similar terms. Hugo Friedrich, one of the last representatives of an outstanding group of Romanic scholars of German origin that includes Vossler, Curtius, Auerbach, and Leo Spitzer, has exercized a great deal of influence through his short book *The Structure of the Modern Lyric*. Friedrich uses the traditional historical pattern, also present in Marcel Raymond's *From Baudelaire to Surrealism*, making French poetry of the nineteenth century and especially Baudelaire the starting point of a movement that spread to the whole body of Western lyric poetry. His main concern, understandably enough in an explicator of texts, is the particular difficulty and obscurity of modern poetry, an obscurity not unrelated to the light-symbolism of Yeats's mirror and lamp. The cause of the specifically modern kind of obscurity—which Friedrich to some extent deplores—resides for him, as for Yeats, in a loss of the representational function of poetry that goes parallel with the loss of a sense of selfhood. Loss of representational reality (*Entrealisierung*) and loss of self (*Entpersönlichung*) go hand in hand: "With Baudelaire, the depersonalization of the modern lyric starts, at least in the sense that the lyrical voice is no longer the expression of a unity between the work and the empirical person, a unity that the romantics, contrary to several centuries of earlier lyrical poetry, had tried to achieve" [*The Structure of the Modern Lyric*]. And in Baudelaire "idealization no longer, as in the older aesthetic, strives toward an embellishment of reality but strives for a loss of reality." Modern poetry—this is said with reference to Rimbaud—"is no longer concerned with a reader. It does not want to be understood. It is a hallucinatory storm, flashes of lightning hoping at most to create the fear before danger that stems from an attraction toward danger. They are texts without self, without 'I.' For the self that appears from time to time is the artificial, alien self projected in the *lettre du voyant*." Ultimately, the function of representation is entirely taken over by sound effects without reference to any meaning whatever.

Friedrich offers no theoretical reasons to explain why the loss of representation (it would be more accurate to speak of a putting into question or an ambivalence of representation) and the loss of self—with the same qualification—are thus linked. He gives instead the crudest extraneous and pseudo-historical explanation of this tendency as a mere escape from a reality that is said to have become gradually more unpleasant ever since the middle of the nineteenth century. Gratuitous fantasies, "the absurd," he writes, "become aspects of irreality into which Baudelaire and his followers want to penetrate, *in order to* avoid an increasingly confining reality." Critical overtones of morbidity and decadence are unmistakable, and the possibility of reading Friedrich's book as an indictment of modern poetry— a thesis nowhere explicitly stated by the author—is certainly not entirely foreign to the considerable popular success of the book. Here again, it is preferable for the sake of clarity to put the value judgment temporarily between brackets. Friedrich's historicist background, however crude, and his suggestion that the evolution of modern literature follows a line that is part of a wider historical pattern allow him to give his essay a genetic historical coherence. A continuous genetic chain links the work of Baudelaire to that of his successors Mallarmé, Rimbaud, Valéry, and their counterparts in the other European literatures. The chain extends in both directions, for Friedrich finds antecedents of the modern trend as far back as Rousseau and Diderot, and makes romanticism a link in the same chain. Symbolist and post-Symbolist poetry appear therefore as a later, more self-conscious but also more morbid version of certain Romantic insights; both form a historical continuum in which distinctions can be made only in terms of degree, not of kind, or in terms of extrinsic considerations, ethical, psychological, sociological, or purely formal. A similar view is represented in this country by M. H. Abrams, for example, in a paper entitled "Coleridge, Baudelaire and Modernist Poetics" published in 1964.

This scheme is so satisfying to our inherent sense of historical order that it has rarely been challenged, even by some who would not in the least agree with its potential ideological implications. We find, for instance, a group of younger German scholars, whose evaluation of modernity would be strongly opposed to what is implied by Friedrich, still adhering to exactly the same historical scheme. Hans Robert Jauss and some of his colleagues have considerably refined the diagnosis of obscurity that Friedrich had made the center of his analysis. Their understanding of medieval and baroque literature—which Friedrich chose to use merely in a contrasting way when writing on the modern lyric—influenced by the kind of fundamental reinterpretations that made it possible for a critic such as Walter Benjamin to speak about sixteenth-century literature and about Baudelaire in closely similar terms, allows them to describe Friedrich's *Entrealisierung* and *Entpersönlichung* with new stylistic rigor. The traditional term of allegory that Benjamin, perhaps more than anyone else in Germany, helped to re-store to some of its full implications is frequently used by them to describe a tension within the language that can no longer be modeled on the subject-object relationships derived from experiences of perception, or from theo-ries of the imagination derived from perception. In an earlier essay, Benjamin had suggested that "the intensity of the interrelationship between the per-ceptual and the intellectual element" ("Zwei Gedichte von Hölderlin") be made the main concern of the interpreter of poetry. This indicates that the assumed correspondence between meaning and object is put into question. From this point on, the very presence of any outward object can become superfluous, and, in an important article published in 1960, H. R. Jauss characterizes an allegorical style as "beauté inutile," the absence of any reference to an exterior reality of which it would be the sign. The "disap-pearance of the object" has become the main theme ["On the Question of the 'Structural Unity' of Older and Modern Lyric Poetry" in H. R. Jauss *Aesthetic Experience and Literary Hermeneutics*]. This development is seen as a historical process that can be more or less accurately dated: in the field of lyric poetry, Baudelaire is still named as the originator of a modern allegorical style. Friedrich's historical pattern survives, though now based on linguistic and rhetorical rather than on superficially sociological consid-erations. A student of Jauss, Karlheinz Stierle, tries to document this scheme in a consecutive reading of three poems by Nerval, Mallarmé, and Rimbaud, showing the gradual process of irrealization dialectically at work in these three texts ("Möglichkeiten des dunklen Stils in den Anfängen moderner Lyrik in Frankreich," in *Lyrik als Paradigma der Moderne*).

Stierle's detailed reading of a late and difficult sonnet by Mallarmé can serve as a model for the discussion of the "idées reçues" that this group of scholars still shares with Freidrich, all political appearances to the contrary. His interpretation of the "Tombeau de Verlaine"—chronologically though not stylistically perhaps Mallarmé's last text—following Benjamin's dictum, consciously analyzes the obscurity of the poem and the resistance of its diction to a definitive meaning or set of meanings, as the interpenetration between intellectual and perceptual elements. And Stierle comes to the conclusion that, at least in certain lines of the poem, the sensory elements have entirely vanished. At the beginning of the sonnet, an actual object—a tombstone—is introduced:

Le noir roc courroucé que la bise le roule

but this actual object, according to Stierle, is "at once transcended into irreality by a movement that cannot be represented." As for the second stanza, "it can no longer be referred to an exterior reality." Although Mallarmé's poetry, more than any other (including Baudelaire's or Nerval's), uses objects rather than subjective feelings or inward emotions, this apparent return to objects (*Vergegenständlichung*), far from augmenting our sense of reality, of language adequately representing the object, is in fact a subtle and successful strategy to achieve complete irreality. The logic of the relationships that exist between the various objects in the poem is no longer based on the logic of nature or of representation, but on a purely intellectual and allegorical logic decreed and maintained by the poet in total defiance of natural events. "The situation of the poem," writes Stierle, referring to the dramatic action that takes place between the various "things" that appear in it,

> can no longer be represented in sensory terms. . . . If we consider, not the object but that which makes it unreal, then this is a poetry of allegorical reification (*Vergegenständlichung*). One is struck most of all by the nonrepresentability of what is assumedly being shown: the stone rolling by its own will. . . . In traditional allegory, the function of the concrete image was to make the meaning stand out more vividly. The *sensus allegoricus,* as a concrete representation, acquired a new clarity. But for Mallarmé

the concrete image no longer leads to a clearer vision. The unity reached on the level of the object can no longer be represented. And it is precisely this unreal constellation that is intended as the product of the poetic activity.

This particular Mallarméan strategy is seen as a development leading beyond Baudelaire, whose allegory is still centered on a subject and is psychologically motivated. Mallarmé's modernity stems from the impersonality of an allegorical (i.e., nonrepresentational) diction entirely freed from a subject. The historical continuity from Baudelaire to Mallarmé follows a genetic movement of gradual allegorization and depersonalization.

The test of such a theory has to be found in the quality of the exegetic work performed by its proponent. Returning to the text, we can confine ourselves to one or two of the key words that play an important part in Stierle's argument. First of all, the word "roc" in the first line:

Le noir roc courroucé que la bise le roule

The movement of this rock, driven by the cold north wind, is said by Stierle to be "at once" beyond representation. As we know from the actual occasion for which the poem was written and which is alluded to in the title, as well as from the other "Tombeaux" poems of Mallarmé on Poe, Gautier, and Baudelaire, this rock indeed represents the monument of Verlaine's grave around which a group of writers gathered to celebrate the first anniversary of his death. The thought that such a stone could be made to move by the sheer force of the wind, and that it could then be halted (or an attempt be made to halt it) by applying hands to it ("Ne s'arrêtera ni sous de pieuses mains / Tâtant sa ressemblance avec les maux humains"), is indeed absurd from a representational point of view. Equally absurd is the pseudo-representational phrase that combines a literal action ("tâter") with an abstraction ("la ressemblance"), made more unreal yet because the resemblance is in its turn to something general and abstract ("la ressemblance avec les maux humains"). We are supposed to touch not a stone but the resemblance of a stone, wandering about driven by the wind, to a human emotion. Stierle certainly seems to have a point when he characterizes this dramatic "situation" as beyond representation.

But why should the significance of "roc" be restricted to one single meaning? At the furthest remove from the literal reading, we can think of the rock in purely emblematic terms as the stone miraculously removed from the grave of a sacrificial figure and allowing for the metamorphosis of Christ from an earthly into a heavenly body; such a miracle could easily be accomplished by an allegorical, divine wind. There is nothing farfetched in such a reference. The circumstance of the poem is precisely the "empty tomb" (to quote Yeats) that honors the spiritual entity of Verlaine's work and not his bodily remains. Verlaine himself, in *Sagesse,* singled out by Mallarmé as his most important work, constantly sees his own destiny as an *Imitatio Christi* and, at his death, much was made of the redeeming virtue of suffering for the repenting sinner. In Mallarmé's short prose texts on Verlaine, one senses his irritation with a facile Christianization of the poet, left to die in poverty and scorned as the alcoholic tramp that he was during his lifetime, but whose destiny becomes overnight a lesson in Christian redemption. This sentimental rehabilitation of Verlaine as a Christ figure, alluded to in the reference to the miracle of the Ascension, making his death exemplary for the suffering of all mankind, goes directly against Mallarmé's own conception of poetic immortality. The real movement of the work, its future destiny and correct understanding, will not be halted ("ne s'arrêtera pas") by such hypocritical piety. The opposition against a conventional Christian notion of death as redemption, a theme that recurs constantly in all the "Tombeaux" poems with their undeniable Masonic overtones, is introduced from the start by an emblematic reading of "roc" as an allusion to Scripture.

What concerns us most for our argument is that the word "roc" thus can have several meanings and that, within the system of meanings so set up, a different representational logic can be expected to function; within the scriptural context of miraculous events we can no longer expect naturalistic consistency. But between the literal rock of the gravestone and the emblematic rock of Christ's tomb, many intermediary readings are possible. In another prose text of Mallarmé's on Verlaine (that Stierle never mentions) Verlaine, later called tramp (vagabond) in the poem, is seen as a victim of cold, solitude, and poverty. On another level, "roc" can then designate Verlaine himself, whose dark and hulking shape can without too much visual effort be seen as a "noir roc." And the black object driven by a cold wind in the month of January suggests still another meaning: that of a dark cloud. In Mallarmé's poems of this period (one thinks of "Un Coup de dés," of "A la nue accablante tu," etc.) the cloud symbolism plays a prominent part and would almost have to enter into the symbolic paraphernalia of any poem—since Mallarmé strives for the inclusion of his entire symbolic apparatus in each text, however brief it may be. The hidden cloud imagery in this sonnet, first perceived by the intuitive but astute Mallarmé reader Thibaudet in a commentary on the poem, which Stierle mentions, reappears in the second stanza and completes the cosmic symbolic system that starts out "here" ("ici," in line 5), on this pastoral earth, and ascends, by way of the cloud, to the highest hierarchy of the star in line 7: "l'astre mûri des lendemains / Dont un scintillement argentera les foules." With a little ingenuity, more meanings still could be added, always bearing in mind the auto-exegetic symbolic vocabulary that Mallarmé has developed by this time: thus the word "roule," written in 1897, suggests a cross-reference to the rolling of the dice in "Un Coup de dés," making the "roc" into a symbolic equivalent of the dice. And so on: the more relevant symbolic meanings one can discover, the closer one comes to the spirit of Mallarmé's metaphorical play in his later vocabulary.

"Noir roc" for a cloud may seem visually farfetched and forced, but it is not visually absurd. The process that takes us from the literal rock to Verlaine, to a cloud and the tomb of Christ, in an ascending curve from earth to heaven, has a certain representational, naturalistic consistency. We easily recognize it for the traditional poetic topos that it is, a metamorphosis, with exactly the degree of naturalistic verisimilitude that one would have to expect in this case. The entire poem is in fact a poem about a metamorphosis, the change brought about by death that transformed the actual person Verlaine into the intellectual abstraction of his work, "tel qu'en lui-même enfin l'éternité le change," with emphasis on the metamorphosis implied in "change." Confining himself to the single literal meaning of "roc," Stierle can rightly say that no representational element is at play in the text, but he also has to lose the main part of the meaning. A considerable extension of meaning, consistent with the thematic concerns of Mallarmé's other works of the same period, is brought about by allowing for the metamorphosis of one object into a number of other symbolic referents. Regardless of the final importance or value of Mallarmé's poetry as *statement,* the semantic plurality has to be taken into account at all stages, even and especially if the ultimate "message" is held to be a mere play of meanings that cancel each other out. But this polysemic process can only be perceived by a reader willing to remain with a natural logic of representation—the wind driving a cloud, Verlaine suffering physically from the cold—for a longer span of time than is allowed for by Stierle, who wants us to give up any representational reference from the start, without trying out some of the possibilities of a representational reading.

In the second stanza of the sonnet, Stierle is certainly right when he asserts that a *summum* of incomprehensibility is reached in the lines

> Ici . . .
> Cet immatériel deuil opprime de maints
> Nubiles plis l'astre mûri des lendemains.

What on earth (or, for that matter, in heaven) could be these nubile folds that oppress a star or, if one follows Stierle's tempting, because syntactically very Mallarméan suggestion that "maints nubiles plis" by inversion modifies "astre" and not "opprime," what then is this mourning that oppresses a star made up of many nubile folds? The word "pli" is one of the key-symbols of Mallarmé's later vocabulary, too rich to even begin to summarize the series of related meanings it implies. Stierle rightly suggests that one of the meanings refers to the book, the fold being the uncut page that distinguishes the self-reflective volume from the mere information contained in the unfolded, unreflective newspaper. The nubility of the book, echoed in the "astre *mûri* des lendemains," helps to identify the star as being the timeless project of the universal Book, the literary paradigm that Mallarmé, half-ironically, half-prophetically, keeps announcing as the *telos* of his and of all literary enterprise. The permanence, the immortality of this Book is the true poetic glory bequeathed to future generations. But "nubile," aside from erotic associations (that can be sacrificed to the economy of our exposition), also suggests the bad etymological but very Mallarméan pun on *nubere* (to marry) and *nubes* (cloud). "Nubiles plis," in a visual synecdoche that is bolder than it is felicitous, underscored by an etymological pun, sees the clouds as folds of vapor about to discharge their rain. The cloud imagery already present in "roc" is thus carried further in the second stanza of the sonnet. This reading, which nowise cancels out the reading of "pli" as book—the syntactical ambivalence of giving "maints nubiles plis" both adjectival and adverbial status is a controlled grammatical device entirely in the spirit of Mallarmé's later style—opens up access to the main theme of the poem: the difference between the false kind of transcendence that bases poetic immortality on the exemplary destiny of the poet considered as a person (in the case of Verlaine, the redeeming sacrifice of the suffering sinner) and authentic poetic immortality that is entirely devoid of any personal circumstances. Mallarmé's prose statements on Verlaine show that this is indeed one of his main concerns with regard to this particular poet, an illustration of his own reflections on the theme of poetic impersonality. The actual person Verlaine, as the first tercet unambiguously states, is now part of the material earth—"il est caché parmi l'herbe, Verlaine"—and far removed from the heavenly constellation of which his work has become a part. The symbol of the false transcendence that tries to rise from the person to the work, from the earthly Verlaine to the poetic text, is the cloud. The misdirected mourning of the contemporaries, the superficial judgments of the journalists, all prevent the true significance of the work from manifesting itself. In the straightforward representational logic of the line, the cloud ("maintes nubiles plis") covers up the star ("opprime . . . l'astre") and hides it from sight. In the dramatic action performed by the various symbolic objects, the set of meanings associated with clouds ("roc," "nubiles plis") denounces the psychological fallacy of confusing the impersonal self of the poetry with the empirical self of the life. Verlaine himself did not share in this mystification, or rather, the correct critical reading of his work shows that his poetry is in fact not a poetry of redemption, sacrifice, or personal transcendence. The "Tombeaux" poems always also contain Mallarmé's own critical interpretation of the other poet's work and he sees Verlaine very much the way Yeats saw William Morris, as a naïvely pagan poet unaware of the tragic, Christian sense of death, a fundamentally happy pastoral poet of earth despite the misery of his existence. In the second part of the sonnet, the imagery shifts from Christian to pagan sources, from the Ascension to the river Styx, with the suggestion that he, Mallarmé, might repeat consciously the experience Verlaine went through in naïve ignorance. Verlaine's death and poetic transfiguration prefigure in a naïve tonality the highly self-conscious repetition of the same experience by Mallarmé himself. Like all true poets, Verlaine is a poet of death, but death for Mallarmé means precisely the discontinuity between the personal self and the voice that speaks in the poetry from the other bank of the river, beyond death.

These brief indications do not begin to do justice to the complexity of this poem or to the depth of the Mallarméan theme linking impersonality with death. They merely confirm that, as one would expect, the sonnet on Verlaine shares the thematic concerns that are present in the poetry and in the prose texts of the same period, including "Un Coup de dés" with its insistence on the necessary transposition of the sacrifical death from the life into the work. It is important for our argument that these themes can only be reached if one admits the persistent presence, in the poetry, of levels of meaning that remain representational. The natural image of the cloud covering a star is an indispensable element in the development of the dramatic action that takes place in the poem. The image of the poetic work as a star implies that poetic understanding is still, for Mallarmé, analogous to an act of seeing and therefore best represented by a natural metaphor of light, like the lamp in Abrams's title. The poem uses a representational poetics that remains fundamentally mimetic throughout.

It can be argued that this representational moment is not the ultimate horizon of Mallarmé's poetry and that, in certain texts that would probably not include the "Tombeau de Verlaine," we move beyond any thematic meaning whatsoever. Even in this poem, the "ideas" that allow for direct statement, however subtle and profound, however philosophically valid in their own right they may be, are not the ultimate raison d'être of the text, but mere pre-text. To say this, however—and the statement would require many developments and qualifications—is to say something quite different from Stierle's assertion that a language of representation is immediately transcended and replaced by an allegorical, figural language. Only after all possible representational meanings have been exhausted can one begin to ask if and by what these meanings have been replaced, and chances are that this will be nothing as harmless as Stierle's entirely formal notions of allegory. Up to a very advanced point, not reached in this poem and perhaps never reached at all, Mallarmé remains a representational poet as he remains in fact a poet of the self, however impersonal, disincarnated, and ironical this self may become in a figure like the "Maître" of "Un Coup de dés." Poetry does not give up its mimetic function and its dependence on the fiction of a self that easily and at such little cost.

The implications of this conclusion for the problem of modernity in the lyric reach further than their apparent scholasticism may at first suggest. For Stierle, following Jauss who himself followed Friedrich, it goes without saying that the crisis of the self and of representation in lyric poetry of the nineteenth and twentieth centuries should be interpreted as a gradual process. Baudelaire continues trends implicitly present in Diderot; Mallarmé (as he himself stated) felt he had to begin where Baudelaire had ended; Rimbaud takes an even further step in opening up the experimentation of the surrealists—in short, the modernity of poetry occurs as a continuous historical movement. This reconciliation of modernity with history in a common genetic process is highly satisfying, because it allows one to be both origin and offspring at the same time. The son understands the father and takes his work a step further, becoming in turn the father, the source of future offspring, "l'astre *mûri* des lendemains," as Mallarmé puts it in a properly genetic imagery of ripening. The process by no means has to be as easy and spontaneous as it appears in nature: its closest mythological version, the War of the Titans, is far from idyllic. Yet, as far as the idea of modernity is concerned, it remains an optimistic story. Jupiter and his kin may have their share of guilt and sorrow about the fate of Saturn, but they nevertheless are modern men as well as historical figures, linked to a past that they carry within themselves. Their sorrow is a life-giving form of understanding and it integrates the past as an active presence within the future. The literary historian gets a similar satisfaction from a rigorous historical method that remembers the past while he takes part in the excitement of a youthful new present, in the activism of modernity. Such a reconciliation of memory with action is the dream of all historians. In the field of literary studies, the documented modernism of Hans Robert Jauss and his group, who seem to have no qualms about dating the origins of modernism with historical accuracy, is a good contemporary example of this dream. In their case, it rests on the assumption that the movement of lyric poetry away from representation is a historical process that dates back to Baudelaire as well as being the very movement of modernity. Mallarmé might in all likelihood have agreed with this, since he himself resorts frequently, and especially in his later works, to images of filial descent, images of projected futurity which, although no longer founded on organic continuity, nevertheless remain genetic.

There is one curious and puzzling exception, however. Many critics have pointed out that among the various "Tombeaux" poems paying tribute to his predecessors, the sonnet on Baudelaire is oddly unsatisfying. The subtle critical understanding that allows Mallarmé to state his kinship as well as his differences with other artists such as Poe, Gautier, Verlaine, or even Wagner seems to be lacking in the Baudelaire poem. Contrary to the controlled obscurity of the others, this text may well contain genuine areas of blindness. In fact, Mallarmé's relationship to Baudelaire is so complex that little of real insight has yet been said on the bond that united them. The question is not helped by such lapidary pronouncements as Stierle's assertion that "Mallarmé began as a pupil of Baudelaire with pastiches of the *Fleurs du mal*. His latest poems show how far he went beyond his starting point." In the early poems, most of all in "Hérodiade," Mallarmé is in fact systematically opposing a certain conception of Baudelaire as a sensuous and subjective poet—which might well be the limit of his own explicit understanding of Baudelaire at that time—while simultaneously responding, especially in his prose poems, to another, darker aspect of the later Baudelaire. The two strains remain operative till the end, the first developing into the main body of his poetic production, the latter remaining more subterranean but never disappearing altogether. The truly allegorical, later Baudelaire of the *Petits poèmes en prose* never stopped haunting Mallarmé, though he may have tried to exorcize his presence. Here was, in fact, the example of a poetry that came close to being no longer representational but that remained for him entirely enigmatic. The darkness of this hidden center obscures later allusions to Baudelaire, including the "Tombeau" poem devoted to the author of the *Fleurs du Mal*. Far from being an older kinsman who sent him on his way, Baudelaire, or, at least, the most significant aspect of Baudelaire, was for him a dark zone into which he could never penetrate. The same is true, in different ways, of the view of Baudelaire held by Rimbaud and the surrealists. The understanding of the nonrepresentational,

allegorical element in Baudelaire—and, for that matter, in Baudelaire's predecessors in romanticism—is very recent and owes little to Mallarmé or
Rimbaud. In terms of the poetics of representation, the relationship from
Baudelaire to so-called modern poetry is by no means genetic. He is not the
father of modern poetry but an enigmatic stranger that later poets tried to
ignore by taking from him only the superficial themes and devices which
they could rather easily "go beyond." In authentic poets such as Mallarmé,
this betrayal caused the slightly obsessive bad conscience that shines through
in his later allusions to Baudelaire. Such a relationship is not the genetic
movement of a historical process but is more like the uneasy and shifting
border line that separates poetic truth from poetic falsehood.

It could not have been otherwise, for if one takes the allegorization of
poetry seriously and calls it the distinctive characteristic of modernity in the
lyric, then all remnants of a genetic historicism have to be abandoned. When
one of the most significant of modern lyricists, the German poet Paul Celan,
writes a poem [*Die Niemandsrose*] about his main predecessor Hölderlin,
he does not write a poem about light but about blindness. (The first stanza
of the poem goes as follows:

> Zur Blindheit über—
> redete Augen.
> Ihre—"ein
> Rätsel ist Rein-
> entsprungenes"—, ihre
> Erinnerung an
> schwimmende Hölderlintürme, möwen-
> umschwirrt.
>
> [Eyes talked into
> blindness.
> Their—"an enigma is
> the purely
> originated"—, their
> memory of
> Hölderlin towers afloat, circled
> by whirring gulls.])

The blindness here is not caused by an absence of natural light but by the
absolute ambivalence of a language. It is a self-willed rather than a natural
blindness, not the blindness of the soothsayer but rather that of Oedipus at
Colonus, who has learned that it is not in his power to solve the enigma of

language. One of the ways in which lyrical poetry encounters this enigma is in the ambivalence of a language that is representational and nonrepresentational at the same time. All representational poetry is always also allegorical, whether it be aware of it or not, and the allegorical power of the language undermines and obscures the specific literal meaning of a representation open to understanding. But all allegorical poetry must contain a representational element that invites and allows for understanding, only to discover that the understanding it reaches is necessarily in error. The Mallarmé-Baudelaire relationship is exemplary for all intrapoetic relationships in that it illustrates the impossibility for a representational and an allegorical poetics to engage in a mutually clarifying dialectic. Both are necessarily closed to each other, blind to each other's wisdom. Always again, the allegorical is made representational, as we saw Jauss and his disciples do when they tried to understand the relationship between mimesis and allegory as a genetic process, forcing into a pattern of continuity that which is, by definition, the negation of all continuity. Or we see ultimate truth being read back into a representation by forcing literal meaning into an allegorical mold, the way Stierle prematurely allegorized a Mallarmé who knew himself to be forever trapped in the deluding appearance of natural images. The question of modernity reveals the paradoxical nature of a structure that makes lyric poetry into an enigma which never stops asking for the unreachable answer to its own riddle. To claim, with Friedrich, that modernity is a form of obscurity is to call the oldest, most ingrained characteristics of poetry modern. To claim that the loss of representation is modern is to make us again aware of an allegorical element in the lyric that had never ceased to be present, but that is itself necessarily dependent on the existence of an earlier allegory and so is the negation of modernity. The worst mystification is to believe that one can move from representation to allegory, or vice versa, as one moves from the old to the new, from father to son, from history to modernity. Allegory can only blindly repeat its earlier model, without final understanding, the way Celan repeats quotations from Hölderlin that assert their own incomprehensibility. The less we understand a poet, the more he is compulsively misinterpreted and oversimplified and made to say the opposite of what he actually said, the better the chances are that he is truly modern; that is, different from what we—mistakenly—think we are ourselves. This would make Baudelaire into a truly modern French poet, Hölderlin into a truly modern German poet and Wordsworth and Yeats into truly modern English poets.

JACQUES DERRIDA

The Double Session

Now, once the crisis of literature has thus been remarked, would any criticism whatsoever—as such—be capable of facing up to it? Would such criticism be able to lay claim to any *object?* Doesn't the project of the χρίνειν [krinein] itself proceed precisely out of the very thing that is being threatened and put in question at the focal point of this remodeling, or, to use a more Mallarméan word, this re-tempering of literature? Wouldn't "literary criticism" as such be part of what we have called the *ontological* interpretation of mimesis or of metaphysical mimetologism?

It is in this de-limitation of criticism that we will henceforth be interested.

If we take into account a certain time lag and some significant historical developments, it can be said that the elements in Mallarmé's text that re-mark these "critical" boundaries have now been recognized. But this recognition cannot be reached by one viewer alone or in one fell swoop. It must be something other than mere recognition, and it must entail a certain stratified repetition. On the one hand, "contemporary criticism" has now recognized, studied, confronted, and *thematized* a certain number of *signifieds* that had long gone unnoticed, or at least had never been treated as such, systematically, for more than half a century of Mallarméan criticism. And on the other hand, the whole formal crafting of Mallarmé's writing has recently been analyzed in detail. But never, it seems, has the analysis of the way the text is assembled seemed to block access to the

From *Dissemination,* translated by Barbara Johnson. © 1981 by the University of Chicago. The University of Chicago Press, 1981.

thematic level as such, or, more broadly, to meaning or the signified as such. Never has an overall meaning system or even a structural semantics seemed to be threatened or thwarted by the very progression or onward *march* of the Mallarméan text, and this according to the workings of a regular law. That law does not apply only to the text of "Mallarmé," even though he "illustrates" it according to a "historical" necessity whose entire field needs to be mapped out, and even though such an illustration entails a general reinterpretation of everything.

What we will thus be concerned with here is the very possibility of thematic criticism, seen as an example of modern criticism, at work wherever one tries to determine a meaning through a text, to pronounce a decision upon it, to decide that this or that *is* a meaning and that it is meaningful, to say that this meaning is posed, posable, or transposable as such: a theme.

It is obvious—and this will later receive further confirmation—that the fact that we have chosen to focus on the "blank" and the "fold" is not an accident. This is both because of the specific effects of these two elements in Mallarmé's text and precisely because they have systematically been recognized as *themes* by modern criticism. Now, if we can begin to see that the "blank" and the "fold" cannot in fact be mastered as themes or as meanings, if it is within the folds and the blankness of a certain hymen that the very textuality of the text is re-marked, then we will precisely have determined the limits of thematic criticism itself.

Is it necessary to point out that *L'Univers imaginaire de Mallarmé* (*Mallarmé's Imaginary Universe*) (1961) [by Jean-Pierre Richard] remains the most powerful of all works of thematic criticism? It systematically covers the whole of the textual field of Mallarmé; or at least, it *would* do so if the structure of a certain crisscrossed groove (the blankness of a fold or the folding of a blank) did not turn the "whole" into the *too much* or the *too little* of the text. And vice versa. Thus, let us say, the whole of Mallarmé's textual field would be covered.

The questions we will ask of this book, for the same reason, will not be directed toward it as a "whole," the "whole" being the imaginary version of a text. They will be addressed to a certain determinate part of its procedure, particularly to the theoretical and methodological formulation of its project: its thematicism. In this, we will be dealing with the book on a level that is still too thematic. But one would not be able to redirect our own critique against us in the end without confirming its legitimacy and its principle.

At the point at which the theoretical project of the book is stated in the preface, it is explained by means of two examples. Although these are given as two examples among many, and although what is exemplary or exceptional about them is never rigorously examined by Richard, it is not without cause that they have found their way to such a key position. The examples in question are precisely the "themes" of the "blank" and the "fold." We must here quote a long and beautifully written page of the preface. Inquiring into "the very notion of a *theme*, on which [our] whole enterprise is based," Richard has just noted the "strategic value" or the "topological quality" of the theme. "Any thematics will thus derive both from cybernetics and from systematics. Within this active system, the themes will tend to organize themselves as in any living structure: they will combine into flexible groupings governed by the law of isomorphism and by the search for the best possible equilibrium. This notion of equilibrium, which first arises out of the physical sciences but whose crucial importance in sociology and psychology has been demonstrated by Claude Lévi-Strauss and Jean Piaget, seems to us to be of considerable utility in the understanding of the realms of the imaginary. One can indeed observe how themes arrange themselves into antithetical pairs, or, in a more complex manner, into multiple compensating systems. In his dream of the idea, for example, Mallarmé appeared to us to oscillate between the desire for an opening (the idea bursting apart, *vaporized* into suggestion or silence) and a need for closure (the idea *summoned*, summed up in a contour or a definition). The closed and the open, the clear and the fleeting, the mediate and the immediate, these are a few of the mental pairings whose presence we believe we have discerned on a number of very diverse levels of the Mallarméan experience. The important thing is then to observe how these oppositions are resolved, how their tension is eased into new synthetic notions or into concrete forms that realize a satisfactory equilibrium. The opposition between the closed and the open thus engenders certain beneficent figures in which both contradictory needs can be satisfied, successively or simultaneously: for example the *fan*, the *book*, the *dancer*. . . . The essence succeeds at once in summoning and in vaporizing itself in a synthetic phenomenon: *music*. At other times the equilibrium is established in a static manner, through a play of forces very precisely pitted against each other, whose total balance amounts to the euphoria of a 'suspension.' It is thus that Mallarmé himself indeed envisioned the internal reality of a poem and the ideal architecture of the objects the poem must reorder within itself: grottos, diamonds, spiderwebs, rose windows, kiosks, shells, all stand as so many images which translate the search for a total correlation of nature with itself, a perfect equalization of all things. The mind or spirit then becomes the keystone of this architecture, functioning as the absolute center through which everything communicates, balances out, and is neutralized (Mallarmé adds 'is annulled'). Thus Mallarmé's thematics itself provides us with the technical tools needed for its own elucidation. What we have tried to do is to see how the profoundest tendencies of reverie succeed in going beyond their inherent conflict toward some state of equilibrium. To that end it was in fact enough to reread the most beautiful of the poems, where that balance is achieved effortlessly and spontaneously, poetic felicity—what is called 'felicity of expression'—being doubtless nothing other than the reflection of lived felicity, that is, a state in which a being's most contradictory needs are all satisfied at once, and even satisfy *each other*, in a harmony composed of connections, oscillations, or fusions."

Let us interrupt the quotation for a moment. Not in order to ask—as Richard does not, throughout the length of the book—what "the most beautiful of the poems, where that balance is achieved effortlessly and spontaneously" might be, but in order to point out a coherent group of concepts: "living structures," "law of isomorphism," "best possible equilibrium," "mental pairings," "beneficent figures," "synthetic phenomenon," "euphoria of a suspension," "total correlation of nature with itself," "happy states of equilibrium," "felicity of expression," "reflection of lived felicity," etc. These concepts belong to a critical "psychologism." Gerard Genette has analyzed the *transitive* character of this approach, along with its "sensualist" and "eudaemonist" postulates ("Bonheur de Mallarmé?" in *Figures*). Using this concept of "reflection" (of "lived felicity"), so loaded with history and metaphysics, such a representative psychologism makes the text into a form of expression, reduces it to its signified theme, and retains all the traits of mimetologism. What it retains in particular is that *dialecticity* that has remained profoundly inseparable from metaphysics, from Plato to Hegel. (If one wishes to identify the specificity of the writing operation or of the operation of the textual signifier [the graphics of supplementarity or of the hymen], one must focus one's critique on the concept of *Aufhebung* or sublation [*relève*], which, as the ultimate mainspring of all dialecticity, stands as the most enticing, the most sublating, the most "relevant" way of [re]-covering [up] that graphics, precisely because it is most similar to it. This is why it has seemed necessary to designate the *Aufhebung* as the decisive target. And since thematicism presents itself not only as a dialectic but also, and rightly so, as a "phenomenology of the theme," let us here recall by analogy the fact that it was the possibility of "undecidable" propositions that presented phenomenological discourse with such redoubtable difficulties.) We have already shown in what way the dialectical structure is incapable of accounting for the graphics of the hymen, being itself comprehended and inscribed within the latter, almost indistinguishable from it, separated from it only by itself, a simple veil that constitutes the very thing that tries to reduce it to nothing: desire.

This dialectical intention animates the whole of Richard's thematicism, reaching its fullest expansion in the chapter entitled "The Idea" and in its subsection "Toward a dialectics of Totality." This dialectics of totality intervenes in the preface just after the passage cited above, precisely in connection with the examples of the "blank" and the "fold": "If one wishes to approach the psychological reality of the theme from another angle, one can do so through that other product of the imagining function: the symbol. In a recent study of the work of M. Eliade, Paul Ricoeur gives an excellent analysis of the different modes of comprehension at our disposal for dealing with the symbolic world: his remarks could be applied with little modification to a phenomenology of the theme. The theme, too, 'makes us think.' To understand a theme is also to 'deploy [its] multiple valences': it is, for example, to see how Mallarmé's dream of the *blank* can incarnate now the ecstasy of virginity, now the pain of an obstacle or of frigidity, now the happiness of an opening, of a liberation, or of a mediation, and then to connect these diverse nuances of meaning into one single complex. One can also, as Ricoeur suggests, understand a theme through another theme, progressing from one to the other following 'a law of intentional analogy' until one has reached all the themes linked by relations of affinity. This would involve, for example, moving from the azure to the windowpane, to the blank paper, to the glacier, to the snowy peak, to the swan, to the wing, to the ceiling, not forgetting the lateral branchings that occur at each point in this progression (from the glacier to the melted water, to the blue eyes, and to the amorous bath; from the white paper to the black marks that cover and divide it; from the ceiling to the tomb, the priest, the sylph, and the mandolin). And finally, one can show how the same theme 'unifies several experiential and representational levels: the internal and the external, the vital and the speculative.' The Mallarméan figure of the *fold,* for example, enables us to join the erotic to the sensible, then to the reflective, to the metaphysical, and to the literary: the fold is at once sex, foliage, mirror, book, and tomb—all are realities it gathers up into a certain very special dream of intimacy."

This passage (in which each connotation calls for analysis) is flanked by two brief remarks. One cannot, it seems, subscribe to it without acknowledging two objections in principle to the phenomenological, hermeneutic, dialectical project of thematicism. The first involves the differential or diacritical character of language: "Then another difficulty arises: to construct a lexicon of frequencies is to suppose that from one occurrence to another the meaning of words remains fixed. But in reality, meaning varies; it is modified both within itself and according to the horizon of meanings that surround, sustain, and create it. Languages, as we now know, are *diacritical* realities; each element within them is in itself less important than the *gap* that distinguishes it from other elements. . . . Neither a mathematical study nor even an exhaustive list of themes can therefore ever account for their intention or their richness; what will above all be left out is the original relief of their system." Out of this fundamental diacriticity whose design should also be further complicated, we will later draw another consequence: a certain inexhaustibility which cannot be classed in the categories of richness, intentionality, or a horizon, and whose form would not be simply foreign to the order of mathematics. Nevertheless, it can be seen that even in the eyes of Richard himself, diacriticity already prevents a theme from being a theme, that is, a nuclear unit of meaning, posed there before the eye, present outside of its signifier and referring only to itself, in the last analysis, even though its identity as a signified is carved out of the horizon of an infinite perspective. Either diacriticity revolves around a nucleus and in that case any recourse to it remains superficial enough not to put thematicism as such into question; or else diacriticity traverses the text through and through and there is no such thing as a thematic nucleus, only theme *effects* that give themselves out to be the very thing or meaning of the text. If there is a textual system, a theme does not exist ("no—a present does not exist"). Or if it *does* exist, it will always have been unreadable. This kind of nonexistence of the theme in the text, this way in which meaning is nonpresent or nonidentical with the text, has in fact been recognized by Richard, however—this is the second of the two remarks mentioned above—in a note dealing with the problems of ordering and classifying themes. These problems are by no means secondary: "We cannot help admitting, however, that this order is far from satisfactory. For in fact it is actually the multiplicity of lateral relations that creates the *essence* of meaning here. A theme is nothing other than the sum, or rather the putting in perspective, of its diverse modulations."

This concession still allows for the hope, the "dream," of reaching a sum and of determining a perspective, even if these are infinite. Such a sum or perspective would enable us to define, contain, and classify the different occurrences of a theme.

To this we would oppose the following hypotheses: the sum is impossible to totalize but yet it is not exceeded by the infinite richness of a content of meaning or intention; the perspective extends out of sight but without entailing the depth of a horizon of meaning *before* or *within* which we can never have finished advancing. By taking into account that "laterality"

Richard mentions in passing, but by going on to determine its law, we shall define the limit otherwise: through the angle and the intersection of a re-mark that folds the text back upon itself without any possibility of its fitting back over or into itself, without any reduction of its spacing.

The fold, then, and the blank: these will forbid us to seek a theme or an overall meaning in an imaginary, intentional, or lived domain beyond all textual instances. Richard sees the "blank" and the "fold" as themes whose plurivalence is particularly rich or exuberant. What one tends not to see, because of the abundance of his sample, is that these textual effects are rich with a kind of poverty, I would even call it a very singular and very regular monotony. One does not see this because one thinks one is seeing themes in the very spot where the nontheme, that which cannot become a theme, the very thing that has no meaning, is ceaselessly re-marking itself—that is, disappearing.

All this in the movement of a fan. The polysemy of "blanks" and "folds" both fans out and snaps shut, ceaselessly. But to read Mallarmé's *éventail* [fan] involves not only an inventory of its occurrences (there are hundreds, a very large but finite number if one sticks to the word itself, or an infinite number of diverse possibilities if one includes the many-faceted figure of wings, pages, veils, sails, folds, plumes, scepters, etc., constituting and reconstituting itself in an endless breath of opening and/or closing); it involves not only the description of a phenomenological structure whose complexity is also a challenge; it is also to remark that the fan re-marks itself: no doubt it designates the empirical object one thinks one knows under that name, but then, through a tropic twist (analogy, metaphor, metonymy), it turns toward all the semic units that have been identified (wing, fold, plume, page, rustling, flight, dancer, veil, etc., each one finding itself folding and unfolding opening/closing with the movement of a fan, etc.); it opens and closes each one, but it also inscribes *above and beyond* that movement the very movement and structure of the fan-as-text, the deployment and retraction of all its valences; the spacing, fold, and hymen *between* all these meaning-effects, with writing setting them up in relations of difference and resemblance. This surplus mark, this margin of meaning, is not one valence among others in the series, even though it is *inserted* in there, too. It has to be inserted there to the extent that it does not exist outside the text and has no transcendental privilege; this is why it is always *represented* by a metaphor and a metonymy (page, plume, pleat). But while belonging in the series of valences, it always occupies the position of a supplementary valence, or rather, it marks the structurally necessary posi-tion of a supplementary inscription that could always be added to or sub-

tracted from the series. We will try to show that this position of the
supplementary mark is in all rigor neither a metaphor nor a metonymy even
though it is always represented by one trope too many or too few.

Let us set the fan down here as an epigraph at the edge of the demonstration.

The "blank" appears first of all, to a phenomenological or thematic
reading, as the inexhaustible totality of the semantic valences that have any
tropic affinity with it (but what is "it"?). But, through a reduplication that
is always represented, the "blank" *inserts* (says, designates, marks, states—
however one wishes to put it, and there is a need here for a different
"word") the blank as a blank *between* the valances, a hymen that unites and
differentiates them in the series, the spacing of "the blanks" which "assume
importance." Hence, the blank or the whiteness (is) the totality, however
infinite, of the polysemic series, *plus* the carefully spaced-out splitting of the
whole, the fanlike form of the text. This *plus* is not just one extra valence,
a meaning that might enrich the polysemic series. And since it has no meaning, it is not *The* blank proper, the transcendental origin of the series. This
is why, while it cannot constitute a meaning that is signified or represented,
one would say in classical discourse that it always has a delegate or representative in the series: since the blank is the polysemic totality of everything
white or blank *plus* the writing site (hymen, spacing, etc.) where such a
totality is produced, this *plus* will, for example, find one of these representatives representing nothing in the blankness or margins of the page. But for
the reasons just enumerated, it is out of the question that we should erect
such a representative—for example the whiteness of the page of writing—
into the fundamental signified or signifier in the series. Every signifier in the
series is folded along the angle of this remark. The signifiers "writing,"
"hymen," "fold," "tissue," "text," etc., do not escape this common law,
and only a conceptual strategy of some sort can temporarily privilege them
as *determinate* signifiers or even as *signifiers* at all, which strictly speaking
they *no longer are*.

This non-sense or non-theme of the spacing that relates the different
meanings to each other (the meaning of "blank" or "white" along with the
others) and in the process prevents them from ever meeting up with each
other cannot be accounted for by any *description*. It follows, then, firstly,
that there is no such thing as description, particularly in Mallarmé's work:
we have already shown through one or two examples that while Mallarmé
was pretending to describe "something," he was *in addition* describing the
operation of writing ("there is at Versailles a kind of wainscotting in scroll-
work tracery"). It follows, secondly, that any description of "themes," par-

ticularly in Mallarmé's work, will always run aground at the edges of this *greater* or *lesser* extent of theme which makes it possible that "there is" a text, that is, a readability without a signified (which will be decreed to be an unreadability by the reflexes of fright): an undesirable that throws desire back upon itself.

If polysemy is infinite, if it cannot be mastered as such, this is thus not because a finite reading or a finite writing remains incapable of exhausting a superabundance of meaning. Not, that is, unless one displaces the philosophical concept of finitude and reconstitutes it according to the law and structure of the text: according as the blank, like the hymen, re-marks itself forever as disappearance, erasure, non-sense. Finitude then becomes infinitude, according to a non-Hegelian identity: through an interruption that suspends the equation between the mark and the meaning, the "blank" marks everything white (this above all): virginity, frigidity, snow, sails, swans' wings, foam, paper, etc., *plus* the blankness that allows for the mark in the first place, guaranteeing its space of reception and production. This "last" blank (one could equally well say this "first" blank) comes neither before nor after the series. One can just as easily subtract it from the series (in which case it is determined as a lack to be silently passed over) or add it as an extra to the number, even if the number is infinite, of the valences of "white," either as an accidental bit of white, an inconsistent discard whose "consistency" will show up better later, or else as another theme which the open series must liberally embrace, or else, finally, as the transcendental space of inscription itself. As they play within this differential-supplementary structure, all the marks must blend to it, taking on the fold of this blank. The blank is folded, is (marked by) a fold. It never exposes itself to straight stitching. For the fold is no more of a theme (a signified) than the blank, and if one takes into account the linkages and rifts they propagate in the text, then *nothing* can simply have the value of a theme any more.

And there is more. The supplementary "blank" does not intervene only in the polysemous series of "white things," but also *between* the semes of *any* series and *between all* the semantic series in general. It therefore prevents any semantic seriality from being constituted, from being simply opened or closed. Not that it acts as an obstacle: it is again the blank that actually liberates the effect that a series exists; in marking itself out, it *makes us take* agglomerates for substances. If thematicism cannot account for this, it is because it overestimates the *word* while restricting the *lateral*.

In his taxonomy of "whites," Richard indeed distinguished the *principal* valences, which he designated by abstract concepts or names of general essences ("the ecstasy of virginity, the pain of an obstacle or of frigidity, the happiness of an opening, of a liberation, of a meditation"), and the *lateral* valences exemplified by material things, enabling one to "move from the azure to the windowpane, to the blank paper, to the glacier, to the snowy peak, to the swan, to the wing, to the ceiling, not forgetting the lateral branchings . . . from the glacier to the melted water, to the blue eyes and to the amorous bath; from the white paper to the black marks that cover and divide it; from the ceiling to the tomb, the priest, the sylph, and the mandolin"). This leads one to believe that some sort of hierarchy lines the lateral themes up with the principal themes and that the former are but the sensible figures (metaphors or metonymies) of the latter, which one could *properly conceive* in their literal meaning. But without even resorting to the general law of textual supplementarity through which all proper meanings are dislocated, one has only to turn to one of Richard's own lateral remarks ("In fact it is actually the multiplicity of lateral relations that creates the *essence of meaning*,") in order to undercut such a hierarchy. And since there is never, textually, anything but a silhouette, one can hold up against any frontal conception of the theme the way in which Mallarmé writes *on the bias,* his *double play* ceaselessly re-marking its *bifax*. Once more: "it will be (the) language whose gambol this is.

"Words, of themselves, are exalted on many a facet known as the rarest or having value for the mind, the center of vibratory suspense; whoever perceives them independently from the ordinary sequence, projected, on the walls of a cave, as long as their mobility or principle lasts, being that which of discourse is not said: all of them quick, before becoming extinct or extinguished, to enter into a reciprocity of fires that is distant or presented on the bias as some contingency.

"The debate—which the average necessary obviousness deflects into a detail, remains one for grammarians." Elsewhere translated as "there is a double-faced silence."

The grammar of the *bias* and of *contingency* is not only concerned with treating lateral associations of themes or semes whose constituted, smoothed, and polished unit would have as its signifier the form of a word. And in fact, the "relation of affinity" which interests the thematic critic only brings together semes whose signifying face always has the dimensions of a word or group of words related by their meaning (or signified concept.) Thematicism necessarily leaves out of account the formal, phonic, or graphic "affinities" that do not have the shape of a word, the calm unity of the verbal sign. Thematicism as such necessarily ignores the play that takes the word apart, cutting it up and putting the pieces to work "on the bias as some contingency." It is certain that Mallarmé was fascinated by the possibilities inherent in the *word,* and Richard is right in emphasizing this, but these possibilities are not primarily nor exclusively those of a body proper, a carnal unit, "the living creature" that miraculously unites sense and the senses into one *vox;* it is a play of articulations splitting up that body or reinscribing it within sequences it can no longer control. That is why we would not say of the word that it has "a *life* of its own"; and Mallarmé was just as interested in the dissection of the word as in the integrity of its life proper. It is a dissection called for by the consonant as much as by the vowel, the pure vocable; called for no less by the differential skeleton than by the fullness of breath. On the table or on the page, Mallarmé treats the word as something dead *just as much as* something living. And how is one to separate what he says of the science of language in *Les Mots anglais* (*English Words*) from what he *does* elsewhere:

"Words, in the dictionary, are deposited, the same or of diverse date, like stratifications: in a moment I will speak of layers. . . . Akin to all of nature and hence comparable to the organism that stands as the depository of life, the Word presents, in its vowels and diphthongs, something like flesh; and, in its consonants, something like a skeleton delicate to dissect. Etc., etc., etc. If life feeds on its own past, or on a continual death, Science will uncover this fact in language: which latter, distinguishing man from the rest of things, will also imitate him in being factitious in essence no less than natural; reflective, than fated; voluntary, than blind."

This is why it is difficult to subscribe to the commentary Richard offers on the sentence from *Les Mots anglais* ("the Word presents . . . to dissect") at the very moment he recognizes that thematicism stops short before Mallarmé's formal analyses, here his work with phonetics: "If one wishes to know completely the profound orientation of a poet, one must perhaps attempt a phonetic phenomenology of his key words. In the absence of such a study, let us at least recognize in the word the mystery of the flesh joined with the felicity of structure: a union that suffices to make the word a complete, closed system, a microcosm." It is difficult to subscribe to this: (1) because such a phonetic phenomenology would always, as such, have to lead back to plenitudes or intuitive presences rather than to phonic differences; (2) because the word cannot be a complete system or a body proper; (3) because, as we have tried to show, there cannot be any such thing as key words; (4) because Mallarmé's text works with graphic differences (in the narrowest ordinary sense of the term) as much as with phonic differences.

While it is far from being the only example, the play of *rhyme* is doubtless one of the most remarkable instances of this production of a new sign, a meaning and a form, through the "two-by-two" (cf. Richard, passim)

and the magnetization of two signifiers; it is a production and a magnetization whose necessity imposes itself against contingency, arbitrariness, and
semantic, or rather semiological, haphazardness. This is the operation of
verse, whose concept Mallarmé, as we shall see, extends and generalizes; it
is *not limited to rhyme* ("Verse, which, out of several vocables, remakes a
total new word foreign to the language and as if incantatory, achieves that
isolation of speech: negating, in a sovereign stroke, the haphazardness remaining in each term despite the artifice of its alternate retempering in sense
and sound." Mallarmé's bias is also worked out with a file (*à la lime;*
rhymes with *à la rime*, "at the rhyme"). (*"Lime:* from Lat. *lima,* related to
limus, oblique, because of the obliquity or curvature of the teeth of a file"
[Littré, from whom we are asking for anything but an etymology here].) The
"total new word foreign to the language": through this (signifying) difference, it is truly the effect of a transformation or displacement of the code,
of the existing taxonomy ("new, foreign to the language"); and it is also, in
its newness, its otherness, constituted out of parts borrowed from the language (the "old" language), to which, however, it cannot be reduced ("total"). But no astonishment at this poetic production of new meaning should
make us forget—and to read Mallarmé is to be sufficiently reminded of it—
that while it works *upon* the language, the total new word foreign to the
language also *returns* to the language, recomposes with it according to new
networks of differences, becomes divided up again, etc., in short, does not
become a master-word with the finally guaranteed integrity of a meaning or
truth. (This at least is the hypothesis on the basis of which we would
question certain formulations in the remarkable analyses Richard entitles
Formes et moyens de la littérature [*The Forms and Means of Literature*].
Formulations like these, for example, concerning the "new word": "this
word is new because it is total, and it seems foreign to our language because
it has been restored to that primordial language of which ours is but a fallen
echo. . . . *New,* that which is of the order of the recreated original, that
is, no doubt, of the eternal." "The pessimism of the word thus gives way
in Mallarmé to a marvelous optimism of verse or sentence, which indeed is
but a kind of confidence in the inventive or redemptive powers of the
mind." "What pours forth here in the form of flowing fabric or a half-open
spiritual strongbox is indeed the certain revelation of meaning." Since the
value of virginity [newness, wholeness, etc.] is always overlaid with its
opposite, it must ceaselessly be subjected—and would indeed submit of its
own accord—to the operation of the hymen. The "presence" of words like
"wholeness," "nativeness," "ingenuousness," etc., in Mallarmé's text cannot be *read* as a simple or simply positive valorization. All evaluations

[optimism/pessimism] immediately pass into their opposite according to a logic that Richard describes elsewhere in its greatest complexity—at least up until the moment when, by a regularly repeated decision, what is undecidable or unprecedented in this logic, in this "almost impracticable" poetics, is reconstituted as a dialectical contradiction that must be gone beyond, that Mallarmé would have wished to overcome through "a perfect synthetic form" [The Book]; through the affirmation, produced by the space of its own absence, of a center of truth; through an aspiration toward unity, truth, "the happiness of a truth that is both active and closed," etc.) The "effect" (in the Mallarméan sense of the word: "to paint not the thing but the effect it produces") of totality or novelty does not make the word immune to difference or to supplement; the word is not exempt from the law of the bias and does not present itself to us squarely, with its own singular face. (From a letter to Cazalis [1864, *Correspondence*]: "I have finally begun my "Hérodiade"—in terror, for I am inventing a language that must necessarily arise from a highly new poetics, which I could define in the following two words: *To paint, not the thing, but the effect it produces.* The line of verse should not then be composed of words but of intentions, and all speech should efface itself before sensation." At that date, the first interpretation of the "highly new poetics" is formulated in a language that is naïvely sensualist and subjectivist. But the exclusion is clear: poetic language will not be a description or imitation or representation of the thing itself, of some substantial referent or of some primal cause, and it should not be *composed* of words taken as substantial or atomic units that are precisely undecomposable or uncompoundable. This letter [which should of course be interpreted with the utmost caution, without falling into retrospective teleology, etc.] seems at any rate to proscribe, under the terms of this new poetics, that a thing or cause in the last instance be what is signified by a text. ["There is no such thing as the true meaning of a text," said Valéry; of Mallarmé, he wrote: "But what one finds pronounced there on the contrary is the most daring and sustained attempt ever made to overcome what I shall call naive intuition in literature."] But it could be asked whether "sensation" or "intention" are not here simply occupying the place vacated by the referent, and are now to be *expressed* rather than *described*. This is no doubt the case, except if, in being placed in radical opposition to *the thing* with all its predicates, which is what Mallarmé is doing, they are in effect being displaced otherwise by a discourse, a practice, a writing.)

In the constellation of "blanks," the place of the semic content remains practically empty: it is that of the "blank" meaning insofar as it refers to the non-sense of spacing, the place where nothing takes place but the place. But that "place" is everywhere; it is not a site fixed and predetermined; not only, as we have already noted, because the signifying spacings continually re- produce themselves ("Indefectibly the white blank returns") but because the semic, metaphoric, or even thematic affinity between "white [blanc]" and "blank [blanc]" (spacing, interval, the *entre,* etc.) means that each "white" in the series, each "full" white thing in the series (snow, swan, paper, virginity, etc.), is the trope of the "empty" white space. And vice versa. The dissemination of the whites (*not* the dissemination of whiteness) produces a tropological structure that circulates infinitely around itself through the incessant supplement of an extra turn: there is *more* metaphor, *more* me- tonymy. Since everything becomes metaphorical, there is no longer any literal meaning and, hence, no longer any metaphor either. Since everything becomes metonymical, the part being each time greater than the whole and the whole smaller than the part, how could one arrest a metonymy or a synechdoche? How could one fix the *margins* of any rhetoric?

If there is no such thing as a total or proper meaning, it is because the blank *folds over.* The fold is not an accident that happens to the blank. From the moment the blank (is) white or bleaches (itself) out, as soon as there is something (there) to see (or not to see) having to do with a *mark* (which is the same word as *margin* or *march*), whether the white is marked (snow, swan, virginity, paper, etc.) or unmarked, merely demarcated (the *entre,* the void, the blank, the space, etc.), it re-marks itself, marks itself twice. It folds itself around this strange limit. The fold does not come up upon it from outside; it is the blank's outside as well as its inside, the complication according to which the supplementary mark of the blank (the asemic spacing) applies itself to the set of white things (the full semic enti- ties), plus to itself, the fold of the veil, tissue, or text upon itself. By reason of this application that nothing has preceded, there will never be any Blank with a capital B or any theology of the Text. (If the *blanc* extends both the marks and the margins of the text, then there is no reason to give any special status to the whiteness of what we think we know literally under the name *page* or *paper.* The occurrences of this type of white are less numerous than others, the white of all the fabrics, the flying wings or foam, the sobs, fountains, flowers, women, or nudes in the night, the agonies, etc. The white involved in spacing slips in between all the others and can be remarked in the word *spacious,* whether it intervenes directly ["what leaps and if more spacious"; "here the spacious illusion intervenes"], or figuratively.) And yet the structural site of this theological trap is nevertheless prescribed: the mark-supplement (le supplément de marque) produced by the text's work- ings, in falling outside of the text like an independent object with no origin other than itself, a trace that turns back into a presence (or a sign), is inseparable from desire (the desire for reappropriation or representation). Or rather, it gives birth to it and nourishes it in the very act of separating from it.

The fold folds (itself): its meaning spaces itself out with a double mark, in the hollow of which a blank is folded. The fold is simultaneously virginity, what violates virginity, and the fold which, being neither one nor the other and both at once, undecidable, *remains* as a text, irreducible to either of its two senses. "The act of folding . . . with respect to the page printed large," the "intervention of folding or *rhythm,* that which initially causes a closed page to contain a secret; silence remains in it," "the folding back of the paper and the undersides this installs, the shadow dispersed in the black lettering," "the virginal folding back of the book" (emphasis mine), such is the closed, feminine form of the book, protective of the secret of its hymen, the "frail inviolability" preceding "the introduction of a weapon, or letter opener, to mark the taking of possession," before "the consummation of any encroachment." We have never been so close to "Mimique," and the femininity of the virgin book is surely suggested by the place and form of the verb "prête" (as a verb, it means "lends," as an adjective, it means "ready" or "willing" in the feminine.—Trans.), clearly ready to offer itself as an adjective with the copula understood ("The virginal folding-back of the book, again, willing/lends for a sacrifice from which the red edges of the books of old once bled"). The masculine is turned back upon the feminine: the whole adventure of sexual difference. The secret angle of the fold is also that of a "minuscule tomb."

But in the same blow, so to speak, the fold ruptures the virginity it marks as virginity. Folding itself over its secret (and nothing is more virginal and at the same time more purloined and penetrated, already in and of itself, than a secret), it loses the smooth simplicity of its surface. It differs from itself, even *before* the letter opener can separate the lips of the book. (On the [anagrammatic, hymenographic] play between *livre* [book] and *lèvres* [lips], read over the development opened up in *Crayonné au théâtre* on the House, the Stage, and the "absent mime.") It is divided from and by itself, like the hymen. But after the fact, it still remains what it was, a virgin, beforehand, faced with the brandished knife ("the fact is, in the actual case, that, for my part, however, on the subject of pamphlets to be read according to common usage, I brandish a knife, like a cook slaughtering fowls"). After the consummation, more folded up than ever, the virginity transforms the act that has been perpetrated into a simulation, a "barbarous simulacrum." What is intact is remarked by the mark that remains intact, an immarcescible text, at the very edge of the margin: "The folds will perpetuate a mark, intact, bidding one to open or close the page, according to the master."

Perpetual, the rape has always already taken place and will *nevertheless* never have been perpetrated. For it will always have been caught in the foldings of some veil, where any and all truth comes undone.

Indeed: if all the "whites" accrue to themselves the blanks that stand for the spacing of writing—the "blanks" that assume importance—it is always by way of a signifying relay through the white canvas or sail, a cloth that is folded and stitched, the surface on which all marks apply themselves, the sheet of paper where the pen or the wing comes to propagate itself ("Our triumphal frolic, so old, out of the crypt-book / Hieroglyphics that so exalt the multitudes / Propagating with the wing a familiar shiver!"). ("Sois, Louys, l'aile qui propages / A quelque altitude ces Pages [Louys, be the wing that propagates / To some altitude these Pages"].) The blanks are always applied, directly or indirectly, to something woven: whether it be "the white solicitude of our canvas" ("Salut"), "the banal whiteness of the curtains" ("Les Fenêtres"), the white in the "Albums" (where "white reflection" rhymes with "simulation") or in the *fan* poems ("wool / . . . white flock"), the white of the bed sheet or the pall, the shroud (extending through a number of texts *between* the "sole fold" in the "Hommage" to Wagner and the vellum in the "Overture" to "Hérodiade" ["She sang out, sometimes incoherently, a lamentable / Sign! the bed with the vellum pages, / Such, useless and so cloistral, is no linen! / Which no longer keeps the cryptic folds of dreams, / Nor the sepulcral canopy's deserted moire"]) in which the book is wound ("The lovely paper of my ghost / Together sepulcher and shroud / Thrills with immortality, a tome / To be unfurled for one alone") or in which the Poet is draped ("The flash of a sword, or, white dreamer, he wears a cope, . . . Dante, in bitter laurel, in a shroud is draped, / A shroud"), icy like the paper, or frigid, (which rhymes, in one dedication, with "Gide": "Awaiting what he himself will add / You sheets of paper now so frigid, / Exalt me as a great musician / For the attentive soul of Gide"). These veils, sails, canvases, sheets, and pages are at once the content and the form, the ground and the figure, passing alternately from one to the other. Sometimes the example is a figure for the white space on which they are inscribed, that which stands out, and sometimes it is the infinite background behind. White on white. The blank is colored by a supplementary white, an extra blank that becomes, as in "Numbers," a blank open on all four sides, a blank that is written, blackens itself of its own accord, a false true blank sense (*sens blanc*), without a blank (sans blanc), no longer countable or totalizable, counting on and discounting itself at once, a blank that indefinitely displaces the margin and undoes what Richard calls "the unitary aspiration of meaning" or the "sure revelation of meaning." The white veil that slips between the blanks, the spacing that guarantees both the gap and the contact, enables us no doubt to see the blanks; it determines them. It could therefore never be lifted without blinding us to death, either by closing or by bursting. But inversely, if it were never lifted, if the hymen remained sealed, the eye would still have no greater capacity to open. The hymen, therefore, is not the truth of an unveiling. There is no *alētheia*, only a wink of the hymen. A rhythmic fall. A regular, *(w)inclined* cadence.

The dream of the "sure revelation of meaning" proposed to us by *L'Univers imaginaire de Mallarmé* thus appears to be a hymen without a fold, a pure unveiling without a snag, a "felicity of expression" and a marriage without difference. But in this wrinkle-free felicity, would there still be such a thing as an "expression," not to speak of a text? Would there be anything beyond a simple parousia of meaning? Not that, in the absence of such parousia, literature would be an infelicity of expression, a romantic inadequacy between expression and meaning. What is in question here is neither a felicity or an infelicity of expression—because there is no longer any expression, at least in the ordinary sense of the word. No doubt the hymen, too, would be one of those "beneficent figures" engendered by "the opposition between the closed and the open," "in which both contradictory needs can be satisfied, successively or simultaneously: for example the *fan*, the *book*, the *dancer*." But such dialectical happiness will never account for a text. If there is text, if the hymen constitutes itself as a textual trace, if it always leaves something behind, it is because its undecidability cuts it off from (prevents it from depending on) every—and hence *any*—signified, whether antithetic or synthetic. (It would be useful to quote in their entirety—and perhaps discuss some of the speculative moments—the analyses put forth by R. G. Cohn concerning what he calls Mallarmé's "antisynthesis" and "dual-polarity" [*L'Oeuvre de Mallarmé*].) Its textuality would not be irreducible if, through the necessities of its functioning, it did not do without (deprivation and/or independence: the hymen is the structure of *and/or*, between *and* and *or*) its refill of signified, in the movement through which it leaps from one to another. Thus, strictly speaking, it is not a true sign or "signifier." And since everything that (becomes) traces owes this to the propagation-structure of the hymen, a text is never truly made up of "signs" or "signifiers." (This, of course, has not prevented us from using the word "signifier" for the sake of convenience, in order to designate, within the former code, that facet of the trace that cuts itself off from meaning or from the signified.)

And now we must attempt to write the word *dissemination*.

And to explain, with Mallarmé's text, why one is always at some pains to follow.

If there is thus no thematic unity or overall meaning to reappropriate beyond the textual instances, no total message located in some imaginary order, intentionality, or lived experience, then the text is no longer the expression or representation (felicitous or otherwise) of any *truth* that would come to diffract or assemble itself in the polysemy of literature. It is this hermeneutic concept of *polysemy* that must be replaced by *dissemination*.

E. S. BURT

Mallarmé's "Sonnet en yx": The Ambiguities of Speculation

Ses purs ongles très haut dédiant leur onyx,
L'Angoisse, ce minuit, soutient, lampadophore,
Maint rêve vespéral brûlé par le Phénix
Que ne recueille pas de cinéraire amphore

Sur les crédences, au salon vide: nul ptyx,
Aboli bibelot d'inanité sonore,
(Car le Maître est allé puiser des pleurs au Styx
Avec ce seul objet dont le Néant s'honore).

Mais proche la croisée au nord vacante, un or
Agonise selon peut-être le décor
Des licornes ruant du feu contre une nixe,

Elle, défunte nue en le miroir, encor
Que, dans l'oubli fermé par le cadre, se fixe
De scintillations sitôt le septuor.

[The onyx of her pure nails offered high,
Lampadephore at midnight, Anguish bears
Many a twilight dream the Phoenix burned
To ashes gathered by no amphora.

On the credence, in the empty room: no ptyx,
Curio of vacuous sonority, extinct
(The Master's gone to dip tears from the Styx
With that unique delight of Nothingness).

But near the vacant northern window, gold
Expires, conformed perhaps to the motif

From *Yale French Studies* no. 54 (1977). © 1977 by Yale French Studies.

Of unicorn flames rearing at a nymph,
She, in the mirror, nude, defunct, although,
Within the framed oblivion at once
Appears, all scintillation, the Septet.]

The most valuable of the body of "secondary" literature which has sprung up about the "Sonnet en *yx*," this first of Mallarmé's "truly hermetic poems" (Robert G. Cohn, *Toward the Poems of Mallarmé*), is suggestive without attempting to be immediately totalizing; it indicates directions or forms links between hitherto unrelated texts. But just as those who attempt to discover the whole of what Mallarmé really meant to say in the sonnet must ultimately leave out much of what he *did* say, so those who interpret the poem in the context of the entirety of the poet's work must eventually cover up the individual sonnet by their reading of the whole. In the first case, the irreducible nature of the poem's particularities is sacrificed immediately to a coherent interpretation. In the second, the poem, as specific self-contained entity, disappears into the larger context of Mallarmé's work. What is gained by putting off interpretation of the poem if such a deferral means that the poem is eventually lost in a totalizing interpretation? The relationships established between poem and poem, word and passage, passage and "thought," point up the ambiguity of their status: meaningful similarities are discovered between texts at the same time as crucial distinctions are forgotten. In establishing these relationships between texts, or noting the differences closing one text off from another, the critic, like the poet, interprets by discovering bridges between one theme and another, one word and another—bridges which permit passage from text to text and fix at the same time the irreducible distance dividing the two contexts. This problem of sense-making as formation of relationships, of leaving out sense and particularity in order to discover sense, is raised directly in the poem by its many ambiguities.

Like the relationships that link one poem to another, ambiguity focuses on the double movement of revealing and concealing, but unlike the former, it operates within the framework of the poem. Ambiguity calls into question the act of privileging univocal meaning, of discovering the coherent whole out of the "sum" of its parts. In other words, while thematic explanations can account for one system of meaning or for another, they depend, in their sense-making process, on the unequivocal—on the one, "true" meaning. In the ambiguities of the "Sonnet en *yx*," however, voices of equal authority vie for supremacy.

There are two distinct kinds of ambiguity in the sonnet which figure this tension: ambiguous syntax, the equivocal word. The ambiguous word, the *ptyx,* may be put into relation with many other images or themes in the poem. It may be interpreted as a seashell, as a writing tablet, as a fold, as a receptacle—depending upon the relationships that the critic chooses to privilege. The ambiguous word is linked to other words by clusters of etymological and sonorous—and even graphemic—connotations. Sense can be made of the *ptyx* only if it is "associated" with other words, only if it is fixed in its context.

Syntactic ambiguities depend explicitly on relationship:

> Quel pivot, j'entends, dans ces contrastes, à l'intelligibilité? il
> faut une garantie—
> 　La Syntaxe—

> [What hinge, I mean, among these contrasts, to intelligibility?
> We must have a guarantee—
> 　Syntax—]

By thematizing intelligibility, syntactic ambiguity questions the very act of making sense of words linked to one another by grammar or by association. The ambiguous word, which means only when put into relation with other words, shows its own insufficiency as self-contained entity. Syntactic ambiguity, which focuses on the relationships between elements, points up the inability of these relationships to explain conclusively. In the first case, the burden of meaning is on the relationships uncovered by the interpreter. The explicit ambiguity of the *ptyx* makes the reader turn to associations with other images, upon which one builds an explanation of the *ptyx* and of the poem. In the second case, the explanation can only be found in the elements that make up the relationship. Only by determining the signification of the sentence's terms can a univocal statement be made about its meaning. But what happens if these two different kinds of ambiguity are juxtaposed? Where would sense lie then? If both the terms and the relationships are ambiguous, our own reading is at the same time necessary and necessarily misleading:

> Tout devient suspens, disposition fragmentaire avec alternance
> et vis-à-vis, concourant au rythme total, lequel serait le poëme

tu, aux blancs; seulement traduit, en une manière, par chaque pendentif.

[Everything becomes suspense, fragmentary disposition with alternation and counterpart, running to the entire rhythm, which would be the poem, silenced, to blanks; only translated, in a manner, by each pendative.]

Although Mallarmé's poems insist on hesitation, on ambiguity, they are not incoherent. Sense may be suspended, may be put into question, but it is also necessarily there:

Tout écrit, extérieurement à son trésor, doit, par égard envers ceux dont il emprunte, après tout, pour un objet autre, le langage, présenter, avec les mots, un sens même indifférent.

[All writing, outside of its treasury, ought, out of respect for those of whom it borrows the language, for, after all, a different object, to present, with the words, even an indifferent meaning.]

In fact, despite the difficulty of the sonnet, the "décor" described, as well as the eye viewing it, can be discovered. The following reading of the scene represented might satisfactorily "explain" the series of reflections and repetitions in the tercets as analogous to what is "seen" in the poem. In a letter to Cazalis, Mallarmé describes the scene of the earlier version of the sonnet:

Par exemple une fenêtre nocturne ouverte, les deux volets attachés: une chambre avec une personne dedans, malgré l'air stable que présentent les volets attachés, et dans une nuit faite d'absence et d'interrogation, sans meuble, sinon l'ébauche plausible de vagues consoles, un cadre belliqueux et agonisant, du miroir appendu au fond, avec sa réflexion stellaire et incompréhensible, de la grande Ourse, qui relie au ciel seul ce logis abandonné du monde.

[For example, an open nocturnal window, the two shutters tied back: a room with a person in it, in spite of the unchanging aspect which the tied shutters present, and in a night made of absence and interrogation, without furniture, except for the plausible outline of indistinct brackets, a bellicose and agonizing frame, of the mirror hung at the back, with its stellar and in-

comprehensible reflection of the Ursa Major, which connects this
lodging abandoned by the world to the sky alone.]

This commentary provides a description of the space seen from outside
of the room. But the final version of the sonnet appears, at least initially, to
depend on a spectator located within. If this is the case, in the first quatrain
the onlooker would turn his gaze to the north, noting the "purs ongles" (the
stars), and the lamp of the moon hung in the sky outside. In the second
quatrain, as he turns to the inside of the room, he remarks on the absence
of furniture and of the *ptyx* in the "salon vide." In the first tercet, he turns
again toward the outside, but this time his eye may be caught as much by a
gleam in the window as by a gold outside the room. The mirror, hung on the
wall opposite the window (according to the letter quoted above), may perhaps be reflected in the glass—or rather, its frame may glitter momentarily
in the "vacant" window casements. Perhaps the gold is the stars, linked only
to the mirror frame by memory, but in either case there is now a relationship
formed between the room and the outer universe. In the final verse, as the
spectator looks again into the room, he catches the reflection of the Big
Dipper fixed in the mirror.

This representation of the scene depends on a spectator (the poet), and
insofar as there is a point of view, this eye must be located. But, as the poem
tells us, there is no I: "Car le Maître est allé puiser des pleurs au Styx."
Indeed, Anguish is the subject of the poem's quatrains, not the first person.
Our reading, then, must remain a tentative one. In fact, it would be possible
to make a strong case for an opposite interpretation, for a spectator looking
in from outside the room as in the letter cited above. Here, he would first
look up at the sky, next into the empty room. Then, catching a glimpse of
the reflected stars in the pane (or perhaps the gold of the mirror seen
through the window) he would peer more closely at the "croisée" and see
through it this time into the mirror which reflects the stars. This latter
reading, like the first, depends on the *alternating* functions of the window as
reflector and as transparent surface. Since the first quatrain contains the
subject, this interpretation would seem to be in line with Mallarmé's prose
description of the scene, and hence more attractive. It would not explain
"une personne dedans," however, and would leave out the suggestive series
of reflections between mirror and window.

A breakdown of the distinction between inside and outside is inscribed
in other possible "points of view." Since glass is both transparent and
reflecting, the poet can see through the glass or in the glass. He can see the
reflections of objects within the room and "representations" of the world

outside passing in through the panes. And were he to turn to the glass of the mirror, he would continue to see the stars and the moon—and perhaps even the décor of the room—reflected in this looking glass. He might also see this room reflected by the glass of the window, and the whole—glass and reflected room—in the mirror. These readings would require that the window contain *at the same time* reflection and representation. Although the window may permit the simultaneity of these two kinds of images, the eye can only focus on each one successively.

It might be possible to synthesize all these plausible readings, to come up with an "explanation" for the "floating eye." If two mirrors face one another, "infinite" reflection occurs only if there is no object, no eye, standing in the way of the point of infinity. In other words, only when the two reflecting surfaces reflect nothing but themselves is there an infinity of reflections. Such reflection, nothing but the sterile repetition of an identity, shows itself to be—literally—a reflection of no thing, of nothing. The fact that this reflection is based on an exclusion of all things, an inclusion of "nothing," would make it a "one-sided" infinity—if one may still speak of infinity in such a case—in Hegel's terms, a "bad infinity."

If a mirror stands in front of an empty window frame looking out onto a nocturnal sky, then a part of the infinity of space may pass through the window to be reflected in the mirror. Here, there is a reflection of something—a part of space—and literally, an exclusion of no thing, since everything may be, indeed must be, included in the reflection of infinity. Unlike the first case, in which the eye must be absent in order for infinite reflection to occur, here it must be omni-present in order to unite the dispersed material and establish the totality of infinity. In this sense, the infinite multitude of "somethings" that pass through the window form a collection; but this collection is not a re-collection, that is, there is no identity but only difference. Such a collection would threaten with absolute difference, relating objects to one another only insofar as they occupy the same space. The limited nature of the infinity involved—which prevents it from including nothing, i.e., the relationship of absolute identity already discussed—would make of it another "bad infinity."

Can the infinite reflection of the two mirrors and the reflection of the infinite universe form together the infinite reflection of infinity? It would seem that such a project would be a central question of the poem. The window to the outside can serve as simultaneously reflecting and transparent surface. But can the eye (I), the mind, hold on to (fix) two contradictory, mutually excluding systems at the same time, or can it entertain them only successively? In order for reflection to occur, the lamp within the room, the

stars outside, must light up the surrounding space. If the light stands between the two mirrors, there is no point of infinity. If it is oblique to them,
the infinity cannot be seen. Similarly, without the stars there is no perception of the infinite multitude of things. But the stars introduce identity into
the infinite difference of space. They light up regions of space to the exclusion of others and create configurations which force the infinity of differences into the background. In other words, the finite sources of light are at
the same time the condition of and the obstacle to the infinite reflection of
infinity. The eye, like the light, must be simultaneously present and absent,
inside and outside, in order to posit what it cannot see. The spectator, like
the light sources, is the condition of the infinities that he stands in the way
of; his eye (I) must "float," must be dispersed, in order for him to conceive
of these mutually excluding infinities at the same time as he attempts to
reconcile them. The final image of the poem, the fixing of the starlight in the
dark mirror would be, then, both a victory and a defeat.

A tension between white and black, or more particularly, between light
and lack of light, characterizes the poem. The polarity is set up in the first
quatrain, between the "purs ongles" and the darker midnight (or even
Anguish who "plants her black flag" in Baudelaire's "Spleen"). In fact, a
similar tension might be discovered between "purs" and the white stars
described in the image, since purity—by definition that which lacks mixture,
that which remains homogeneous—is in conflict with the white heterogeneous light of the fingernail-stars. On a "referential" level, black, the absence of light and color, and white, the presence of light and all color, are
both to be found in the onyx, a translucent precious stone containing parallel and concentric layers of different colors. The stone most often appears
to be black, but when turned to the light, these various layers of color are
revealed. In terms of his own "logic" of sonority, Mallarmé notes elsewhere
"la perversité conférant à *jour* comme à *nuit*, contradictoirement, des tim-
bres obscur ici, là clair" [the perversity conferring to day (*jour*) as to night
(*nuit*), contradictorily, obscure tones here, light there]. The "clear" vowel *i*
and the darker *o*, the vowels recurring most often in the poem, are both to
be found in this single word, "onyx."

The suspension of the two colors that occurred in "onyx," may also be
found in the second line. (This suspension is also suggested by the "licorne"
whose horn is striped black and white.) "Minuit," the hour of greatest
darkness, is formed of two "clear" vowels while, temporally, it marks the
time half-way between the disappearance and the reappearance of the sun.
"Lampadophore," which ends the first line, also participates phonetically in
the darkness. And, if understood as being in apposition with "Angoisse," it

can be seen as a mere repetition of the black associated with this figure. But
the lamp carried by Anguish must be a light—the moon perhaps. In one
sense, a certain crossed structure has been set up. The white fingernails give
way to the darker onyx in the first line; in the second, dark Anguish and
midnight become the light of the lamp. But a reading of connotations in-
termingles each color with its opposite, suspending them in a kind of endless
repetition. "Purs ongles," "onyx," "minuit," "lampadophore"—each contains elements on a referential or phonetic level of light and lack of light.

The static quality of the first quatrain seems to be due to similar repetitions. The two verbal forms, "soutient" and "dédiant," occur in parallel
places and are both present tense forms. Not only do the terms that indicate
color occur at the beginnings and endings of the two lines, but also the
present participial construction "très haut dédiant" indicates the same vertical upward movement of "soutient" that is also suggested by one of the
Greek roots of "lampadophore"—"bearer." In addition, "ang" repeats
phonetically the "ong" of the first line. Even within the graphemic and
phonetic structure of the first line there is repetition—"pURs
ONgles" / "leUr ONyx"; and the second line shows a similar pattern—
"L'ANgoisse" / "LAMpadophore." In one sense, the second line might be
considered a kind of reflection on the first—from the crossing over of the
color terms noted above. But in another sense, this first line is only a transformed repetition of its predecessor. A certain distancing from the first
image has been accomplished through transformation: the fingernails are
"higher up" than Anguish. And, in addition, the cruelty connoted by "ongle"
and "onyx" through their common Greek root, "claw," is here transformed
into an Anguish in *relation* to that cruelty, and to the distant and pure stars
that figure it. These cruel fingernails are made of precious stone; they are
foreign to the personified Anguish and of a different material than the black
space which they light up. Similarly, Anguish, properly "narrow" from the
Latin "angustus," is divided as contraction from the vastness of the dark
universe.

In the first line, the universe is transformed in terms of the subject; the
stars are *her* fingernails. Here, in the second line, it is no longer a natural
phenomenon that is personified, subjectified, but a physical and mental state
of a human being that is objectified. The consciousness that has imposed a
human order on the universe distances itself first of all from its own parts,
but secondly, from its own pathos. The coldness and distance that Cohn
notes in this quatrain may be partly due to the objectification of an affective
state into the almost sculpted figure of "Angoisse." The static quality of the
stanza, as well as the abundance of words with Greek roots and connota-

tions of Greek religious rites would link Anguish to figures in classical art. This statue of "Angoisse" holding her hands up to the heavens is reminiscent of Atlas who bears the universe on his broad shoulders. As in a certain notion of classical art, the physical form and the ideal content seem to be in harmony. Anguish, the feeling of anxiety in the face of danger, is one with the hour of midnight, the moment of highest tension in the solar drama of which Gardner Davies speaks (*Mallarmé et le drama solaire*). Anxiety, in terms of this drama, arises in part because the darkness threatens to swallow up the dedicatory offering of the stars, but perhaps also because the daylight that will follow menaces the human elements in the drama. Anguish and her fingernails figure this tension, this menace.

But if this harmony of form and idea would link the sculpted Anguish to the classical Atlas, there are also several important differences between them. To begin with, the personified form given to the character in this drama is "inscribed" in a space as dark as itself. In other words, there is no sculpture, there is only the positing of such a figure. Anxiety participates in both the light and the dark that she fears. Perhaps more important, Anguish is an apprehension of death which springs into being in the face of the pure, physical and infinite universe, at the same time as it is threatened with extinction by this boundless space. In classical art, it is rather the finished physical form that contrasts with and points toward the grandeur of an ideal, infinite spirit. Unlike Atlas, Anguish does not hold up the world, but rather the burned dreams of what might have been a world. In addition, the personification of a feeling would be in direct contradiction with what Hegel terms the character of the ancient gods: "In their calmness and their serenity they cannot permit themselves to indulge in pleasure, in enjoyment, nor in what we especially term satisfaction." Anguish appears precisely on that (eudaemonic) level of pleasure and pain that is forbidden to these statues of the ancient gods. She is afraid of that which the classical statues represent—the menacing calmness and serenity of the universe. In question here is the negation of the human consciousness and not the transitory nature of the sensuous form.

But the relationships that we have noted—of "onyx" with "ongle," of "ongle" with "Angoisse," with "lampadophore" and finally with "amphore"—are merely formal ones; that is, the phonetic, etymological and graphemic properties of the signifier, or the physical properties of the "referent," form the basis for the patterns of repetition and transformation in this quatrain. The inner, subjective "content" is not grasped, is not "collected" in these images: "Que ne recueille pas de cinéraire amphore." The amphora, both art object and funerary urn whose shape is reminiscent of the statue of Anguish holding up the dreams, the stars and the lamp, is only a "purified" residue of "lAMpadoPHORE." Consciousness is threatened in that it is constantly receding in relation to the multitude of forms, the excess of objectified materiality which it itself has "created." In this sense, the figure of Anguish resembles Mallarmé's conception of Hamlet's role:

> Hamlet extériorise, sur des planches, ce personnage unique d'une tragédie intime et occulte, son nom même affiché exerce sur moi, sur toi qui le lis, une fascination, parente de l'angoisse. . . . L'œuvre de Shakespeare est si bien façonnée selon le seul théâtre de notre esprit, prototype du reste.

> [For that is precisely, uniquely the kind of character that Hamlet externalizes on the stage, in an intimate and occult tragedy; his name, even when posted, has a fascination for me, and for you who read it, which approaches anguish. . . . This work of Shakespeare is so well patterned on the theater of the mind alone—this being the prototype of all the others.]

Like Hamlet, Anguish is the dramatic character who cannot seize herself: "mais avance *le seigneur latent qui ne peut devenir* [And now here comes the *prince of promise unfulfillable*]." Both Anguish and Hamlet are characters in a play, in a spectacle. Their task is to render their affective states in a series of pictures to be picked up and understood by an audience. But they are limited by the one-sidedness of their roles. Hamlet reappears night after night and repeats the same words, the same indecision, performs the same actions, and dies the same death. Hamlet (as character, as role) cannot be said to "profit" from his own lesson, to have grasped himself or to have "understood" his play.

The Phoenix is cast in a similar role in this poem, as elsewhere in "Sauvegarde [Safeguard]":

> Cette rumeur, plutôt, qui en fait des élus murés dans la survivance—comme rameau la syntaxe nue d'une phrase, attentifs à la dalle funèbre du dictionnaire, que jonchent les mots épars: ou si, quant à leur métaphore, les inquiète le trépas en double emploi et réel de l'un d'eux, tout de suite ils gravissent un tréteau où le successeur achève par des traits compris d'elle seule l'ombre malséante et invite au carquois vidé de quelque autre, pour paraître invulnérable. Le spectacle, à l'assistance, impose un ex-

ploit mythique, peut-être du Phénix recouvré de sa cendre tel que le peuvent jouer les humains.

[That rumbling, however, which turns them into the elected encrypted in living on—as a bough, the naked syntax of a sentence—paying attention to the gravestone of the dictionary, strewn by the scattered words: or if, as to their metaphor, the pleonastic and actual decease of one of them upsets them, all of a sudden they climb onto the stage where the successor finishes off the unseemly shadow, with barbs that only the shadow can understand, and invites another's emptied quiver to the sport, in order to appear invulnerable. The spectacle impresses a mythic exploit upon the audience, perhaps that of the Phoenix recovered from his own ashes, at least as far as humans can play it.]

The Phoenix, the mythical bird that destroys itself every five hundred years in order to be born again, is indeed the figure for the repetition that we have discussed. It is eternally itself, and yet needs to "transform" its own exterior form in order to insure its survival. Emblem of immortality and of renascence, it also guarantees its own lineage. Like Anguish and Hamlet, the Phoenix performs an exploit for an audience, repeats its own drama in such a way that its transformation yields no self-consciousness to it, but rather only renewed self-identity. It steps out of its own ashes in a form identical to the one it has just shed. The suspension that characterizes Hamlet is proper to the Phoenix as well: "Son solitaire drame! et qui, parfois, tant ce promeneur d'un labyrinthe de trouble et de griefs en prolonge les circuits avec le suspens d'un acte inachevé . . . car il n'est point d'autre sujet, sachez bien. [The lonely drama that he plays! This walker in a labyrinth of agitation and grievance so prolongs its windings with his unfinishing of an unfinished act.]" That the Phoenix can be identified with the "incompleteness" of the drama of Hamlet or of *Igitur* also points to another link between it and the theater. The Phoenix is concerned with relationships, with its antecedent and with its successor. As such, Mallarmé links it to syntax, to the line of discourse which guarantees formally the continuity of sense. In the "Sonnet en *yx*," the Phoenix appears between two syntactic ambiguities: the antecedent for "lampadophore," as Abastado has suggested ("Lecture inverse d'un sonnet nul"), may be either "Angoisse" or "rêves"; "Que ne recueille pas de cinéraire amphore" may depend on either the "Phénix" or on "rêves." The mythical creature that is reborn identical to itself, and yet steps out of its own ashes, is comparable in a sense to the putting into question of formal relationships which occurs in these ambiguities. Whether "Angoisse" or "rêves" serves as the antecedent for "lampadophore" is, grammatically speaking, indifferent. The "naked syntax" would make sense of either, for syntax concerns itself—like the theater, like the Phoenix—with roles. And yet the "renewal" of the system of grammatical relationships— through the suspension provided by ambiguity—points to another path toward meaning at the same time as it draws attention to this indifference of grammar to sense-making. Machine for interpreting the world, grammar shows its capacity to manipulate the meanings of the terms that it relates. It threatens simultaneously with an excess of sense (since there is no necessary formal relationship between "Angoisse," "lampadophore," and "rêves") and with a lack of sense (since it proves itself inadequate to establish differences except by relationship). But what is the effect of ambiguity on the system of repetitions and transformations noted earlier? The answer lies in the examples.

If Anguish is the antecedent for "lampadophore," then it holds up the fingernail-stars and the ashes of the burned dreams in addition to the lamp. "Lampadophore" may, however, be linked with "rêves," since Mallarmé occasionally anteposes appositions. Then the dreams, carried by Anguish, would bear the lamp. This lamp, which Cohn associates with the moon, may also be linked profitably with the commonplace image of the lamp as consciousness, especially in view of the fact that "Angoisse" is at the same time a projection of the human consciousness and "lamp-bearer," carrier, of that consciousness. Consciousness would then reside in the forms and relationships that it has created. Such a reading would establish an identity between Anguish and the lamp. If the dreams hold up the lamp, then they would also carry the Anguish that carries them. A kind of crossing over of terms occurs here. In the first reading, Anguish bears the lamp and the dreams. Since the lamp and Anguish are images for the same consciousness, in a second reading the dreams would bear both of them. The crossed terms are the subject and the object. Such a reversal of terms interrupts the static quality of the first quatrain, providing several possibilities of relating the dreams, Anguish and the lamp to one another. Anguish is the carrier of consciousness, that recognition in the face of death which causes consciousness to spring up, and at the same time she is "born" of consciousness, carried by the dreams—dreams which on the one hand are the manifestations of consciousness lit up by its "lamp," and on the other serve as its very foundation. Contradictory relationships which exist simultaneously in the syntax but which can only be read successively are revealed by this chiasmic reversal. The system of formal relationships which would permit the chiasmus points to an excess of meaning, to a simultaneity of sense, at the same time as it reveals its inadequacy to account for this sense. The form—which can permit these two contradictory meanings to co-exist "within" it—cannot permit both of them to be read at the same time. On the other hand, grammar also shows its inability to express the "true" relationship between subject and object to which it points. Syntactic ambiguity puts into question the system of formal relationships, which points to a single sense at the same time as it refuses univocal meaning, and simultaneously shows a richness of meaning and admits its own inability to express such equivocalness. The chiasmus, a particularly fruitful way of linking terms ambiguously, directs the search for meaning away from the network of relationships and onto the constitutive terms of these relationships by identifying subject and object with one another. Such an identity is, as has been shown, a problematic one, since it depends on a simultaneity of readings which are mutually exclusive. The subject cannot be both subject and object at the same time—at least so long as the verb is nonreflexive. The chiasmus, which establishes the identity of "Angoisse" and "rêves," is also dependent on the difference between them—a difference maintained formally by the syntactic functions performed by the terms. But, in showing their inability to express adequately the subject that has created them, these successive forms exteriorized by the subject open the way to the reflexiveness of the second quatrain. Through these successive readings the syntactically ambiguous statement finds the system of relationships and of antecedents insufficient to bear the burden of meaning. This load is thrown back onto the words themselves, onto the subject that hides "content" in it. The Phoenix that sheds its old form to take on a new one performs a transformation that only point up its identity with itself. For the Phoenix, preoccupied with this change of skin, there is renewal, difference. But the spectator might note that this rebirth seems peculiarly static in quality, that the Phoenix has not changed a whit in all the flurry of its activity. What then is the Phoenix in itself, the word by itself? This question is taken up by the second quatrain—and by the *ptyx*.

The movement away from the scene outside toward the interior of the room is accomplished in the first line: "Sur les crédences, au salon vide: nul ptyx." In contrast to the first stanza, the limits of the space are clearly defined, the "place" of the second quatrain located by the two prepositions. The focal point is an object, the absent *ptyx*. The final image in the last line of the first quatrain—the amphora—is of a container which does not contain. Here, the "empty" room contains "l'ébauche plausible de vagues consoles [plausible outline of indistinct credences]," according to the letter to

Cazalis, as well as an object called up out of "la magie de la rime [the magic of rhyme]." These contents of the circumscribed space are injected with more than a small dose of nothingness. "Vide," "nul," "ptyx" (since *ptyx* does not exist in French), "aboli," "inanité" (which comes from the Latin "inanus"—"empty"), the past tense "est allé," "Styx" (the river that winds around Hades and is poison to those who drink of it), and "Néant"—the words of this second quatrain participate overwhelmingly in negativity. In addition to these indices of emptiness, the subject and object of the sentence that ends in the second quatrain both appear in the first stanza. The value of the second quatrain is merely that of a qualifying statement. Neither "independent" sentence nor dependent clause, it serves to expand the "complete" sentence of the first quatrain. The statue of Anguish inscribed in the darkness of space, the stars seen as extensions of the hand, are both projections of the subject onto an already present form. Similarly, Anguish and the dreams may be considered as performing primarily grammatical functions. In the second quatrain, this subservience to given syntactic necessities is no longer the rule. The function of the parenthesis is precisely to interrupt the syntax of the sentence, to permit the digressive or the incidental statement. The problematic punctuation and the ellipsis of the first lines may indicate more freedom from rigid grammatical constraints.

The relative freedom attained in syntax can be related to another problem of the second stanza. The multitude of images of the first quatrain here gives way to a solitary object. This object, "ce seul objet dont le Néant s'honore," is not only an "invented" word, it is also evoked out of the emptiness of the room. Why mention the *ptyx* if, in fact, it is not there? Like the digressive parenthetical remark, the *ptyx* is not a presence in need of interpretation or explanation in terms of a subject. It comes out of nowhere into the empty room; yet it remains absent. No longer a projection of the self imposed on an already extant natural universe, it is posited as a possible object that might begin to fill up the empty space.

But the *ptyx* is a problematic object. Evoked out of nothing, it also participates in that nothingness. The *ptyx,* which has meaning in Greek, does not exist in French; it is a word taken out of a past context and inserted in one foreign to it. Less word at its source than word irrevocably lost because of its pastness, because its context has disappeared, the *ptyx* reintroduces the problem of excess and lack of sense. Interpreters of the poem have had to deal with this question. They have proposed many meanings for the *ptyx* (and there are more to be discovered). Indeed, so many senses are hidden in this word that, taken together, they would make *no* sense. Most critics would choose a single interpretation out of many. Gretchen Kromer prefers the signification of "writing tablets," linking the *ptyx* to "le Livre." Others give the *ptyx* the meaning of seashell, a container, relating it to the amphora. Henry Grubbs leaves it its meaninglessness, adding that "something is created out of nothing." It would also be possible to give it the vague meaning of "fold." The poem provides evidence to support all these interpretations. A proponent of the seashell theory could cite the knickknack [or, curio] and the amphora. One might also suggest that "licorne" and "lampe" are shellfish, mentioning that "ongles" may be "divers opercules des coquilles." Such a definition would also fit in nicely with the "fiole" from which the character of *Igitur* drinks poison—and one might cite the Styx as poisonous substance, the unicorn's horn as antidote to the poison, and the credenzas [or credences] (from the Italian "credere"—"to believe"), as the consoles on which the liqueurs to be served to the princes of the Renaissance were placed before being tasted for poison. Finally, a "coquille" in French may mean "printing error" and it is as misprint that the *ptyx* may first strike us. It has also been associated with the "repli de la rime [the folding back (reply) of the rhyme]" by Robert Nelson, as well as with "pyx," an English word signifying the container in which the Eucharist is kept, by A. R. Chisholm ("Mallarmé: "Ses purs ongles' "). (If Mallarmé did find "pyx" in an English dictionary, he might also have seen an entry under "Pyxis"—a constellation in the Southern Hemisphere. The "Phénix" and the "licorne," as well as the Big Dipper referred to in the last line, are also constellations.) In line with the overwhelming negativity of the second quatrain, the *pty* of *ptyx* might be linked to "emPTY." In his article, Pierre Citron relates the *ptyx* to the horn of the unicorn and to the "onyx," a suggestive link since the antelope's name resumes the rhyme scheme ("Sur le sonnet en -yx de Mallarmé").

While many of these definitions are plausible and even attractive, the *ptyx* is first of all a group of letters that means nothing. The second line— "Aboli bibelot d'inanité sonore"—which is in apposition to the *ptyx,* comments on this function. The *ptyx* is a sonorous inanity, a misprint that fills out a difficult rhyme scheme. To put the *ptyx* into relationship with other texts in Mallarmé's work, to bring in its Greek meanings or to find English look-alikes, tempting though it may be, is also to forget part of the peculiarity of the word's status. In a sense, one can say that the *ptyx* reflects nothing more than itself. It is fully adequate to itself in that its only referent is itself, in that the signifier and the signified are one and the same, in that what it names is exactly itself. In these senses, the *ptyx* stands alone. The fact that it is found in the middle of a poem permits hypotheses on possible relationships with other things in that poem. But insofar as the *ptyx* is only related to itself, equals only itself, it has no parallel, and no relationship, with any other image in the sonnet. It is linked to the credenzas in the first line, but only to affirm that it has no relation to them. That it reflects only itself is suggested by a reading of the second line—not only in terms of meaning, but also by the reversed letters found inside the words themselves: the *oli* of "abOLI" becomes *ilo* in "bIbeLOt"; *ina* reflects *ani*, *on* reflects *no* in "INANIté sONOre." In each case, the reversed letters turn around a pivotal letter.

The *ptyx* is pure tautology. In that sense, it collapses the distinction between subject and object, relegating them to a shadowy world. The reflection in which it engages is merely a tautological repetition of its own adequacy to itself. That is, the private voice that has found a word expressing itself so completely as to be without relationship to anything else, can only repeat itself over and over. This word invented by the rhyme, which one might see as a residue of other phonetic or semantic elements found in the first quatrain—the "Phénix" and the "onyx," for example, or the "amphore" because of its shape—does not point up these relationships. It is a private word whose status as residue reflecting on itself gives it a self-sufficiency and a "re-collection" of itself that is missing in the first stanza. The *ptyx* is first of all no thing. It is divorced from the form and shape of the objective world so entirely that what it grasps when it seizes itself is precisely its own nature, that of being no thing, nothing. In its adequation to itself, it seems to have no contact with the exterior, objectified world of the first quatrain. In that it contains itself, it renders the distance between subject and object meaningless.

But the *ptyx* is also residue—phonetic and graphemic remains of the poem, residue of Greek civilization. It exists only by virtue of its material and sensuous components. In that it has no referent, in that it is an image of no thing, the *ptyx* seems to form an adequate relationship (i.e., no relationship but rather identity) between its meaning and its form. But, because the *ptyx* is an image, even if only an image of itself, because it is created by and dependent on its materiality as sheer meaningless signifier in order to attain this perfect adequation to itself, the tautology of the *ptyx* shows itself to be self-defeating. The word's meaninglessness, which on the one hand frees it from all materiality, referentiality and exterior form, on the other hand serves to stress its nature as physical object: "ce seul objet dont le Néant s'honore." Kenneth Burke formulates succinctly the impossibility of "conceiving of nothing": "Insofar as an *idea* of "Nothing" involves an *image,* it must be an image of "something," since there can be no other kinds of image" (*The Rhetoric of Religion*).

With the reemergence of the *ptyx* as object, the distinction between subject and object also reappears. The *ptyx* in its fixity is an inadequate expression of the subject in that it is incapable of any relationships but one-sided "relationships" of identity. Tautological repetition does not account for the capacity of the subject to recognize and establish differences, to create formal links between objects. The series of transformations performed by the subject in the first quatrain has provided the necessary point of departure for the *ptyx,* the background against which it must be set. These transformations threatened ultimately to become meaningless as the subject exteriorized fragments of itself without being able to establish an identity between them. Here, inanity is promised by the inability of the subject to distinguish difference.

Sonorous inanity also describes the *ptyx.* Although it is related to other words musically through the rhyme scheme, it is a note struck only once in this quatrain—unlike the homonyms "sonore" / "s'honore" and the "Styx" which repeats the letter *s.* As a single note, it is significant that it is formed of a whole series of "stops" in Mallarmé's terms and indeed is set off by itself between two punctuation marks. That it is a word in Greek, meaning something in a classical text or in a dictionary, but that has been set down in a context which takes away its meaning—a French poem—only serves to heighten this isolation. The single musical tone that it strikes may be held (although with difficulty, due to its phonetic makeup), in which case it becomes a monotone, an irritation that, if listened to long enough, will become so familiar as to disappear. And if struck only once, as a staccato, it will also rapidly die away. A solitary "note" is not only not music, it also has no meaning. Music necessitates memory, that is to say, relationship. For the "chord to be struck" in a subject, at the very least several notes must be played. There can be no "re-collection" until there is repetition, but that repetition must also include difference—again, relationship. It is in the second line, the more "musical" of the two, that the necessity of the musical phrase is made apparent. Unlike the collected consonants of the *ptyx,* this line abounds in vowels which turn around pivotal letters. In the sense that music implies a remembering, a synthetic moment of a present note and a "forgotten" past one that must be separated by at least one different note in order to establish identity, this second line succeeds where the first fails in providing sonorous "recollection." The second line is in apposition with the *ptyx,* however, and as such is related only to it. The *ptyx* as musical word has a capital importance in terms of memory, insofar as "music" is made up of a series of *ptyxes,* that is to say, meaningless, nonreferential sounds. But it has also shown its inability (in terms of the "musical word") to preserve

that entirely nonreferential status in that its excess of materiality would give
back to it the burden of signification. Hence, the *ptyx* "is" a seashell, a
unicorn's horn, a book, a fold. The second line also tells us what the *ptyx*
is. It unfolds the "meaning" of the *ptyx*—its meaninglessness. But by the
very fact that it is in apposition with the *ptyx*, it also points up that object's
insufficiency in itself, in its proclaimed meaninglessness, by putting it into
relation with another element that makes it signify something—"aboli bibelot d'inanité sonore." Because the *ptyx is* something, it is not without
meaning. The *ptyx* is indeed a "folding" in on itself in that it achieves a
momentary adequation to itself which disappears again as it is "unfolded."
This solitary sign dropped into a context takes on meaning; it is linked to
other words, to other groups of meaning. The *ptyx*, then, is both a total lack
of meaning, in that it is adequate to itself, and an excessive meaningfulness
since it also proves to be inadequate.

The second line, which comments on this meaninglessness at the same
time as it shows that meaning can and must be attached to the *ptyx*, also
points to its musical nature and to its failure as a single note. But this second
line, while achieving a certain "musicality" that links sounds through memory, can be put in relation to the *ptyx* only in terms of its ambiguous status
as excess and lack of meaning. Because the *ptyx* is excessively meaningful,
because it can be linked to elements throughout the poem, the second line
is inadequate to its task of "explaining." It has no phonetic relationships to
the "residue" of the *ptyx* except the *t*, and although "knickknack" may
indeed suggest seashell, or "BIBeLOT" invoke book, these indices are only
part of the network of meanings in which the *ptyx* is involved. And, as
paucity of meaning, as word standing alone adequate to itself, the second
line means too much for the *ptyx*. In its apposition to the ptyx, to the "no
thing" that the ptyx "represents," it is excessive modification and meaning.
It puts into relationship, unfolds the music which the *ptyx* contains within
itself.

The *ptyx*, then, is the ambiguity of a non-sense word that at the same
time has excessive sense, which in turn threatens to become no meaning. It
expands sense, reverberates and vibrates throughout the poem, but at the
same time it tries to dispense with meaning entirely. The private word with
no "sens réel," "created" by the rhyme, is both more and less than the
meaningful words that surround it: "Le souhait d'un terme de splendeur
brillant, ou qu'il s'éteigne, inverse. [The desire for a term of brilliant splen-
dor, or, inversely, that it is put out.]" But if the word is a "centre de suspens
vibratoire," this vibration must put other words into relation, must, in the
poet's terms, find "avant extinction, (à) une réciprocité de feux distante ou

présentée de biais comme contingence [before extinction, (to) an exchange of distant fires or obliquely presented as a contingency]." Although the *ptyx* shows the failure of the word to contain itself indefinitely, it does achieve a certain isolation that implies, in this most private of words, the disappeareance of the subject. By taking himself out of a system of relationships, out of the representational world of the first quatrain, the poet "creates" a private voice—simultaneously of lack and excess—that throws the burden of signification back onto the relationships that can be found between words. The most subjective word, the *ptyx*, also becomes the most "objective" one, the word least tainted by layers of meaning imposed on it by a subject. But it is also the word most susceptible to being read as "meaning," the word that puts the brunt of creating relationships on the reader. In its isolation and meaninglessness, it does not permit a single explanation to be "abstracted" out of it, to be imposed on it. Rather, it sets in "motion" the surrounding words, demanding to be related to them while at the same time installing a nonreferentiality, an impossibility of certain meaning at the center of the poem:

> L'œuvre pure implique la disparition élocutoire du poëte, qui cède l'initiative aux mots, par le heurt de leur inégalité mobilisés; ils s'allument de reflets réciproques comme une virtuelle traînée de feux sur des pierreries, remplaçant la respiration perceptible en l'ancien souffle lyrique ou la direction personnelle enthousiaste de la phrase.

> [The pure work implies the disappearance of the poet as speaker, yielding his initiative to words, which are mobilized by the shock of their difference; they light up with reciprocal reflections like the virtual stream of fireworks over jewels, restoring perceptible breath to the former lyric impulse, or the enthusiastic personal directing of the sentence.]

The continual grouping and regrouping of images, collecting and recollecting of "reflets," begins with the *ptyx* (which most critics would directly or indirectly make the focal point of the poem). But the *ptyx* needs to be contained by the context of antiquity, of the amphora, of the sonnet, in order for these links to become apparent. Like memory, the *ptyx* must "unite" disparate moments, establish relationships of identity among the dispersed images of the poem. But both memory and the *ptyx* are inadequate to *create* any relationships but one-sided relationships of identity. The words, the pictures that they link must include a necessary difference—

established through the chain of syntax, through representation, to insure that such relationships do not become mere tautologies.

The tercets seem to offer a solution, or at least a possible tempering of the "failure" of the first two quatrains. They are in opposition to the quatrains: the words linked to classical civilization have given way to terms connoting the Middle Ages and European Christianity. "Nixe," for example, comes from German. The "croisée" is reminiscent of the cross from which it originally came. "Licorne" is distanced from Latin by a change from "unicornis" through the Italian "alicorno." The emblems of the Middle Ages permit a link between the unicorn and Christ. And the change in rhyme scheme, from *yx/ore* to *ixe/or*, also points to this opposition. Finally, a new color term appears, the gold. This gold may refer back to the vesperal setting of the sun—"un or agonise." But it may also be a looking forward to a future sunrise: gold is linked to Aurora in *Les Dieux antiques* [*The Ancient Gods*]":

> Inutile de dire qu'Aurore est la déesse du matin. . . . Remarquez seulement que ce nom correspond à quelque chose dans la mythologie orientale: il se rattache au sanscrit Ushas, un nom de l'aurore, issu d'une racine commune au latin *aurum*, l'or, et *urere*, brûler.

> [Useless to say that Aurora is the goddess of the morning. . . . Notice only that this name corresponds to something in Oriental mythology: it is linked to the Sanskrit Ushas, a name of the dawn, sprung from a root common to Latin *aurum*, gold, and *urere*, to burn.]

The gold of the sunset and of the dawn would then be linked through the "rêves brûlés" and the "or." At the same time referring back to the "past" sunset, this gold is also a first appearance, or rather, a dramatic reappearance, of the sun.

Phonetically and graphemically these tercets show both a similarity to and a difference from the first two quatrains. The transformations discussed in terms of the first quatrain occur here also. Related anagrammatically to "Angoisse," "Agonise" is also the death menacing the forms. "PHENIX" is repeated in "FEU contre une NIXe" and in "FIXe," "aBOLI" might be linked to "OuBLI." But in the first quatrain there was a tendency toward a "purifying" transformation, with a consequent contracting movement— from "lAMpadoPHORE" to "AMPHORE," for example. Here, as is shown by the resemblance between "Phénix" and "feu contre une nixe," the movement may also be expansive. At the same time, it may contract—"feu contre une nixe" becomes "fixe." The reflections noted in the second quatrain occur here: "AU NOrd," "vACAnte." But whereas the "reflecting" letters of the second quatrain turned around a pivotal letter, here they also occur separately, as terms whose parallel structure shows a crossing over: "pROche la cROisée au nORd vacante un OR" is perfectly symmetrical and it is reflected. Similarly, the two *ti* of "scinTIllaTIons" are reversed in "sITôt." The parallels, the reversals, the transformations and the identities that could be pointed out within these tercets or between the tercets and the quatrains are innumerable. But more important, both kinds of phonetic and graphemic repetition are present, and both work on one another. "Oubli" is at the same time a repetition of "aboli bibelot," a transformation of it, and a transposition of some of its letters. In the same way "pROChe," "CROisée," "déCOR," "liCORnes," "COntRe," and "enCOR" show a number of different relationships. These phonetic and graphemic phenomena explain nothing, of course; at most they would indicate a direction to be taken. A certain synthesis of the quatrains, which permits a working together of the representational aspects of the first stanza and the "vivifiant effluve qu'épand la musique [quickening effluvium which music scatters]" of the second, has been effected. What does this synthesis consist of and to what extent is it "successful"? A discussion of a doubly ambiguous line in this last part of the poem may point out some of the answers.

In the line "Elle, défunte nue en le miroir," "nue" may be either an adjective describing the substantive "défunte," or it may be a noun described by the adjectival "défunte." In the first case, "défunte nue" would be "naked dead one," in the second, "dead cloud." As for "elle," most critics have seen the nixie as its antecedent. Even should it refer to this nymph alone, the grammatical construction of the line remains problematic. As Henry Grubbs has noted, "the 'elle' (is) left hanging without a verb." If "elle" does refer to the nixie on the mirror frame (as suggested by the letter to Cazalis), her disappearance into the mirror would suggest that, although perhaps ("peut-être") reflected in the window, she is not reflected by the mirror. If, however, "elle" is in apposition with "croisée," it may be the window that is "défunte" in the looking glass. Or, perhaps the "elle" would once again be in apposition with what follows it, the cloud. In other words, the game of transparence and reflection discussed at the beginning, in reference to the represented scene, would be unfolded by this one line: nonreflection of the nymph, reflection of the vacant window, or in the sky outside passing in through the window—all are interpretations permitted by this suspended sentence.

The previously-discussed ambiguities and their functions are so interwoven in this line that they become dependent on one another. For example,
if one begins interpretation with the syntactical ambiguity of "défunte nue,"
ambiguity would appear on a semantic level: "dead cloud" or "naked dead
one." This ambiguity would, in turn, set in motion the grammatical ambivalence of the referent of "elle." The equivocal status of this pronoun would
force the reader to look closely at one of the possible antecedents. Or,
looking elsewhere in Mallarmé's work, it might be seen that: "Les Nymphes,
charmées de la cour qui leur est faite, ce sont les nuages blancs arrêtés dans
les cieux au dessus du bouquet d'arbres. [The nymphs, charmed by the court
which is paid to them, are the white clouds, stopped in the skies above a
grove of trees.]" One might find a woman at/in the window in "Sainte":

> A la fenêtre recelant
> Le santal vieux qui se dédore
> De sa viole étincelant
> Jadis avec flûte ou mandore,
>
> Est la Sainte pâle.
>
> [At the window ledge concealing
> The ancient sandalwood gold-flaking
> Of her viol dimly twinkling
> Long ago with flute or mandore,
> Stands the palid Saint.]

One might also discover that the nymph Callisto was changed into one of
the stars of the Great Bear. And finally, one might uncover links between
nudity and clouds:

> Le nuage autour exprès: que préciser. . . . Plus, serait entonner le
> rituel et trahir, avec rutilance, le lever de soleil d'une chape
> d'officiant, en place que le desservant enguirlande d'encens, pour
> la masquer, une nudité de lieu.
>
> [The cloud expressly around: to be precise. . . . More, would be
> to strike up the ritual and to betray it by reddening the sunrise of
> a celebrant's cope, instead of the officiating minister engarlanding
> with incense, in order to mask it, a nakedness of the place.]
>
> la trop lucide hantise de cette cime menaçante d'absolu, devinée
> dans le départ des nuées là-haut, fulgurante, nue, seule.

[the too lucid obsession by that threatening peak of the absolute, divined in the departure of the clouds up there, thundering, naked, alone.]

These quotations are not meant to illuminate the poem, but rather to serve as examples of what the reader of Mallarmé is invited to do in his or her interpreting. As one finds a link between two words that seems to "explain" an ambiguity already noted, a momentary triumph may be felt. But a closer look at the citations that one has chosen reveals, in most cases, such complexity of structure, so many possible meanings, that they must be interpreted once again to find out how these words are linked.

The synthesis of syntactic and semantic ambiguities in the poem has achieved something, however. If nothing else, these ambivalences reveal themselves as a constant suspension of a "definite" answer, as a multiplicty of meanings, and as none. They also begin to take on characteristics of one another. The *ptyx*, suspended word, is isolated in the same sense as the suspended syntactic unity, the clause ("elle, défunte nue"). The semantic ambiguity of "défunte nue" is dependent on the syntax. But this ambiguity of words also creates relationships, forming a group reminiscent of the sky of the first quatrain and the "death" in the second—"dead cloud"—as well as a group related to the denuded purity of Anguish and her fingernails and the nothingness of the Styx quatrain—"naked dead one."

The juxtaposition of cloud and nudity in the citation from "Richard Wagner" shows a certain relevance to the final effect of these interwoven ambiguities: "la trop lucide hantise de cette cime menaçante d'absolu, devinée dans le départ des nuées là-haut, fulgurante, nue, seule." Here, the clouds are at the same time what hides and what seems to permit the "hantise," the menacing pinnacle of an absolute. They are simultaneously the condition of, and the obstacle to its discovery, even to its possibility. That which is alone and sufficient to itself, the *ptyx*, has shown itself to be dependent on the representational, on the "objective" meanings and images of the poem. Similarly, the syntactic relationships of "lampadophore" to its two antecedents, which seem to "cloud" the meaning, throw the weight of sense back onto the words themselves, demanding that they mean something by themselves. In both cases, through a veiling of meaning, an insufficiency is discovered, a meaning laid bare.

It is not surprising, then, that the critics—all critics—are constantly thrust back and forth from the lateral meanings to be culled from the rest of Mallarmé's work, onto the poem itself, onto its adequacy to itself. The poem that seems to cut itself off so cleanly from other poems, that achieves a final fixation of a musical image in the mirror, manages to compress a maximum of signification, of ambiguous and therefore excessively meaningful moments, into its own "frame." But, like the *ptyx,* its self-sufficiency is put into question by its own character. As frame, as signifier, it is insufficient, dependent on its materiality, on its links with a space outside of its own closed container. As such, it demands continual relationship with the "outside," with the stars of the last tercet, with the etymologies and layers of meaning to be gleaned from the Littré, with the totality of Mallarmé's work.

ROGER DRAGONETTI

"Le Nénuphar blanc": A Poetic Dream with Two Unknowns

I t is a strange adventure that joins the fiction of a voyage with a more essential immobility!

Thus could one sum up the adventure that is traced by the writing of the poem and erased in the same gesture.

The title of the poem does not seem to allude to this imaginary voyage and appears only to retain the metaphoric goal of this "quest for water flowers (quête de floraison d'eau)": a water-lily whose hollow whiteness envelopes a "nothingness."

The voyage described is made in a "yole," a light boat whose obsolete name, if we are to believe Mallarmé, ought to furnish a clue to the comprehension of the poem: "Notice the fact that the least used words often act as guides, unexpected and precious, between a distant double meaning of two considerable terms."

The passage we have just quoted is part of the text which serves as an introduction to the "Table" of word families in the *Mots anglais*. Strangely enough, in looking over this "Table," we find, under the letter *F,* and in particular in the group headed by *Far,* the word "wherry" which Mallarmé translates by "yole" (skiff [yawl]).

This discovery permits us to glimpse in the phonic nature of the word *nénuphar* the promise of a trip to distant places (to fare). Understood thus, the title would condense remarkably the course of the quest and its object. Besides, this trip which seems to deny itself twice (at any rate if one interprets as a double negation the first two syllables of the word *né-nu-phar*)

From *Yale French Studies* no. 54 (1977). © 1977 by Yale French Studies.

supports admirably, as an imaginary voyage—whose appearances only
would be preserved—the adjective "blanc" (white or blank), in the sense it
has in the expression "mariage blanc" (unconsummated marriage).

Mallarmé hesitated for quite a while about the spelling of the word,
nénuphar or *nénufar* ("Notes"), but the poet's opting in favor of the splitting of the letter *f* into *ph* establishes perhaps a supplementary relationship
with the words wherry and yole, whose initial letters admit graphic division
($v \to w$; $i \to \ddot{y}$).

Note that Mallarmé extracts the sense of an oscillation from the splitting of the letter *W:*

> The senses of oscillating (which would seem due to the vague
> doubling of the letter, then of floating, etc. . . . of water and
> humidity; of fainting and flight; then, of weakness, of charm and
> of imagination) melt in astonishing diversity.
>
> ("Table")

In reading this passage, would not one think he was in the atmosphere
of the poem whose location is figured by a point of suspension on the water,
the site of the oscillation of the *yole?* And does not this doubled initial reflect
both the doubling in the word *wherry* as well as that of the initials engraved
on the *two* oars?

> Je ne vérifiai l'arrêt qu'à l'étincellement stable d'initiales sur
> les avirons mis à nu, ce qui me rappela à mon identité mon-
> daine.
>
> (I only verified the halt by the steady sparkling of the initials on
> the raised oars, which called me back to my worldly identity.)
>
> ("Nénuphar blanc")

This halt in the navigation is thus doubled by the stopping of a flight,
and the oars, like wings, transpose "into the region of luminous phenomena" the oscillation and the aquatic stability both metamorphosed into a
"steady glittering."

Here one thinks of the possibilities of meaning which Mallarmé attributes to the letter *F* when added to the letter *L:*

> It forms with *L* most of the sounds representing the act of flight
> or beating the air, even transposed by rhetoric into the area of
> light phenomena, as well as the act of flowing, as in the classical
> languages.

Evidently, it is the English language which is in question here, but the signifying impulses of isolated letters could constitute the basis of onomatopeia, a process in which, according to Mallarmé, the power of invention has taken refuge: "[onomatopeia] perpetuates in our idioms a process of creation which was perhaps the first of them all" (*Mots anglais*).

In other respects, when Mallarmé declares that the letter *F* "indicates in itself a strong and fixed embrace," how can we not see another analogue to the grasp of the rower entirely turned in upon himself, "les yeux au dedans fixés sur l'entier oubli d'aller" ("Nénuphar")?

Thus, the words "yole" and "nénuphar" seem to have inherited from their immemorial past "a thousand certain and mysterious intentions of language" that one rediscovers within the context of the poem and which "too much [philological] rigor," as Mallarmé again emphasizes, would have "transgressed" (*Mots anglais*).

The following text proves that Mallarmé's reflections are valid as much for English as for French:

> More than one criticism will aim at the translation of this vo-
> cabulary into French: sometimes giving the primitive and now
> least used meaning or molding a thousand every-day nuances
> into a strict generality; it had to be done. It is even common, in
> order to relate a known word to some distant relative, to show
> only an almost accessory nuance of the meaning of this first
> word.

Our analysis will take Mallarmé's reflections into account. They have bearing in a more general way on a new science which opposes to the rigor of traditional philology the poetic instinct of language, thanks to which success can be measured by an *impression* more than by the correctness of an etymology: "A link, so perfect between the meaning and form of a word that it seems to cause only one impression, that of its success, on the mind and the ear." This is why Mallarmé despairs of reaching certain readers, "already too accustomed to the habits of the philologists for this suggestion to reach them," when it will be necessary, for example, to warn his listeners to guard against the historical explanation of certain apparently arbitrary parallels: "no historical relation, in English (at least) and it is to an imme-morial common origin that we must look for resemblances authorizing an apposition." This chimerical science, into which Mallarmé ventures grop-ingly, aims at the "absolute meaning" of letters of the alphabet, "sometimes guessed, sometimes misunderstood" by men, whereas the poet, endowed with a superior instinct, has more of a chance to approach it:

It will be the lot of the poet or even the knowing prosateur, by a superior and free instinct, to bring together terms united with so much more advantage to compete with the charm and music of language as they come as from more fortuitous distances: this is the process inherent in the northern genius, and of which so many famous lines show us so many examples: ALLITERA-TION.

Certainly, a reading of "Nénuphar blanc" will be enriched if one takes into account these fortuitous pairings in which chance takes the place of knowledge. It is thus, for example, that the phonic intensities of the stressed syllable of *fiole, viole, yole* will lead us to discover affinities of meaning despite the difference in kind of these objects; in each of the three cases, there is a hollow envelope containing an essence, be it a perfume, a rhythm, or the intimate being of the rower-magician who identifies himself with the *yole,* as the "soul" of the instrument merges with the viola (viole):

> Courbé dans la sportive attitude . . . je souris au commencement d'esclavage . . . que ne signifiaient pas mal les courroies attachant le soulier du rameur au bois de l'imbarcation, comme on ne fait qu'un avec l'instrument de ses sortilèges.

> (Bent over in the sportive stance . . . I smiled at the beginning of enslavement . . . which the straps attaching the shoe of the rower to the wood of the boat signified fairly well, as a man becomes one with the instrument of his enchantments.)
>
> ("Nénuphar")

A whole analogical network is organized about the idea of a hollow which leads us to other "exquisite emptinesses (vacances)" (*vacances* also gives us the sense of "leisure," "availability," which is associated in the text to the theme of the relaxation of the pleasure trip) like that of the water lily or of the bubble of foam which could reveal the presence of the marauder:

> partir avec: tacitement, en déramant peu à peu sans du heurt briser l'illusion ni que le clapotis de la bulle visible d'écume enroulée à ma fuite ne jette aux pieds survenus de personne la ressemblance transparente du rapt de mon idéale fleur.

> (to leave with it: silently, by rowing backwards little by little, without by the shock breaking the illusion and without the lapping of the visible bubble of foam enrolled in my escape throw-

ing up at anyone's arriving feet the transparent likeness of the abduction of my ideal flower.)

And is it not from the disappearance of this wake of foam that the verse appears in its radical negation?

> "Rien, cette écume, vierge vers."
> ("Salut")

These metaphors are basically only variations of a hollowness in the work of writing whose "cast of the die" (dés) (or of the "d," pronounced in French) will produce, by a successful effect, the relationship between *ramer* and *déramer, row* and *row backwards.* For it is really by the poetic game of language that Mallarmé makes us hear the negative force of the cast of the "die (des)" in such oppositions as *astre/désastre, livre/délivre,* and here *ramer* and *déramer,* two words whose contrary action is the pure product of a poetic invention.

Taken in the context of the "Nénuphar blanc," *ramer* and *déramer* designate respectively the setting out on and return from the trip, whereas the *Littré* only mentions *déramer* (a word which has disappeared from the *Larousse*) in the sense of the "action of removing a cocoon of a silkworm from the branches." With respect to this meaning, fallen into disuse, the other appears manifestly as a happy "coup de dés" of Mallarmean invention and all the more fortunate in that it allows the opposite sense of *déramer,* that is, to spin a cocoon, to flow over onto *ramer.*

The poem thus presents itself as the secretion of a thread (fil) of silk (soie) (or of oneself) (soi) which the poet produces in a state of half-sleep. It is the work of the silkworm (ver(s)) (or line of verse) into whose envelope the true identity of the poet has disappeared, as the other identity, from which the steady *sparkling* of the letters frees itself, is only exterior, worldly. In this context of "spinning (filature)," the skiff, miniscule boat (navire) which carries the *rameur* or the *dérameur,* is metamorphosed into a shuttle (navette), and the back and forth of its shuttling imitates a movement of incessant return to the point of oblivion between two imaginary courses:

> J'avais beaucoup ramé, d'un grand geste net assoupi, les yeux au dedans fixés sur l'entier oubli d'aller, comme le rire de l'heure coulait alentour. Tant d'immobilité paressait que frôlé d'un bruit inerte *où fila jusqu'à moitié la yole,* je ne vérifiai l'arrêt qu'à

l'étincellement stable d'initiales sur les avirons mis à nu, ce qui
me rappela à mon identité mondaine.

("Nénuphar")

(I had rowed much, with a great, clean, sleepy gesture, my eyes
within fixed on the entire forgetting of motion, as the laughter of
the hour flowed about me. So much immobility idled about that
brushed by a dull noise *into which the boat half veered,* I only
verified my stopping by the steady sparkling of initials on the
raised oars, which brought me back to my worldly identity.) (My
italics.)

It is thus that the poem of the "Nénuphar" begins. It paradoxically
takes its departure from its arrival, which results in a confusion of the signs
and a scintillation, which blurs the contours of things and letters:

Je ne vérifiai l'arrêt qu'à l'étincellement stable d'initiales sur les
avirons mis à nu, ce qui me rappela à mon identité mondaine.

Whether it be a question of his worldly identity or the other, through
the luminous or aquatic vibrations, depth is only perceptible in the confused
shimmer of the surfaces.

The stream of revery which has carried the rower to this crucial point
is itself only an *interval* between dormant vegetation:

Il fallut, pour voir clair en l'aventure, me remémorer mon départ
tôt, ce juillet de flamme, sur l'intervalle vif entre ses végétations
dormantes d'un toujours étroit et distrait ruisseau.

(It was necessary, to see the adventure clearly, to recall my early
departure, this flaming July, on the bright interval between the
dormant vegetation of an always narrow and distracted stream.)

As soon as the images doubled by their own reflection have arisen, the
"impartial oar-stroke" destroys their ephemeral consistency:

Sans que le ruban d'aucune herbe me retînt devant un paysage
plus que l'autre chassé avec son reflet en l'onde par le même
impartial coup de rame.

(Without the ribbon of any grass holding me in front of one landscape more than another dispelled with its reflection in the water by the same impartial oar-stroke.)

Forward stroke of the rower (rameur), which aims to make the vegetation and the branches (Mallarmé appears to allow the play in the word *rame* of its homonym [*rame* in Old French means "branch of a tree"]. In retaining this sense, the rower's stroke [*coup de rame*], which erases the ephemeral branches reflected in the pool, produces the effect of a narcissistic gesture. Another homonym, *ramer*, means in Old French, "to return [reciprocate] love.") where the thread of silk or self of the dreamy worm or line of verse (vers rêveur) could spin itself, disappear, and consequently *return stroke of the rower*, desirous of erasing its traces down to the least vestige of this seam, bubble of foam, which could have taken on the consistency of a cocoon:

> partir avec: tacitement, en déramant peu à peu sans du heurt briser l'illusion ni que le clapotis de la bulle visible d'écume enroulée à ma fuite ne jette aux pieds survenus de personne la ressemblance transparente du rapt de mon idéale fleur.

This is really the fundamental mark of the Mallarmean poem whose projection safeguards in its trace the movement of its own disappearance. As in *Igitur,* the poet "proffers the word to plunge it back into its inanity" (*Igitur*).

As with the oar-stroke, the rhythm in the poem puntuates the discourse of this destruction by the blank spaces in the text: intervals of silence with which the writing composes and imitates the play of its oscillation about the critical point. A series of questions brings together the blanks which scan this musical partition in three moments. The first introduces a development on the early part of the trip:

> Qu'arrivait-il, où étais-je?

> [What was happening, where was I?]

The second marks the rhythmic punctuality of the present:

> Le pas cessa, pourquoi?

> [The step ceased why?]

The third bears upon the return trip:

Conseille, ô mon rêve, que faire?

[Counsel, o my dream, what to do?]

The initial question is double: it concerns as much the event (what was happening) as the place (where was I?), practically making time and space concurrent, as well as the present and the past, for, if the first imperfect has the value of a present, the other "where was I" which precedes the remembering of the departure, retains the ambiguity of these two poles of temporality.

Split and reassembled by this question which appears from this stopping-point on the water, time and space will produce, under other forms, the extremes of poetic fluctuation, and not without an effect of confusion. From the *present* to the *past* and vice-versa, the oscillation from "being (étant)" to "been" (été)" engenders first the image of a season, summer (été), "this flaming July," temporal point of departure and then the spatial image of a pond (étang) as an arrival point.

As an effect of these interferences, the *pond,* end-point of the trip, confuses its image with that of a source:

> Je venais échouer dans quelque touffe de roseaux, terme mystérieux de ma course, au milieu de la rivière; où tout de suite élargie en fluvial bosquet, elle étale un nonchaloir d'étang plissé des hésitations à partir qu'a une source.

> (I had just run aground in a clump of reeds, mysterious end of my trip, in the middle of the stream, where immediately enlarged into a watery thicket, it spreads out the nonchalance of a pond rippled with a spring's hesitations at departure.)

One reads almost by transparency the metaphorization of writing's double movement, both linear and undulating: the stream, *interval* between two banks, becomes an interval between two points and reabsorbs them like a flow of ink in this spot which in spilling over hides the true point of origin, that is, the purpose of the quest.

As always, the failure of writing translates itself into hesitations to start out again, but the repetition of the trip will not eliminate for all that the interferences of a new fluctuation.

Whatever the oscillation may be, it plays itself out more fundamentally between the *chance* of the adventure of the marauder "searching for water flowers" and the *calculation* of the rower who left with:

un *dessein* de reconnaître l'emplacement occupé par la propriété de l'amie d'une amie à qui [il] devait improviser un bonjour.

(A *plan* to explore the emplacement occupied by the property of the friend of a friend to whom [he] was supposed to improvise a greeting.) (My italics.)

Two movements intertwine: on the one hand, the desire of the marauder (or the narrator) to wander, which supposes an openness favorable to the turns and detours, on the other hand, the desire to arrive at the goal to *explore* the place. The indeterminateness which affects the identity of the two friends corresponds to this disjunction of desire.

Indeed, how are we to know who is the recipient of the greeting, the unknown or the other? By virtue of its ambiguous position, the relative pronoun *qui* (whom) makes any identification problematic: "la propriété de l'amie d'une amie à qui je devais improviser un bonjour."

Here again, *improvisation* is mixed with the *calculation of the project* as the both dreamy and precise gesture of the rower is compounded into one:

J'avais beaucoup ramé, d'un grand geste *net assoupi*. (My italics.)

In the same way the fixity of the rower or the lazy immobility of the atmosphere, by contrasting themselves to the passing of the hour and the gliding of the boat, participate in the same counterpoint which underlies the entire poem:

. . . comme le rire de l'heure coulait alentour. Tant d'immobilité paressait que frôlé d'un *bruit inerte* où fila jusqu'à moitié la yole.

(the hour's laughter flowed about me. So much immobility idled about that brushed by the *dull noise* where the boat half drifted.) (My italics.)

For whom is this poem, verse of circumstance or this greeting both improvised and premeditated? For Madame X or for the unknown Y?

The figures of these two letters, as well as that of the two friends, scarcely come to the surface of the poem. In the silence of the three dots, the worldly identity of the known friend has erased itself so well that the same incognito surrounds the two women:

> Simplement le parc de Madame . . . l'inconnue à saluer.

(Simply the park of Madame . . . the unknown to be greeted.)

The unknown woman opposed and made parallel to the other becomes by this fact a differentiation of the same.

Correlatively the respective places are presented as a "pretty neighborhood" whose "obstacle of greenery" occupies the undecipherable interval and precisely that point which assures the contiguity and separation of an X spread out on the surface and a Y which plunges its roots into the depths of the water like a water lily:

> L'inspection détaillée m'apprit que cet obstacle de verdure en pointe sur le courant, masquait l'arche unique d'un pont prolongé, à terre, d'ici et de là, par une haie clôturant des pelouses. Je me rendis compte. Simplement le parc de Madame . . . l'inconnue à saluer.
>
> Un joli voisinage.

> (Detailed inspection taught me that this tapering obstacle of greenery on the current masked the single arch of a bridge prolonged on land on both sides by a hedge enclosing lawns. Then it became clear. Simply the park of Madame . . . the unknown to be greeted.
>
> A pretty neighborhood.)

Now, this obstacle, against which the edge of the boat has just brushed, is, as the text says, the "mysterious end of [the] trip." The exploration of the place will be done by a measuring glance which joins in the poet's eyes the level of the surfaces to that of the depth. And everything takes place as though the "dormant vegetation," "the ribbons of any grass" reassembled in the rippling of the stream stood up in a "watery thicket (bosquet)," in this "clump of weeds (roseaux)," or even better in a "bouquet of water rushes (ros(e)/eau)," first image of the "ideal flower," water lily or *rose,* uniquely present in the vibration of the noun "roseaux" whose bouquet is stripped of "known calyxes":

> I say: a flower! and out of the oblivion where my voice relegates any contour, as something other than the calyxes that are known, musically arises an idea itself and fragrant, the one absent from all bouquets.
>
> (Crise de vers)

Both known and unknown, the friend, or the ideal flower, hides itself behind this *thicket* or in the watery depths of its root. That is why the eye of the rower, now a marauder, oscillates between the horizontality of the space projected by this point until it meets the divergent prolongation of the "hedges closing the lawns" and the depth which opens into the "single arch (arche)," privileged location of the arcana of this "feminine possibility" that the poet would prefer completely "lustral," or which he hopes to find unexpectedly inhabiting the area.

One obtains thus a constant wavering between the two friends and in such a manner that the frequency of the movement flowing back upon itself as soon as it has touched one of the extremities will prevent our fixing on one or the other.

This is why the limpid look of the two inhabitants of the "damply impenetrable" dwellings, *chilling* the willow leaves, transforms them into a mirror *clouded* with this same look which proceeds from inhabited surfaces or their depths:

> Un joli voisinage, pendant la saison, la nature d'une personne qui s'est choisi retraite aussi humidement impénétrable ne pouvant être que conforme à mon goût. Sûr, elle avait fait de ce cristal son miroir intérieur à l'abri de l'indiscrétion éclatante des après-midi; elle y venait et la buée d'argent glaçant les saules ne fut bientôt que la limpidité de son regard habitué à chaque feuille.
>
> Toute je l'évoquais lustrale.

> (A pretty neighborhood, during the season, the nature of a person who has chosen a retreat so damply impenetrable only being more to my taste. Surely, she had made this crystal her inner mirror, protected from the glaring indiscretion of the afternoons; she came there, and the silver mist chilling the willows was soon merely the limpidity of her glance accustomed to each leaf.
>
> All I evoked her lustral.)
>
> ("Nénuphar")

The whole *pond (étang)* metamorphosed into a crystal mirror protected from the *summer (été)* becomes a point of convergence, haunted by the double presence, both positive and negative, of a *person*. Through the "steady glistening" of these reflections, the two unknown women are copresent, as two letters X and Y superimposed, in this point from which the guiding lines, which open the fictive space of the *impenetrable* landscape, diverge.

Tucked in his boat, and even more than in the beginning, in an almost total immobility, the rower leaning toward the bottom of the boat comes to join his own reflection at this unifying point, and seems with the *yole* to make a double screen for the "joli voisinage":

> Courbé dan la sportive attitude où me maintenait de la curiosité, comme sous le silence spacieux de ce que s'annonçait l'étrangère, je souris au commencement d'esclavage dégagé par une possibilité féminine: que ne signifiaient pas mal les courroies attachant le soulier du rameur au bois de l'imbarcation, comme on ne fait qu'un avec l'instrument de ses sortilèges.

> (Bent over in the sportive stance in which curiosity kept me, as if under the spacious silence of the stranger's announcing herself, I smiled at the beginning of enslavement loosed by a feminine possibility: which the straps attaching the shoe of the rower to the wood of the boat signified fairly well, as a man becomes one with the instrument of his enchantments.)

By the use of a remarkable modulation, the poet here effectuates a transition from seeing to hearing. If the *yole* was able to suggest the idea of a place, receptacle of essences, it appears at present as an instrument, a sort of viola whose soul, in the technical and other sense of the term, has identified itself with the soul of the rower attached to the depths of the wood.

From interferences of space and time, we pass over, imperceptibly even here, to a crossing-over of space and of rhythm which is announced in the expression "spacious silence." The attention first given to the appearance of figures is displaced after the fact toward the sudden appearance of a rhythm, in sum toward this "step (pas)" of the stranger, and of which we do not know, moreover, if it really comes from elsewhere or from this "nudge with the thumb" or we should say with the "toe," well protected in the shoe of the rower, which becomes one with "the instrument of his enchantments." Chance, or, as Mallarmé implies elsewhere, trickery? "No sense, consequently, of trickery, and introduce, the gentle nudge, which rather, remains the statuary caress, creator of the idea" ("Confrontation").

Just as in the "Démon de l'analogie" the wire breaks on the "zero sound" ("Démon de l'analogie"), here this "step (pas)" of "any one (personne)," brusquely interrupted, seems to actualize that virtual negativity that the two noun substantives have in common with the homonymous negations: "ne . . . pas," "personne . . . ne." Thus the interruption excludes the appearance of any "feminine possibility" driven up from the edges or the depths:

> Aussi bien une quelconque . . . allais-je terminer. Quand un imperceptible bruit me fit douter si l'habitante du bord hantait mon loisir, ou inespérément le bassin.
> Le pas cessa pourquoi?

> ("As well any woman" . . . I was going to conclude. When an imperceptible noise made me doubt whether the inhabitant of the bank haunted my leisure or, beyond all hope the pond.
> The step ceased, why?)

> ("Nénuphar")

The game of poetic repetition begins again, starting from a halt. If, at the beginning of the poem, the rower, roused from his half-sleep *verified* by a glance rather than *heard* the halt of the rhythm, giving rise to a visualization of rhythmic space, here, on the contrary, the visual aspect of space invaded by silence is reduced to this sole "property," that is, to this "situation" of the soul of the boat tensed to listen.

The remembering of the rhythm and its break is therefore going to play a role in this conflict of foam and laces or cambric (batistes) which circumscribe the listening place with a mysterious boundary, or, who knows, the birthplace of the artifice of that boundary.

"In the doubt of the final game," one could say with Mallarmé, the notion of baptism (which the word "batistes" evokes here) is linked with that of blasphemy, provoking this combat of whiteness and blackness, of innocence and ruse which is the same combat as that of writing. Worked like a black lace by the white of the Verse, or negatively defined as a white lace on a night background, writing is above all this game of a "garland with the same," a compromise of ingenuity and calculation.

These interchangeable doubles, frequent in Mallarmean poetry, take on in the "Nénuphar blanc," a little before the reabsorption of the extent of the word into its point of silence, the figure, both confused and inverted by the play of the mirror, of a skirt that, while brushing the ground, seems to emerge from the water. For the back and forth oscillation of the boat is substituted here the more secret oscillation of feet:

> Subtil secret des pieds qui vont, viennent, conduisent l'esprit où le veut la chère ombre enfouie en de la batiste et les dentelles d'une jupe affluant sur le sol comme pour circonvenir du talon à

l'orteil, dans une flottaison, cette initiative par quoi la marche
s'ouvre, tout au bas et les plis rejetés en traîne, une échappée, de
sa double flèche savante.

(Subtle secret of feet which go, come, lead the mind where desires the dear shadow hidden in the cambric and the laces of a
skirt flowing down on the ground as if to surround from the heel
to the toe, in a watermark, this initiative by which the gait opens
for itself, right beneath and the folds held back in a train, a path,
by its double knowing arrow.)

But the rhythmic coming and going is more a march in place which resembles immobility. The *initiative* of the walk is hidden from perception and
only leaves to view the "path" of a division of "worldly" *initials,* only
vestige, one could say, of the imaginary wake of the *yole* and of the way it
is written.

Again the rippling of the source could open up into trails, in seams, in
intervals between two banks or between two points, but these are going to
situate themselves now on the vertical axis.

One might observe that the closed space of the rippled pond, where the
spreading out of the stream came to be reabsorbed, was at the origin of the
divergence of the hedges. By an opposite movement, the watermark which
circumscribes the walk tightens the circle of the new image of the source
whose ripples will be, on the contrary, thrown behind in a double arrow.
This image, one might say, announces the end of the poem, the return trip
seen as a double possibility. Before reaching that, it must be pointed out that
this mixture of foam and lace hides a superposition of images: that of the
skirt masking the step of the "stranger" linked with the image of the boat
concealing the shoe of the rower.

Gradually the closed space (pond, boat, skirt, straps attaching the shoe)
tends to tighten itself around an invisible point that the *buckle* of the "belt
(ceinture)" now closes. (*Ceintures* also contains the sense of "enceinte";
enclosure.)

In its upward projection, this "belt buckle" suggests the image of the
female waist (taille) or of a clump (taillis) of reeds, whereas from its reflection in the water the image of a diamond buckle seems to be born, closing
even "more authentically" the space of the "belts."

Whatever the space reduction might be, its *place* escapes view, except
that in spite of all these vertically superimposed screens, the rower, whose
glance was first "fixed inwardly," after having "bent [himself] into a sport-

ive stance," not only has almost identified himself with the instrument, but receives now all its vibrations in a sort of unison. "With [his] ear at the level of the mahogany," the poet will have no need of vision to detect the presence which he will capture solely in the "rustling of an arrival." This is why he can ignore the features of Madame which might tend to distract him from that "charm of something underneath," which resounds in the rower's ear in all its folds and grooves. All the preceding images of enclosed space are concentrated here in this new image of the buckle (= ear) which hangs over the rhythmic site.

> A quel type s'ajustent vos traits, je sens leur précision, Madame, interrompre chose installée ici par le bruissement d'une venue, oui! ce charme instinctif d'en dessous que ne défend pas contre l'explorateur la plus authentiquement nouée, avec une boucle en diamant, des ceintures.

> (To whatever type your features conform, I sense that their precision, Madame, interrupts something fixed here by the rustling of an arrival, yes! this instinctive charm of something underneath which is not defended against the explorer by the most authentically closed, with a diamond buckle, of belts.)

Strange hero of the mirror, this Narcissus who refuses to see himself in the features of his "feminine possibility" and thus defers his own death!

> Si vague concept se suffit: et ne transgressera le délice empreint de généralité qui permet et ordonne d'exclure tous visages, au point que la révélation d'un (n'allez point le pencher, avéré, sur le furtif seuil où je règne) chasserait mon trouble, avec lequel il n'a que faire.

> (Such a vague concept suffices: and will not transgress the delight marked with generality which permits and orders the exclusion of all faces, to the extent that the revelation of one (do not tilt it, well-established, over the stealthy threshold where I reign) would chase away my emotion, with which it has no connection.)

To preserve the music of the poem means therefore keeping the *suspense* which destroys all consistency of the image of *Echo* to only retain the *echo* of a "rustling."

Such, summarized here, is the entire poetics of the "Nénuphar," whose title, as we have suggested, "as something other than the known calyxes," is a receptacle of musical virtualities, in the same way the *yole,* more than a boat, becomes by its name the instrument of the poet's enchantments.

Seen thus, the fiction of the trip is an aggregate of projections and rejections of meanings found in the "creux néant musicien," of words, in the folds of their immemorial source. Oscillations, then sparklings, or vibration gathered by the ear at this point of "crisis of verse" where, as Mallarmé again says: "All becomes suspense, fragmentary disposition with alternation and opposition, uniting in the total rhythm, which would be the unspoken poem, at the blank spaces" ("Crisé de vers").

After that, how can one know if this "exquisite emptiness" with which the poem regales us, is a trip of *relaxation* (*détente*), where one goes at the behest of adventure, or rather the site of a *waiting* (*attente*) or an *understanding* (*entente*), even of a "perfect harmony"?

It remains that the poem sparkles with all these meanings combined, as the games of calculation and chance are combined in the image of the vagabond watcher and as the anagrams of the words *rameur* and *dérameur* are entwined in the word *maraudeur.*

It is thus that through the fortuitousness of adventure now appears the calculation of the marauder who measures his gestures, watches and spies. It then seems that chance was only an excuse and this casual "dress" a disguise designed to reinforce the effect of verisimilitude:

> Ma présentation, en cette tenue de maraudeur aquatique, je la peux tenter, avec l'excuse du hasard.

> (I can attempt my introduction, in this dress of an aquatic marauder, with the excuse of chance.)
>
> ("Nénuphar")

One notices simultaneously that the turns and twists of this trip are merely ways of shaping a discourse spoken not to be heard:

> Que de discours oiseux en comparaison de celui que je tins pour n'être pas entendu, faudra-t-il, avant de retrouver aussi instinctif accord que maintenant.

> (How many discourses, idle in comparison to that which I uttered in order to be unheard, will be necessary, before finding a harmony as intuitive as this one.)

The maneuver of the well-calculated watch can thus take the appearance of a wandering. Even the spontaneity of the improvised greeting is *foreseen* in case the watcher of signs is surprised in his hiding place. This effect of surprise would give to his "introduction" a remarkable natural-ness, all the more credible if it is compared to a polite "phrase" pronounced on the occasion of a visit. This is what would authorize the poet to proffer a greeting in a movement of "inspiration":

> mieux que visite, suivie d'autres, l'autorisera.

> (better than a visit, followed by others, would authorize.)

But, *inspiration* being equally the act by which one takes in one's breath, it follows that these two contrary movements are neutralized at the bound-aries of silence and speech, at this positive and negative limit of a nothing (rien), of a not (pas), and of a nobody (personne), all made of "intact dreams" and "breath withheld"

> dans la peur d'une apparition.

> (in fear of an appearance.)

From this "moving limit" alone can the question, which allows the alternative, loom up:

> Conseille, ô mon rêve, que faire?

The first alternative aims at the total erasure of the poem, the other concludes the "maneuver" of which it was the object.

If the trip proceeded at the beginning as the remembering of a dream, here the poet rewinds the thread of the dreamy silkworm (verse) (ver(s) rêveur) with the sole object of keeping intact the memory of this non-trip, of which the water lily (né-nu-phar) is the hidden sign:

> Résumer d'un regard la vierge absence éparse en cette solitude et comme on cueille, en mémoire d'un site, l'un de ces magiques nénuphars clos qui y surgissent tout à coup, enveloppant de leur creuse blancheur un rien fait de songes intacts, du bonheur qui n'aura pas lieu et de mon souffle ici retenu dans la peur d'une apparition, partir aved: tacitement, en déramant peu à peu sans du heurt briser l'illusion ni que le clapotis de la bulle visible d'écume enroulée à ma fuite ne jette aux pieds survenus de personne la ressemblance transparente du rapt de mon idéale fleur.

(To resume in a glance the virgin absence sprinkled in this solitude, and as one plucks, in memory of a place, one of those
magical closed lilies which suddenly rise up, enveloping with
their hollow whiteness a nothing, made of intact dreams, of
happiness which will not take place and of my breath held here
in the fear of an appearance, to leave with it: silently.)

Here indeed is what is meant in the proper sense of the word *déramer,*
by "the action of removing a cocoon." As for the other sense of *déramer,*
which designates the backwards maneuver and thus the rhythm of erasing,
Mallarmé invents it by this ingenious "coupd de *dé*" which creates the
opposition to the sense of *ramer.*

Everything that could denounce the "abduction" or even better the
theft (vol) of this rhythmic beat must disappear, including even the least
seam of the idle discourse. (*Voler,* of course, is both "to steal" and "to fly.")
Only the closed lily remains, with petals folded in like the useless wings
which anticipate the image of a swan's egg whose "flights have not flown."

Such is the maneuver which has the *idle* discourse veer off toward a
discourse of birds (*oiseux/oiseaux*) in the second alternative: the "quest of
water flowers" changes into a quest for *swans (cygnes)* or for *signs (signes)*
which brings to light another aspect of the marauder or of the writer. These
latter only follow the opening out of the flight or the writing to discover the
nest or the rhythmic source:

> Si, attiré par un sentiment d'insolite, elle a paru, la Méditative ou
> la Hautaine, la Farouche, la Gaie, tant pis pour cette indicible
> mine que j'ignore à jamais! car j'accomplis selon les règles la
> manœuvre: je dégageai, virai et je contournais déjà une ondula-
> tion du ruisseau, emportant comme un noble œuf de cygne, tel
> que n'en jaillira le vol, mon imaginaire trophée, qui ne se gonfle
> d'autre chose sinon de la vacance exquise de soi qu'aime l'été à
> poursuivre, dans les allées de son parc, toute dame, arrêtée parfois
> et longtemps, comme au bord d'une source à franchir ou de
> quelque pièce d'eau.

> (If, drawn by a feeling of something unusual, she appeared, the
> Meditative or the Haughty, the Fierce, the Gay lady, so much the
> worse for that inexpressible face that I shall never know! for I
> completed the maneuver according to the rules: I pushed off,
> turned and was already rounding a curve in the stream, carrying
> away like a noble swan's egg, such as from which no flight will

spring, my imaginary trophy, which does not swell from anything except the exquisite emptiness of itself which every woman,
in summer, loves to pursue, in the avenues of her park, halting
sometimes and for a long time, as if on the edge of a spring to be
crossed or of some pond.)

Certainly, the intention remains the same in spite of the divergence of the
arrows, but do not the contours of the idle discourse run the risk of stiff-
ening in allowing to be seen, in this non-erased poem, the face of "some
friend or other": the Meditative, Haughty, Fierce or the Gay. Four faces to
which correspond respectively four moments of the poem which can be
detailed in the following manner: fixation of the inward glance, resurgence
of the watery copse, stopping of the step, enjoyment of the confused intimacy.

There lies the risk that occurs in following the outline of the composition, whose established meanings Mallarmé has tried to destroy to preserve this "Figure que nul n'est" ("Richard Wagner, rêverie"), joined to the
incognito of this "inexpressible face which he will never know." We realize
the any "ordinary" appearance would thus cancel this "feminine possibility" of Self that the poet attempts to throw back into the scope of the text's
virtualities.

This "exquisite emptiness of [it]self" which figures in the conclusion of
the poem, as a common pursuit of the poet and the friend, can only be
understood if one sees that it is a game of doubles, which the surface of the
mirror would limit in their "confused intimacy."

It remains that if a too-great precision of features could endanger the
oscillations of the writing, it is to conjure away this peril that the poet
invents this double ending where the everything and the nothing of the
appearance of the poem remain the two possibilities of an alternative whose
oscillation should suffice to neutralize the precision and thus to safeguard
the essential indetermination.

Rather than claiming to formulate any essence of Mallarméan poetics,
my analysis aimed rather to pick up this game of "fragmentary disposition
with alternation and opposition" in the poem.

If I have happened to play with words, it is because the "prose poem"
requires this particular attitude of observation and of illumination to see
what makes a *critical* poem of the prose poem:

The breaks in the text, rest assured, take pains to concur, with
sense and only inscribe blank space as far as their points of
illumination: a form, perhaps, emerges, present, permitting that

> which for a long time was the prose poem and our study, to end
> up as a critical poem, if one joins the words better.
>
> (*Notes*)

I have also gone so far in my exploration as to scrutinize the figure of letters in words such as *yole* for example. To *yole* we could add the word "joli" (pretty) which presents in the alternation of descending (j) and ascending (l) rhythms, hollows (o) and fullnesses (i), of its letters, a condensed figuration of the poem, which presents itself as a quest not of *beauty,* but of its *surroundings,* admirably expressed by the form and the meaning of "joli."

However, we did not want to venture farther on the paths of this cabbalistic science which Mallarmé himself considers as chimerical:

> Such a magisterial effort of the imagination touches one of the
> sacred or perilous mysteries of Language; and which it will be
> prudent to analyze only on the day when Science, possessing the
> vast repertoire of idioms ever spoken on earth, will write the
> history of the letters of the alphabet through all the ages and
> what was almost their absolute meaning, sometimes guessed,
> sometimes misapprehended by man, creators of words: but there
> will no longer be, in this time, either Science to sum this up, or
> some one to say it. Chimera, let us be satisfied, for now, of the
> light which magnificent writers throw on this subject.
>
> (*Mots anglais*)

It is really in the spirit of this last sentence that we have conducted our analysis! All the more that in this game of chance and calculations where the poet, as Poe says, is also a mathematician, we would have little chance of succeeding. For, not only does the poet foresee the calculations of *others* but he speculates on the intuition of the *other* and goes beyond by a divining whose mark is unique. Evidently, we are referring to the three characters of the *Purloined Letter,* the inspectror, the minister and Dupin, whose leaps beyond the respective ruses culminate in the figure par excellence of the Poet who is reborn indefinitely in the game of his inventions.

Thus every reader who tries to guess the poem is always and more astutely guessed by it.

HANS-JOST FREY

The Tree of Doubt

The initial lines of "L'Après-midi d'un faune" did never rouse much interpretive effort, probably because the situation at the beginning of the poem seemed to be clear enough. Examining his past the Faun is uncertain whether the nymphs he remembers were actually present or whether they were only a dream.

> Aimai-je un rêve?
> Mon doute, amas de nuit ancienne, s'achève
> En maint rameau subtil, qui, demeuré les vrais
> Bois mêmes, prouve, hélas! que bien seul je m'offrais
> Pour trimophe la faute idéale de roses.

> [Did I dream that love?
> My doubt, the hoard of ancient night, divides
> In subtle branches, which, the only woods
> Remaining, prove, alas! that all alone
> I triumphed in the ideal fault of roses.]

> (ll. 3–7)

The traditional reading of this passage sees the proof of the nonexistence of the nymphs in the fact that the woods are still there. In Robert G. Cohn's words: "The most direct meaning is that the reality of the woods—as opposed to the nonexistent nymphs (represented perhaps only by roses which he mistook for them)—proves his 'fault' (love-act) was only an 'ideal' or unreal one, with a sort of 'spectre of a rose,' as in Gautiers's familiar poem"

From *Yale French Studies* no. 54 (1977). © 1977 by Yale French Studies.

(*Toward the Poems of Mallarmé*). If such were the Faun's argument, he would be reasoning rather poorly. The presence of the real woods could perhaps prove that there are no nymphs now (a fact which doesn't have to be proved), but it does not prove that they were never there. Their present absence does not contradict their past presence. They can very well have been present in the past and be absent in the present. If this is true, the Faun's doubt as to the reality of the nymphs cannot be removed by the reality of the woods. Also, it remains unresolved if we accept the ambiguity of the verb *s'achever* which means not only that doubt comes to an end, but also that it is completed and culminates in the boughs. This second meaning is supported by an earlier version of the poem which has in its place the verb *se prolonger* [to extend].

Nevertheless, something is proved. The Faun verifies "que bien seul je m'offrais / Pour triomphe la faute idéale de roses." This seems to suggest that the Faun is now sure of the illusionary nature of the nymphs. But the sentence cannot be reduced to the question of whether they were real or not. Words like *s'offrir, triomphe, faute,* with their affective and moral implications, show that the problem has to be considered on a second level which is that of the Faun's relationship to the nymphs. This relationship is expressed in the initial question: "Aimai-je un rêve?" The Faun is not interested in presence as such. He wants the nymphs to be present because he loves them. Their presence is important because they mean something to him. One does not love something simply because it's there, but because it is meaningful to oneself. This meaning founds the Faun's relationship to the nymphs, a relationship which is not subject to doubt. The question "Aimai-je un rêve?" implies that it is possible to love a dream. The Faun's love is therefore independent of the status of the nymphs. It is based only on their meaning. The question of whether the nymphs were real or not concerns the nymphs insofar as they are meaningful and become the object of the Faun's love. To the extent that they have meaning the nymphs are language. They are language independently of the question whether they are referentially real or not. Referential reality is not important as such, but only to the extent that it becomes meaningful. The Faun's question ultimately concerns the status of language and his own relationship to it.

The certainty the Faun reaches amounts to his having been alone with his "fault." This loneliness stems from the fact that the outside world became meaningful to him. To the extent that things mean they cease to be what they are in themselves. Meaning is bestowed upon them from the outside, by the person to whom they become meaningful. Meaning introduces an absence into their presence, because through it they now refer to what they are not. Meaning undermines the presence of things. What is does not yet mean, and what means is no longer what it was.

This is what is proved, and we must now consider how the evidence is established. Most of the time, interpreters have attributed the power of proof to the actual presence of the woods. But the syntactical structure of the passage shows at once that such a reading is not correct. In the sentence: "maint rameau subtil, qui, demeuré les vrais / Bois mêmes, prouve," the subject of "prouver" is "maint rameau subtil," "les vrais bois mêmes" being only an apposition to it. The proof is not therefore established by the real woods, but by the insight into the peculiar relationship between "maint rameau subtil" and "les vrais bois mêmes," a relationship which is determined as sameness and difference at the same time.

"Maint rameau subtil" is a metaphor for doubt. Doubt as a state of hovering between several undecidable possibilities is well represented by the ramification of a tree whose boughs don't lead anywhere but end up in a void. Mallarmé liked this image and used it again in the prose poem "La Gloire" where, in connection with a visit to the forest of Fontainebleau, he speaks of "mainte indécise flottaison d'idée désertant les hasards comme des branches [many a vague and drifting thought falling from the boughs of chance]" and of "les bras de doute envolés [the wings of doubt flew up]." If the tree becomes the image of the undecidable alternative of doubt, it becomes meaningful. The tree means the Faun's doubt. This meaning does not depend on the actual presence of the tree. The mental representation of its structure is sufficient. On the other hand, the real tree is not affected by the fact that it now means the Faun's doubt. It remains what it was before ("demeuré les vrais / Bois mêmes"). The Faun, however, is preoccupied with the relationship between the real tree and the metaphorical tree. The tree as such has no meaning. To the extent that the Faun bestows meaning upon it, it becomes language and ceases to be the real tree which remains the meaningless object it was.

The proof is established by the analogical transference to the nymphs of the insight gained by means of considering the status of the metaphor with respect to the real tree. The question of whether the nymphs were real or not remains open. Be that as it may, the Faun was alone with what the nymphs meant to him. Insofar as the nymphs mean they have no extralingual existence, but they are the Faun's language. The act of bestowing meaning is an isolating act. Meaning is not in things, but it is given to them by us. What is outside of ourselves does not mean, and what means is not outside of ourselves.

Outside reality is rarefied and vanishes in proportion to its becoming

meaningful. This is Mallarmé's interpretation of the myth of Syrinx. The
nymph, transformed into a reed, becomes the Faun's flute whose sound puts
to flight the nymphs:

> Et qu'au prélude lent où naissent les pipeaux
> Ce vol de cygnes, non! de naïades se sauve
> Ou plonge.

> [And when the pipes are born in slow
>   prelude,
> A flight of swans, no! naiads hastens off
> Or dives.]

> (ll. 30–32)

The sound of the instrument as the ultimate metamorphosis of the nymph
coincides with her disappearance. Meaningless reality and the unreality of
meaning appear in the poem as the opposition between the inertia of nature
and art that dissolves the reality after which it strives.

> Inerte, tout brûle dans l'heure fauve
> Sans marquer par quel art ensemble détala
> Trop d'hymen souhaité de qui cherche le *la*.

> [Inert, all burns in the tawny hour
> With no sight of the miles by which escaped
> That nuptial surfeit the musician sought.]

> (ll. 32–34)

Etymologically, inertia is the lack of art. The inertia of the Faun's surroundings is the incapacity of corresponding to his earlier invitation by which he
called upon them to speak (*CONTEZ que* . . .) and to confirm his own
language. Nature does not speak, unless it is transformed into language, by
which transformation it ceases to be what it is. This is exactly what the
Faun's art achieves. It makes reality disappear by making it meaningful. The
relationship between inertia and art is the same as that between the real, but
meaningless woods and the meaningful, but unreal boughs of doubt.

   Once the Faun recognizes that the nymphs are language and mean
something, the next question is to know what they mean. A possible answer
to this question is considered in the following lines.

> Réfléchissons . . .
>   ou si les femmes dont tu gloses
> Figurent un souhait de tes sens fabuleux!

[Reflect . . .

  or if the women you malign
Configurate your fabled senses' wish!]
(ll. 8–9)

The nymphs are here interpreted as a figure of the Faun's desire. The easiest way of reading this would be to say that desire produces the image of its object and that the image of what is desired becomes the figure of desire itself. But it is obvious, here again, that the figurative nature of the nymphs does not depend on whether they are imaginary or real. As far as the Faun's relationship to them is concerned they are figurative language in both cases.

The fact of the nymphs' being language must not be considered only in itself. It has a bearing on the status of the Faun's speech. The nymphs are not only language that means the Faun's desire, but they also are the object of the Faun's actual speech. The Faun talks about that which talks about himself. His language is therefore language about language. This is why he characterizes his own language as glossing. The gloss is language whose object is another language it tries to explain.

The relationship between the nymphs as language and the language about the nymphs can be seen in a still more precise way if we take into account the meaning of the nymphs. They mean the Faun's desire. It is because desire sets them as the image of its object that they are turned into language and come to mean desire. Desire is possible to the extent that its object is missing. But it always is the desire to reach its object and to transform into real presence what is given only as language. This desire also presides over the Faun's actual speech which is motivated by the wish to perpetuate the nymphs. It is true that an ambiguity is introduced here which we shall have to explore. As soon as the nymphs are recognized to be the figure of desire, to perpetuate them does not only mean to prolong their presence by means of their linguistic representation, but it also means to preserve them as the figure of desire, and so to preserve desire itself. In spite of this complexity of the Faun's desire an analogy between the two levels of language becomes visible. The Faun's speech about the nymphs means the desire for their presence, but the nymphs themselves already mean this same desire. In both cases, language means the wish to overcome language. This analogy implies that when the Faun talks about his relationship to the nymphs, he talks about his relationship to his language. His relationship to the nymphs can therefore be considered as the figurative expression of his relationship to his own speech.

This provides us with a basis for a better understanding of at least one aspect of one of the poem's more difficult passages. I mean the long story (ll. 62–92) in which the Faun relates his real or imaginary adventure with the two nymphs. The difficulty of the episode lies in its anecdotal profusion which is a temptation to take the related facts simply as facts and to qualify their evocation with the Faun's own words as "d'idolâtres peintures [idolatrous depictions]" (l. 55), by means of which he tries to conjure up his lost past. But it is clear that this story is not told for its own sake, but for its meaning. My limited purpose is to examine it only in its relationship to the Faun as its narrator.

The Faun remembers having found in the woods two sleeping nymphs embracing each other. He snatches them up and takes them to the sun without separating them. But in order to possess them he has to divide them, which he does. Because he is unable to concentrate upon one and to let go the other, they both escape from his grasp and leave him frustrated. By somewhat simplifying the structure of the story we may say that the Faun after having discovered the nymphs succeeds in getting hold of them and loses them again. A distance is momentarily overcome and reestablished. This pattern within the related story also governs the relationship between the Faun as narrator and the story he tells. In the final version of the poem Mallarmé italicized the first and last part of the text and put it between quotation marks, whereas the middle section is printed in Roman characters. The story is a remembered one. The Faun who is telling it is separated from his past self. In the italicized passages he is well aware of this distance. He knows that the past is present only through language. The story here is what he calls his "feinte" (l. 58). But the Faun's intention is to overcome language and to reach the reality of what he says. He is "avide d'ivresse [wild to be drunk]" (ll. 60–61). A full recovery of the past is only possible if the Faun believes his language to be what it says. This happens in the central section where he forgets his language and reaches an illusionary identification with his past self. This moment of oblivion, when distance is abolished, coincides with the moment in the story when he holds the nymphs, whereas the distance is reestablished when he comes to relate how he separated the nymphs and lost them. This parallelism shows that the story of the Faun's relationship to the nymphs functions as a metaphor for his relationship to his telling this story.

The starting point of this analysis was the Faun's reflection in lines 8 and 9:

ou si les femmes dont tu gloses
Figurent un souhait de tes sens fabuleux!

We now must return to these lines in order to consider an aspect of the Faun's speech which has been neglected up to now. The explanation they offer for the nymphs is not presented as an affirmation, but as a hypothesis. The sentence is introduced by *ou si*. This indicates that the Faun is considering one possibility among others. But there is no other possibility, because the *ou* cannot be referred to anything except to the blank that precedes it. The *ou* postulates an alternative, but the alternative is missing. The alternative which is no alternative allows of no decision. The Faun must remain suspended in the impossibility of verifying his hypothesis. What is suspended, is the true meaning of the nymphs. This meaning depends on the Faun's desire, through which they become meaningful to him. But this desire is of a strange kind. Its object are two nymphs. If the Faun's problem were nothing but the fulfillment of a sexual desire, one woman would be enough. She could very well figure "un souhait de tes sens fabuleux." Why then are there two nymphs?

In the story of the Faun's encounter with the nymphs, the latter appear as another undecidable alternative. The Faun loses them both, because he is incapable of making his choice. While he tries to rape one of them, he refuses to let go the other. If the union with the first nymph is fulfillment, the Faun's attempt at keeping hold of the second one can only mean that he refuses to renounce desire in the moment of fulfillment. He wants desire and fulfillment at the same time. But fulfillment is the annulment of desire, and desire is the lack of fulfillment. The Faun is suspended between desire and fulfillment. If this is true, what do the nymphs mean? Can we still say that they figure the Faun's desire? Such a statement is true and false at the same time, because the meaning of the nymphs remains suspended. Any attempt at laying down this meaning must necessarily be one-sided and insufficient. To accept the Faun's desire as the meaning of the nymphs is legitimate only insofar as we realize that by doing so we shift the problem to the meaning itself, desire being suspended between the desire for fulfillment and the desire for desire. Desire has exactly the same status as doubt in the lines examined before. The tree means doubt and the nymphs mean desire. But to doubt and to desire is to hover in suspense. If there is any certainty, it can only be the impossibility of reaching the meaning of what is meaningful.

The suspension between what means and what is meant is the *ou*. As the undecidable alternative it is the explication—in the double sense of the word—of the complex structure of the Faun's desire in the episode of the nymphs. It unfolds the indecision inherent in this desire and makes it explicit on the level of the Faun's speech, and in doing so it glosses the text that the nymphs are, explaining their meaning which is not this or that, but the impossibility of reaching this or that. The *ou* says the impossibility of not being in between.

All that has been said concerns the Faun's relationship to his objects. The Faun as a subject does not seem to be questioned. Everything that is said is attributed to him and is said from his point of view. As the origin of his speech he seems to be something which is beyond language and cannot be interpreted anymore. But is there a point of view where there is only the suspense of doubt, hesitation and desire? And is not the Faun as the speaker of what is said, a fiction of Mallarmé's poem? If the appearance of a Faun in the text is meaningful, the Faun himself is language, and we must try to understand what he means. The Faun is a mixed being, neither buck nor man, something between nature and man. And here is what he means:

> Nous ne pouvons pas ne point voir dans les Satyres le phénomène
> de vie qui semble animer les bois et faire danser les branches des
> arbres, au tronc noueux effrayant les voyageurs.

> [We couldn't not see in the satyrs the phenomenon of life which
> seems to animate the woods and make tree branches dance,
> frightening voyagers with the gnarled tree trunk.]

The Faun is the tree that becomes the metaphor of the horror of man faced with the opaqueness of meaningless nature. The Faun's act of bestowing meaning upon the tree is also the act by which the Faun as a metaphor is created. If the Faun is the tree that has become language, he himself is the metaphor by which his speech constitutes itself. "Mon doute" is then not only the doubt I have, but also the doubt I am. The text cannot be traced back to the Faun as its source because it also says the Faun as language. It is the Faun's language as well as the Faun as language. It can be reduced neither to the one nor to the other, but it floats in between. This hovering of the text which undermines and disintegrates the coherence of the poem's fiction, is most clearly perceptible in the double sense of the word *fabuleux* which means not only that the Faun is full of the fables he produces, but also that he himself is a fabulous being.

Mallarmé's Faun is the suspense between tree and man. He is the relationship between nature and man in language.

> Pan
>   tronc qui s'achève en homme

> [Pan
>   trunk which is finished in man]

But what does *s'achever* mean? The Faun has neither ceased to be a tree nor has he become man, but he is the tree that has become man's language. In his undecidable nature he is the condensed figure of that which his speech unfolds.

BARBARA JOHNSON

Poetry and Performative Language:
Mallarmé and Austin

*Surely the words must be spoken "seriously" and so as to be taken
"seriously"? This is, though vague, true enough in general—it is an
important commonplace in discussing the purport of any utterance
whatsoever, I must not be joking, for example, nor writing a poem.*
—J. L. AUSTIN, *How to Do Things with Words*

THE CRY OF THE OCCASION

*The poem is the cry of its occasion,
Part of the res itself and not about it.*
—WALLACE STEVENS,
"An Ordinary Evening in New Haven"

While rocking lazily in their landau through the late afternoon sun, an
elegant lady and her escort happen upon a somewhat dilapidated but mysteriously crowded fairground. There, in an empty stand, the lady remedies
the absence of any proper performer by waking up the drummer, setting her
escort up as a fee-collecting barker, and mounting a table to enigmatically
exhibit herself to the crowd. The gentleman, instantly comprehending his
duty in this tricky situation, glances at the lady's hair and recites a sonnet,
after which, lifting her down from the table, he adds a more plain-folks
explanation of the spectacle. The two then make their way, amid the puz-
zled approbation of the onlookers, back toward their carriage through the
now-dark open air, cozily discussing the performance they have just given.

So runs, more or less, the "plot" of Mallarmé's prose poem "La
Déclaration foraine." The questions raised by this text are legion. What (if

From *The Critical Difference: Essays in the Contemporary Rhetoric of Reading*.
© 1980 by the Johns Hopkins University Press.

anything) is being declared (about poetry?) and how does it relate to other
moments in Mallarmé's writings? What is the relation between the sonnet
and the lady on the one hand, and between the verse and the prose on the
other? How does the narrative frame motivate the existence of the verse
poem? In other words, *when,* according to this text, does it make sense that
there be a poem?

On its most obvious level, "La Déclaration foraine" is the story of an
improvised side show composed of two parts: a motionless woman and a
spoken poem. In the context, the relation between the two seems deceptively
transparent: the sonnet ("La chevelure vol d'une flamme") is simply, as
Robert Greer Cohn describes it, "a celebration of a woman whose looks,
featuring magnificent hair, need no outer adornment" (*Toward the Poems
of Mallarmé*). The poet's act would thus seem to bear out Remy de
Gourmont's affirmation that "all things in life having been said thousands
and thousands of times, the poet can no longer do anything but point to
them, accompanying his gesture with a few murmured words" (*Promenades
littéraires*). In its simultaneous act of naming and exhibiting, the poem can
thus be said to relate to the lady as a sign to its referent.

But if that is the case, how does this poem fit in with the rest of
Mallarmé's poetics of "suggestion," which he explicitly opposes to literal
denomination? If one recalls Mallarmé's repeated insistence on poetry's
abolition of simple referentiality, on the "vibratory near-disappearance" of
the real object "on which the pages would have trouble closing," one begins
to suspect two things: that the traditional reading of Mallarmé's
nonreferentiality is inadequate and that the lady's hair is only the apparent
subject of the sonnet, the "indifferent" or "surface" meaning that both
hides and reveals something to which it remains "exterior." Mallarmé's
own highly ambiguous statement of the noncorrespondence between the
obvious and the true in his own work is probably responsible for the universal critical tendency to give the hair a symbolic meaning, to find the
"pure notion" or "idea"—Poetry, ideal Beauty, naked Truth, Promethean
fire, provocative Femininity—behind the materiality of the *chevelure*. The
prose poem, in fact, expressly invites a reading of this type by calling the
lady a "living allegory," which further problematizes, but does not eliminate, the question of the poem's referentiality.

But whatever may be said about the lady's flaming mane, it is not the
hair or any of its symbolic substitutes that is being discussed in the concluding dialogue of the piece, but rather the conditions of possibility of the
emission and reception of the sonnet itself. Poetry, if it is indeed the "subject" of the poem, becomes here not some ideal and statuesque concept, but

a function of a specific interlocutionary situation, an *act of speech,* the lady banteringly tells her escort, that

> vous n'auriez peut-être pas introduit, qui sait? mon ami, le prétexte de formuler ainsi devant moi au conjoint isolement par exemple de notre voiture—où est-elle—regagnons-la;—mais ceci jaillit, forcé, sous le coup de poing brutal à l'estomac, que cause une impatience de gens auxquels coûte que coûte et soudain il faut proclamer quelque chose fût-ce la rêverie . . .
>
> —Qui s'ignore et se lance nue de peur, en travers du public; c'est vrai. Comme vous, Madame, ne l'auriez entendu si irréfutablement, malgré sa réduplication sur une rime du trait final, mon boniment d'après un mode primitif du sonnet, je le gage, si chaque terme ne s'en était répercuté jusqu'à vous par de variés tympans, pour charmer un esprit ouvert à la compréhension multiple.
>
> —Peut-être! accepta notre pensée dans un enjouement de souffle nocturne la même.

> (you would perhaps not have introduced, who knows? my friend, the pretext of formulating thus before me in the joint isolation for example of our carriage—where is it—let's return to it;—but this spews forth, by force, from the brutal punch in the stomach caused by an impatience of people to whom at all costs and suddenly something must be proclaimed even a reverie . . .
>
> —Which does not know itself and hurls itself naked with fear through the audience; that's true. Just as you, Madame, would not have heard and understood it so irrefutably, in spite of its reduplication on a rhyme in the final thrust, my spiel composed after a primitive mode of the sonnet, I bet, if each term of it had not bounced back to you off a variety of eardrums, to charm a mind open to multiple comprehension.
>
> —Perhaps! accepted our thought in a cheekiness of night air the same.)

The story of the recitation of an occasional poem thus concludes with a discussion of what constitutes a poem's occasion; the two ex-performers are interested not in what the poem means, but in how it means, and in how it managed to come into being at all. Two conditions, whose significance we will discuss later, appear necessary for the poem to occur: audience and violence. Without them, the poet would "perhaps," "who knows?" not

have introduced the "pretext of formulating" his poem into the silent, isolated togetherness of the rocking coach. In fact, the prose poem, which ends
by discussing the necessary conditions for the production of speech, begins
by triply insisting on a state of *absence* of speech:

> *Le Silence!* il est certain qu'à mon côté, ainsi que songes, étendue
> dans un bercement de promenade sous les roues assoupissant
> l'interjection de fleurs, *toute femme,* et j'en sais une qui voit clair
> ici, *m'exempte de l'effort à proférer un vocable:* la *complimenter
> haut* de quelque interrogatrice toilette, offre de soi presque à
> l'homme en faveur de qui s'achève l'après-midi, *ne pouvant* à
> l'encontre de tout ce rapprochement fortuit, *que suggérer la dis-
> tance* sur ses traits aboutie à une fossette de spirituel sourire.
> (Emphasis mine here and passim.)

> (Silence! it is certain that at my side, as maybe dream, lying back
> in a rocking drive while the wheels are assuaging the interjection
> of flowers, any woman, and I know one who sees through this,
> exempts me from the effort of proffering a single vocable: to
> compliment her aloud on some interrogative toilette, offer of self
> almost to the man in favor of whom the afternoon draws to a
> close, serving with respect to all this fortuitous closeness only to
> suggest distance on her features ending in a dimple of bantering
> smile.)

The simple juxtaposition between the "declaration" in the title and the
"Silence" in the opening line should thus, from the beginning, warn us that
"to speak or not to speak" is, in some way, the question. Moreover, a glance
at the vocabulary of the text reveals an overwhelming number of references
to speech acts: verbs ("exempter," "proférer," "complimenter," "suggérer,"
"consentir," "nommer," "témoigner," "proposer," "conjurer," "dégoiser,"
"dire," "soupirer," "diffamer," "observer," "ajouter," "communiquer,"
"introduire," "formuler," "proclamer," "gager," accepter"), nouns
("déclaration," "interjection," "vocifération," "explication," "convoca-
tion," "exhibition," "présomption," "affectation," "approbation"), and
even adjectives ("interrogatrice," "appréciative"). This list resembles nothing so much as the concluding chapter of J. L. Austin's *How to Do Things
with Words,* in which an attempt is made to draw up a list of what Austin
calls "performative utterances."

   In order to determine whether the notion of the performative can shed
any light on our poem (and vice versa), let us now turn briefly to Austin's

description of its principal characteristics. First, a sentence is called performative if it can be shown that "to utter the sentence . . . is not to *describe* my doing of what I should be said in so uttering to be doing or to state that I am doing it: it is to do it. . . . The name [performative] is derived, of course, from 'perform,' the usual verb with the noun 'action': it indicates that the issuing of the utterance is the performing of an action" (emphasis in original). Thus, for example, the sentence "I declare war" is itself the act of declaring war, whereas "I kill the enemy" is only a report of the act of killing the enemy. In addition, according to Austin, the action performed by the utterance must in some way belong to "an accepted conventional procedure having a certain conventional effect." And finally, "it is always necessary that the *circumstances* in which the words are uttered should be in some way, or ways, *appropriate.*" One finds the performative, then, whenever, in a given situation, *saying* something is *doing* something recognizable.

Without further qualification of these criteria, it could be said that the very recitation of the sonnet in "La Déclaration foraine" could be classed as a performative utterance: to utter the poem is visibly to perform the action of uttering a poem which, unorthodox as it may be, is uncontestably made to fit into its side show circumstances. As for the act's conventionality, the poet himself calls it a "lieu commun d'une esthétique." Obviously, some further qualification of the specificity of a performative utterance is needed to distinguish it from the mere act of speaking, for, as Austin himself inquires, "When we issue any utterance whatsoever, are we not 'doing something'? " In his attempts to find a formula inclusive of all speech acts in which saying is doing, Austin passes from considerations of grammatical form and transformational rules to considerations of semantic content and interpersonal effects. In the course of the inquiry, the original binary opposition between performative and constative language inevitably breaks down. The impossibility of defining the linguistic specificity of the performative utterance (for which we will try to account later on) leads Austin to draw up a new set of analytic terms focusing not on the intrinsic characteristics of an utterance but on its actual function in an interlocutionary situation. Abandoning the performative/constative dichotomy, Austin proposes to analyze any utterance according to three "dimensions": (1) the *locutionary* (sound, sense and reference), (2) the *illocutionary* (intentional and conventional force), and (3) the *perlocutionary* (actual effect).

Since these notions, though not without their usefulness, are at least as problematic as the notion of the performative, subsequent thinkers have preferred to return to the search for a set of stable linguistic criteria for the isolation of the performative. By choosing these criteria in such a way as to eliminate all but what Austin himself calls *"explicit* performatives" (emphasis in this paragraph in original), this task becomes relatively simple: explicit performatives are verbs in the first (or impersonal third) person singular present indicative active which possess "an *asymmetry* of a systematic kind [with respect to] other persons and tenses of the *very same word.*" That is, to use Austin's example, "I bet" is the actual performance of the act of betting, whereas "he bets" is only a report of an act of betting. The performative is only operative if the action performed is "at the moment of uttering being done by the person uttering." The performative, then, acts like a "shifter" in that it takes on meaning only by referring to the instance of its utterance. The French linguist Emile Benveniste, adding a self-referential semantic dimension to the definition, effectively eliminates any remaining uncertainty when he asserts that "an utterance is performative insofar as it *names* the act performed. . . . The utterance *is* the act; the utterer performs the act by naming it" [*Problems in General Linguistics*].

This elimination of uncertainty is also, of course, an elimination of the unstated philosophical question behind the whole inquiry, of which the least that can be said is that it has something to do with the role of language in human power relationships. That is, Austin's original question was undoubtedly not, When do we know for sure that an utterance is performative? but, What kinds of things are we really *doing* when we speak? But before discussing the way in which our poem relates to this immense question, let us first examine the role of its "explicit," self-referential performative expressions.

Considered in the most restricted terms of the definition, only one of our numerous performative verbs can actually be classed as a "live" performance. This verb, as it happens, is precisely the verb *I bet* ("je le gage"), with which the poet closes his argument. Is it by chance that Mallarmé should choose this particular verb as the only operative performative in this text? In view of the relation between a bet and, say, a throw of dice, one suspects that it is not. But before pursuing this train of thought further, let us examine the function of the nonoperative performative expressions on our list.

Of these, most are temporally deactivated by being reported in the infinitive ("proférer," "complimenter," "suggérer") or in the third person ("toute femme . . . m'exempte") or in the past tense ("proposa," "consentit," "accepta"). That is, the speech act to which they refer is not being performed but only named or reported. The name of the deactivated speech act therefore functions like any other noun, even to the point of serving as a metaphor for something totally unrelated to a literal speech act ("l'*interjection* de fleurs," "*comme une vociération*"). Thus, if a performative utterance is originally a self-referential speech act, its production is simultaneously the production of a new referent into the world. This, however, is tantamount to a radical transformation of the notion of a referent, since, instead of pointing to an external object, language would then refer only to its own referring to itself in the act of referring, and the signifying chain would end in an infinitely self-duplicating loop. A variant of this difficulty has, in fact, been pointed out by Paul Larreya, who, in attempting to fit a performative utterance into a Chomskyan tree diagram, finds that "to develop the tree it would be necessary to repeat the symbol [designating the performative] an infinite number of times" ("Enoncés performatifs, cause, et référence"). The performative utterance is thus the *mise en abyme* of reference itself.

We have now arrived at a predicament similar to that described by Richard Klein in his study of metaphors of metaphor ("Straight Lines and Arabesques: Metaphors of Metaphor"), but we are still a long way from showing what a poem has to say about the relation between this predicament and the characteristics of language in general. In pursuit of this question, let us examine some further implications of the self-referentiality of the performative utterance. If the performative refers only to itself, it would seem that it does not refer to any exterior or prior origin. In actual analysis, however, we see that this is never considered to be the case. For although the sense and the reference of the speech act are its own utterance, that very fact presupposes the presence of the utterer, who then becomes the necessary origin of the speech act in question. Some sign of the speaker's presence to his utterance is considered indispensable if the performative utterance is to be what Austin calls "felicitous." But in this prose poem, the intentional continuity between the speaker and the utterance is being questioned by the poet and his lady, for the "rêverie" that has been proclaimed to the crowd "*s'ignore* et se lance nue de peur," just as the call to the crowd to enter the booth in the first place had been "obscur pour moi-même d'abord." Indeed, if what the poet has spewed forth, "forcé, sous le coup de poing brutal à l'estomac," can in any way be called self-expression, it is so only in the etymological toothpaste-tube-like sense of the word. The poem is not generated naturally by the poet's subjective intentionality; it is, on the contrary, from the poet's mouth untimely ripped. This, of course, is totally consistent with Mallarmé's much-discussed elimination of the poetic subject: "L'oeuvre pure implique la disparition élocutoire du poéte, qui cède l'initiative aux mots. [The pure (poetic) work implies the elocutionary disappearance of the poet, who leaves the initiative to words.]" Indeed, the active production of this discontinuity between the speaker and his words, far from eliminating the performative dimension of Mallarmé's poetry, may itself constitute that poetry's truly revolutionary performativity.

However, if we return now to how this elimination of subjectivity is actually evoked at the end of "La Déclaration foraine," we find that even this formulation of the relation of speaker to speech is oversimplified. For the assertion of the nonintentionality of the poem is itself so tortuously noncommittal that by the time it ends in an unequivocal "c'est vrai," it has already practically qualified itself out of existence. While naming the impatience of the crowd as the explicit "cause" only of the figurative "punch in the stomach" that makes the poem "squirt out" of the poet, the lady neither totally excludes the possibility of the poem's having occurred in the carriage (into which the poet would only "perhaps," "who knows?" not have introduced it), nor does she articulate in any way the relation between punch and squirt, which cannot even be said to meet on the same rhetorical level.

Turning to the circumstances surrounding the utterance of the one true performative expression "je le gage," we find a similar problematization of the nature of the act performed. For if, according to Austin, a bet can only be said to occur if it is accepted by a taker, the "peut-être!" with which this taker "accepts" the poet's bet effectively suspends its application and thus its ability to function as a true act. Moreover, what is or is not being wagered here seems itself internally inconsequent, since the "irrefutability" of the poet's spiel is dependent not on the clear univocality of its meaning, but, on the contrary, on the uncontrollable multiplicity of its repercussions.

Thus, while "c'est vrai" and "je la gage" explicitly mark the places of the constative and the performative respectively, what happens in between is that what is stated is the problematization of the conditions of performance, while what is wagered is the problematization of the possibility of statement.

Austin's theory, of course, contains no provision for this type of ambiguity. Its elimination is, in fact, one of the main motives behind the explicitation of a performative expression, since "the explicit performative rules out equivocation." But behind the question of ambiguity, something much more unsettling is at stake, for it is not only equivocation that is ruled out by Austin's discussion of performative utterances: it is nothing less than poetry itself.

SPLITTING THE THEORETICAL HAIR

The points at which Austin dismisses poetry from his field of vision are frequent but usually parenthetical. One of these has been cited as our epigraph; the following is another:

> We could be issuing any of these utterances, as we can issue an utterance of any kind whatsoever, in the course, for example, of acting a play or making a joke or writing a poem—in which case of course it would not be seriously meant and we shall not be able to say that we seriously performed the act concerned. If the poet says "Go and catch a falling star" or whatever it may be, he doesn't seriously issue an order.
>
> ("Performative Utterances" in *Philosophical Papers*).

The argument against poetry, theater, and jokes thus stems from the fact that the utterer's relation to his utterance is not "serious." He is not "seriously" doing what he would normally be doing in so uttering. But is this "etiolation" of language, as Austin dubs it elsewhere, a mere accident, a simple infelicity? Consider the example given: the poet says "Go and catch a falling star." In the context of Donne's poem, this order is not only not serious: it is explicitly impossible. It is a *rhetorical* imperative whose function, like that of a rhetorical question, is to elicit an impasse without naming it. The very nonseriousness of the order is in fact what constitutes its fundamental seriousness; if finding a faithful woman is like catching a falling star, according to Donne's poem, this is apparently very serious indeed.

But what about nonrhetorical poetic instances of performative expressions? When Virgil says "Arma virumque cano," is he not doing what he is saying? When Whitman says "I celebrate myself and sing myself," is this not a self-referential utterance? And when Pound asserts "I make a pact with you, Walt Whitman," does it really matter whether or not Whitman is listening? In affirming that "a performative utterance will be *in a peculiar way* hollow or void if said by an actor on the stage, or if introduced into a poem" (emphasis in original), Austin is really objecting not to the use of the verb but to the status of its subject; in a poem, according to this argument, the intersubjective situation is fictionalized. The speaking subject is only a persona, an actor, not a person. But if one considers the conventionality of all performative utterances (on which Austin often insists), can it really be said that the chairman who opens a discussion or the priest who baptizes a baby or the judge who pronounces a verdict are persons rather than personae? This is precisely what Austin is admitting when he says "I do not take orders from you when you try to 'assert your authority' . . . on a desert island, as opposed to the case

where you are the captain on a ship and therefore genuinely have authority."
The performative utterance thus automatically fictionalizes its utterer when
it makes him the mouthpiece of a conventionalized authority. Where else, for
example, but at a party *convention* could a presidential candidate be nomi-
nated? Behind the fiction of the subject stands the fiction of society, for if one
states that society began with a prohibition (of incest) or a (social) contract,
one is simply stating that the origin of the authority behind a performative utterance is derived from a previous performative utterance whose ultimate origin is undeterminable. By using these *tu quoque* arguments, it is, of course,
not our intention to nullify all differences between a poem and, say, a verdict,
but only to problematize the assumptions on which such distinctions are
based. If people are put to death by a verdict and not by a poem, it is not because the law is not a fiction.

The nonseriousness of a performative utterance "said by an actor on
the stage" results, then, not from his fictional status but from his duality,
from the spectator's consciousness that although the character in the play is
swearing to avenge his dead father's ghost, the actor's own performative
commitments lie elsewhere. But the performative utterance itself is here just
as "serious" within the context of its surrounding fiction as it would be in
the context of the fiction we call real life. · Indeed, the question of
seriousness attends the act of interpretation of *any* performative utterance.
Rhetorical imperatives, for example, are far from being restricted to poetry;
a large proportion of our ordinary conversational devices consists of such
expressions as "Go jump in a lake," "Go fly a kite," and other more
frequent but less mentionable retorts. The question of seriousness, far from
marking the borders of the performative, is found to inhabit the very core
of its territory. This is, in fact, one of the main factors behind Austin's
recourse to the notion of illocutionary force. And this question, as it
happens, is explicitly brought up by a line in our sonnet itself, to which we
now turn:

> La chevelure vol d'une flamme à l'extrême
> Occident de désirs pour la tout déployer
> Se pose (je dirais mourir un diadème)
> Vers le front couronné son ancien foyer
>
> Mais sans or soupirer que cette vive nue
> L'ignition du feu toujours intérieur
> Originellement la seule continue
> Dans le joyau de l'oeil vérdique ou rieur

Une nudité de héros tendre diffame
Celle qui ne mouvant astre ni feux au doigt
Rien qu'à simplifier avec gloire la femme
Accomplit par son chef fulgurante l'exploit

De semer de rubis le doute qu'elle écorche
Ainsi qu'une joyeuse et tutélaire torche.

The attempt to translate as many as possible of the ambiguities of this poem introduces the following monstrosity, in which the reader is invited to choose only one of the boxed words at a time, but to accept all permutations of these choices that are grammatically possible. Punctuation may be added as needed.

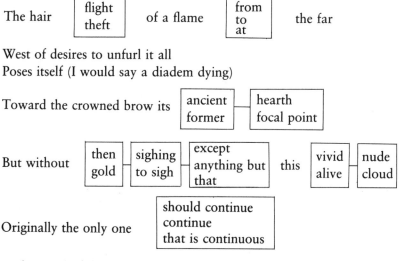

The hair [flight / theft] of a flame [from / to / at] the far

West of desires to unfurl it all
Poses itself (I would say a diadem dying)

Toward the crowned brow its [ancient / former] [hearth / focal point]

But without [then / gold] [sighing / to sigh] [except / anything but / that] this [vivid / alive] [nude / cloud]

Originally the only one [should continue / continue / that is continuous]

In the jewel of the truthful or laughing eye

[To extend a / A tender] nudity of hero defames

The one who not moving star nor fires on her finger
Nothing but by simplifying with glory the woman
Accomplishes by her head, dazzling, the exploit

Of sowing with rubies the doubt she skins
Like a joyful and tutelary torch.

Here, it is the "oeil véridique ou rieur," roughly equivalent to the "naive or ironic reader," that raises the question of seriousness. By naming the prob-

lem of interpretation in terms of an alternative between seriousness and
irony, the sonnet places itself between two incompatible readings of its own
illocutionary force. Readers of "La Déclaration foraine" are indeed often
sensitive to the mocking way in which the poet seems to treat his own
creation; in her very helpful discussion of this prose poem, Ursula Franklin,
for example, uses the word *irony* and its derivatives no less than fourteen
times. But behind the question of illocutionary force lies the question of
intentionality, which, as we have already seen, is here being subverted by the
involuntary, blind relationship between the poet and his poem. We would
therefore expect that the sonnet itself would somehow escape the simple
dichotomy that it evokes between seriousness and irony as, indeed, the poet
says it does when he speaks of its "compréhension multiple." Let us therefore examine the text of the poem in order to follow the precise functioning
of this interpretative multiplicity.

   This poem has been "read" many times. There seems to be little doubt
that it is "about" the woman standing behind it, and in particular, about her
hair. But if one attempts to make explicit not the reference itself but the
sense of the reference—what the poem is saying about the woman—one
finds that the actual affirmations made by the poem are very difficult to pin
down. In attempting to pursue even the simplest of interpretative strategies—the isolation of all the verbs in the present tense, for example—one
stumbles over the word *continue*, which may be not a verb but an adjective
and, even if it is a verb, may be either transitive or intransitive. But a
tenative grammatical skeleton might run something like the following.

> La chevelure
> Se pose
>
> (choose one) {
> Mais sans soupirer que cette nue continue dans
>   le joyau de l'oeil
>
> Mais sans rien soupirer (à l'exception de cette nue),
>   l'ignition du feu continue
>
> Une nudité de héros diffame
> Celle qui accomplit l'exploit

By teasing out three possible "declarations" from the reinsertion of this
skeleton into the poem, we can conclude that the poem is saying that:

   1. The hair is just sitting there, but the lighting of the interior fire
continues in the spectator's eye. The mere presence of the hero maligns this
glorious simplification.

2. The hair sets itself down, but if the hero does not express the hope that this cloud (the fire or hair) continue in the spectator's eye, his tenderness maligns the lady.

3. The hair is posed. But, without gold, to sigh that this cloud extends the hero's naked tenderness to the spectator's eye is to malign the lady.

As if these affirmations were not already incompatible enough, the very word *diffamer* can be split into two diametrically opposed meanings; behind its ordinary performative sense of "to malign" stands the etymological, simple cognitive meaning "to reveal, divulge." The substitution of *reveal* for *malign* in our three readings effectively results not only in three more readings almost directly contrary to the original three, but in the passage from a performative to a constative function of those meanings.

This still oversimplified exposition of what the poem is saying should at least serve to demonstrate that the sonnet is talking less directly about the lady than about its relation to the lady. It is less about *something* than about *being about.* Simultaneously asserting both the necessity and the undesirability of its own existence, the poem refers to its own referring and not directly to its referent. But, it may be objected, is this not because that referent is itself so successfully "simplifying the Woman" that it does not need the poem? Is the lady's "exploit" not still being presented as a dazzlingly self-evident act in its own right? The poet's parting words to the crowd, indeed, appear to be saying just that.

> La personne qui a eu l'honneur de se soumettre à votre jugement, ne requiert pour vous communiquer le sens de son charme, un costume ou aucun accessoire usuel de théâtre. Ce naturel s'accommode de l'allusion parfait que fournit la toilette toujours à l'un des motifs primordiaux de la femme, et suffit.

> (The person who has had the honor of submitting herself to your judgment, does not require in order to communicate to you the sense of her charm, a costume or any ordinary accessory of the theatre. This naturalness is accommodated by the perfect allusion furnished by a toilette always to one of the primordial motifs—or motives—of the woman, and suffices.)

Three hidden difficulties attend the reader who would take this explanation at face value. First, the meaning of "ce naturel" is ambiguous, since it refers back to the absence of theatrical accoutrements but forward to the allusive function of the lady's dress. "Ce naturel" becomes a central meaninglessness around which the presence and absence of allusions play. Second, this entire speech is introduced as "une *affectation* de retour à l'authenticité du spectacle," indicting that anyone who takes all this as the "meaning" of the sonnet—and almost every exegete has done so—is being taken in by a mere affectation. And third, the actual "exploit" referred to in the sonnet is not, as it is often misread, "simplifier la femme" but "semer de rubis le doute qu'elle écorche," the meaning of which is very far from being self-evident. The simplification of the woman is itself only an accessory to the highly problematic exploit of strewing rubies over a skinned doubt. Whatever this may mean, it is unlikely that it is an example of simple reference.

However, reference is not denied: it is problematized beyond reconciliation. The lady remains the referent of the poem, but only insofar as the poem says absolutely nothing about her. The moment she begins to stand for anything, including herself, she is no longer a referent but a sign. We can thus only see her as the poem's referent at the moment she ceases to be the poem's referent. This public display of (the lack of) that about which nothing can be said is described by Mallarmé elsewhere in similar terms:

> Jouant la partie, gratuitement soit pour un intérêt mineur: exposant notre Dame et Patronne à montrer sa déhiscence ou sa lacune, à l'égard de quelques rêves, comme la mesure à quoi tout se réduit.

> (Playing the game, gratuitously or for minor interest: exposing our Lady or Patroness to show her dehiscence or her lack, with respect to a number of dreams, as the measure to which all is reduced.)

If we now hazard a formulation of what the poem is saying, it would run something like this:

> The hair *is,* but the poem's existence maligns and/or reveals the one who, by simplifying the Woman, accomplishes the act of aggravating and/or embellishing the uncertainty over the possibility and/or meaning of the poem's existence.

If this appears to be a reading that no reader in his right mind could possibly intuit, let alone accept, that is precisely the point. What is revolutionary in Mallarmé's poetics is less the elimination of the "object" than this very type of construction of a systematic set of self-emptying, nonintuitive meanings. Mallarmé's famous obscurity lies not in his devious befogging of the obvious but in his radical transformation of intelligibility itself through the ceaseless production of seemingly mutually exclusive readings of the same piece of language. *This* is what constitutes Mallarmé's break with referentiality, and not the simple abolition of the object, which would still be an entirely referential gesture. Reference is here not denied but suspended. The sonnet simultaneously takes on and discards meaning only to the extent that its contact with the lady's presence is contradictorily deferred. The "poème tu," the Book of *relations,* is not a simple absence of meaning; it is the systematic, dynamically self-subverting juxtaposition—*"rime"*—of what becomes "true" only through its radical incompatibility with itself.

As we have seen, this "suspension" of meaning may occur through the simultaneous presence of contradictory affirmations. But if, as in the case of the word *diffame,* the play of contradictions lies in the very separation ("déhiscence") of a word from itself, this is a highly unsettling factor. The diachrony that has moved *diffamer* from the constative *divulge* to the performative *malign* is at work in any utterance whatsoever; quite apart from the question of seriousness, for example, the illocutionary force of an utterance is subject to the same kind of temporal fading and conventionalizing that produces "dead" metaphors and clichés. Benveniste's attempt to exclude "simple formulas" like "je m'excuse" and "bonjour" from consideration as "live" performatives is doomed by the very nature of "living" language itself.

That the logic of language renders some kind of discontinuity between speaker and speech absolutely inescapable is in fact demonstrated precisely by Austin's attempt to eliminate it. For the very word he uses to name "mere doing," the very name he gives to that from which he excludes theatricality, is none other than the word that most commonly *names* theatricality: the word *perform.* As if this were not ironic enough, exactly the same split can be found in Austin's other favorite word: *act.* How is it that a word that expresses most simply the mere doing of an act necessarily leads us to the question of—acting? How is it possible to discuss the question of authenticity when that question already subverts the very terms we use to discuss it? Is it inevitable that the same split that divides the referent from itself the moment language comes near it should divide language from itself in the very same way? And can language actually refer to anything other than that very split? If Austin's unstated question was, What are we really *doing* when we speak? it becomes clear that, whatever else we may be doing, we are at any rate being "done in" by our own words. And it is precisely the unknowable extent to which our statement differs from itself that performs *us.*

Decidedly, "leaving the initiative to words" is not as simple as it sounds. Left to their own initiative, the very words with which Austin excludes jokes, theater, and poetry from his field of vision inevitably take their revenge. But if, in the final analysis, the joke ends up being on Austin, it is, after all, only Poetic justice.

BONNIE J. ISAAC

"Du fond d'un naufrage": Notes on Michel Serres and Mallarmé's "Un Coup de dés"

> Vainement ma raison voulait prendre la barre;
> La tempête en jouant déroutait ses efforts,
> Et mon âme dansait, dansait vieille gabarre
> Sans mâts, sur une mer monstreuse et sans bords!
>
> [*Vainly my reason for the helm was striving:*
> *The tempest of my efforts made a scorn.*
> *My soul like a dismasted wreck went driving*
> *Over a monstrous sea without bourn.*]
> —BAUDELAIRE, "Les Sept Vieillards"

Shipwreck is always the risk of navigation. In Mallarmé's "Brise marine," the narrator asks:

> Et peut-être, les mâts, invitant les orages
> Sont-ils de ceux qu'un vent penche sur les naufrages
> Perdus, sans mâts, sans mâts, ni fertiles îlots.
>
> [And perhaps the masts, inviting tempests,
> Are of those which a wind bends over shipwrecks
> Lost, without masts, without masts or fertile isles.]

Vasco da Gama, passing the cape "Sans que la barre ne varie [with the helm holding steady]," is nevertheless threatened by "Nuit, désespoir [Night,

From *Modern Language Notes* 96, no. 4 (1981). © 1981 by the Johns Hopkins University Press.

despair]"; the ship of poets in "Salut" risks "Solitude, récif [Solitude, reef]. And yet the words elided from the above two verses, "pierrerie" ["gem"] and "étoile" ["star"], announce the hope of the shipwreck of "Un Coup de dés." The Master of the vessel attempts to pit "sa petite raison virile [his little virile mind]" against the elements; "Un Coup de dés . . . quand bien même lancé dans des circonstances éternelles du fond d'un naufrage [A dice-throw . . . even when cast in eternal circumstances from the depths of a shipwreck]" would, in "cette conjonction suprême avec la probabilité [this supreme conjunction with probability]," attempt to transform chance into necessity: the dice-throw, "l'unique Nombre qui ne peut pas être un autre [the one Number that can be no other]" would be transfigured into the Constellation, glimmering above the tempest, "un destin et les vents [a destiny and the winds]."

"Un Coup de dés" has most often been read in terms of relatively straightforward oppositions (chance and necessity, the real and the ideal, the success or failure of Mallarmé's enterprise): interpretations which tend toward a synthesis, whose goal, like that of the dice-throw, might be to "en reployer la division et passe fier [close its gap and go proudly]." Robert Greer Cohn, in his seminal "exegesis" of "Un Coup de dés," maintains that the traditional interpretation, embodied by Thibaudet, emphasizes Mallarmé's failure to attain the *Grand Oeuvre,* the absolute; the Master would renounce his lifetime illusion, which fact would at least explain the title: "Un Coup de dés jamais n'abolira le hasard [A dice-throw never will abolish chance]." Thibaudet's analysis is however more nuanced: the attempts to attain necessity, pure logic, are doomed to failure, but the work would figure less a shipwreck, an unsuccessful battle against the sea, than a battle against enigma, in the domain of the spirit: the fact that in "Un Coup de dés" there is no first-person narrator, as in Baudelaire's "Les Sept Vieillards," might tend to support this view. On the level of an abstract combat, Deleuze's assessment, from a Nietzschean perspective, is much less optimistic. If, for Nietzsche, the dice-throw demands a strict interdependence of chance and necessity—chance being the dice before the throw, sea and waves; necessity the dice after the throw, the constellation—Mallarmé is ultimately unable to maintain this disjunctive simultaneity. His failure would result from a supposed necessity to exclude chance, contingency being necessarily subservient to the pure idea.

The movements of "Un Coup de dés"—both textual and metaphorical—would tend to undercut such polarities. The writings of Michel Serres on thermodynamics, information and game theory, the mathematics of large populations and atomism exploit a certain kind of multiplicity which, though to my knowledge, Serres has never explicitly analyzed Mallarmé, resonate with a strange persistence with many Mallarméan metaphors, particularly those of "Un Coup de dés." I by no means wish to suggest the imposition of a "scientific" model on a "literary" work, particularly given Serres's frequently reiterated cautions against the passage from the "local" to the "global"; I wish to explore a fluid, mobile relationship, its movement and flow. The local connections suggested by shared concepts and metaphors, by similar configurations and dynamics, would not point to any generalizable conclusions, such as "theories of science in Mallarmé." I would wish rather to approach a confluence, a convergence of rivers which flow, swirl, form eddies, whirlpools and turbulences, in uncertain times and uncertain places, suggesting that combination of indeterminateness and rigor which Mallarmé, in his formulations of the nature of *le vers,* might wish to attain.

For Serres, the basis of any system—linguistic, theoretical or scientific—is a stock, reservoir, chaos, *chora:* the "lieu" perhaps of "Rien n'aura en eu lieu que le lieu [Nothing will have taken place but the place]" of "Un Coup de dés." It is, as in Plato's *Timaeus,* a receptacle, womb: that which changes names but has no name, that which undoes or separates through condensation or compression, clouds, fog or running water, displacement or liquidation. It is anterior to all movement, difference, nomination, form: a topogical space where "tous les chemins, tous les sens sont frayables, possibles [all paths, all directions and meanings are passable, possible]"; it is the space before meaning, direction (*sens*), circulation (*Hermès IV: La Distribution*). It is the space where atoms flow in a "chaos-verseau [chaos-outpouring]" or fluctuate in a "chaos-nuage [chaos-cloud]," displaced, at uncertain times and at uncertain places, by the *clinamen*, "écart à l'équilibre [deviation from equilibrium]," the "différentielle, la fluxion, la foudre qui traverse la chute de la pluie [differential, the swell, the lightning that flashes across the downpour]," a stochastic, aleatory "turbulence" in an "orderly" chaos, a spiralling motion which creates the possibility of order, of relationships [*La Naissance de la physique dans le texte de Lucrèce: fleuves et turbulences;* all further references to this text will be abbreviated as *NP*].

It is perhaps no accident that for Mallarmé, the way one would read differently, perceiving words "independently of ordinary succession," is "on a bias, contingently." The "meteorology" of the "crise de vers [crisis of verse]" is a storm, the reflection and refraction of raindrops and lightning. Analogously, the relationship between music and letters is also "meteorological": alternations of light and shadows characterize "le moderne des météores, la symphonie [the modern among meteors, the symphony]" provoking "intempéries [inclemencies]" of "divers ciels [changing skies]," per-

haps the same "circonstances" of "Un Coup de dés." Language, at great
risk, would extract a direction (*sens*) from "la chute des sons nus [the
downpour of naked sounds]" for Serres as well, "meteorology" indicates
risk—unpredictability, storm, shipwreck and tempest, "nuages, trombes,
chutes de grêle ou giboulées, direction et force du vent. Accident, circonstances. Voisinage hasardeux, environnement événementiel de l'essentiel, de
la stance [clouds, waterspouts, hailstorms or sudden showers, the direction
and force of the wind. Accident, circumstances. Dangerous proximity, the
incidental surroundings of the essential, the stance]."

If atoms are letters, then the text, information, can be born from the
same kind of turbulence, as Mallarmé also suggests:

> Le livre, expansion totale de la lettre, doit d'elle tirer, directement,
> une mobilité et spacieux, par correspondances, instituer un jeu,
> on ne sait, qui confirme la fiction. Rien de fortuit, là, où semble
> un hasard capter l'idée.

> [The book, a total expansion of the letter, must draw from it,
> directly, a mobility, and spacious, by correspondences, must in-
> stitute a game, who knows?, that confirms the fiction. Nothing
> fortuitous here, where chance seems to overtake the idea.]

For Serres, atom-letters "s'associent en phrases, se rassemblent en volumes
[group as phrases, assemble in volumes]"; their aggregate is words, and
meaning is formed by the oblique flash of the *clinamen* across background
noise. The poem is "coupé d'éclairs. . . . Hachures inclinées qui dictent,
temps par temps, une nouvelle pente . . . ses tourbillons de mots conjoints,
sur un talweg coupé de catastrophes [streaked by lightning . . . Slanted
streaks that dictate a new slope tense by tense, time after time . . . its eddies
of linked words, on a thalweg cut by catastrophes]." For Mallarmé, the flow
of words ("charroi [cartage]," "courant [current]") necessitates some kind
of textual spacing.

For Serres, information is characterized by its rarity in the face of the
constant flow of atoms, of the constant movement of the cloud he names
"distribution." "Le message y est chaotique, un nuage de lettres. Mieux,
d'éléments quelconques, peut-être pas encore de lettres . . . le bruit qui
tourbillonne . . . au profit de la turbulence [The message is chaotic, a cloud
of letters. Better, of undefined elements, perhaps not yet letters . . . whirling
noise . . . promoting turbulence]" (*La Distribution*). Information attempts
to emerge as archipelagoes in a sea of noise, a risky navigation which
engages a potential emitter-receiver in a violent world. Mallarmé, in "Le

Mystère dans les lettres," recognizes the impossibility of a "neutral" discourse, the necessity of "diving" into a text. For Serres as well, "Nous
baignons dans des entrelacs de canaux . . . plongé[s] dans les fleuves objectifs.
Récepteur, en son lieu, émetteur sous tous angles. Battu, frappé, blessé . . .
douloureux. [We bathe in a network of interlocking channels . . . (we are)
immersed in objective flows. (We are a) receiver in (our) emplacement, a
transmitter from every angle. Beaten, stricken, hurt . . . pained . . .]" The
text is one circulation among others, "Naufrage, inclinaison de texte, chute
des atomes et cataracte des lettres [A shipwreck, a textual inclination, a fall
of atoms, and a cataract of letters]." In any such atmosphere, any information, communication, would appear miraculous. Discourse is a *clinamen*,
among the cataract of atom-letters, creating a turbulence through which one
must carefully navigate:

> On ne gouverne jamais un vaisseau que par l'angle d'inclinaison
> donné au gouvernail, autour de quoi les filets d'eau laissent leurs
> turbulences: alors l'éclair cligne et claque comme un *clinamen*
> perceptible, autour de quoi les vents et les nuages forment leurs
> tourbillons.

> [A ship can only be steered by the angle of inclination of the
> rudder, around which turbulences are created by the stream;
> then lightning flickers and cracks like a perceptible *clinamen*
> around which the wind and clouds form eddies.]

(NP)

Between turbulences and whirlwinds, it is the relationships between words
which make language possible: "en-deça de la relation, il n'y a que nuages
dans le vide, lettres ou atomes [before the relationship, there is nothing but
clouds in the void, nothing but letters or atoms]" (NP).

It is that relationship which attempts to halt or reverse the other consequence of the *clinamen:* irreversible time, entropy. The *clinamen* may
describe the smallest possible angle of deviation, but it also forms the greatest possible angle of descent, declining toward a new equilibrium; a necessary movement so that invariance does not mean repose, constancy stasis:
stability itself can approach movement. Language and writing attempt to
resist the current of the river of entropy, resist inclination, decline, the usury
of time, by the assembly of atom-letters into the conjunction and interstices
of their combinations, signals emerging from noise. Their relationships are
for Serres, as for Mallarmé, embodied in a kind of music: "Comment la
chute déviée introduit-elle du réversible dans l'irréversible? D'où vient cette

musique, par rapport au chaos-bruit de fond, d'où vient le rythme par rapport à l'écoulement sans retour du verseau? [How does a fall that has deviated introduce reversibility into the irreversible? How can chaos-background noise give rise to music? How can an irreversible outpouring (*verseau*) give rise to rhythm?]" (NP). The inclination of the *clinamen* produces direction, vector, *le vers*. In the interstices of that movement, local effects, turbulences, permit reversibility. There are two kinds of music: that of the river; that of the sea:

> La musique va. Elle commence, elle s'achève. Ou plutôt une musique va. Elle va du silence au silence, elle a comme une source et un point de terminaison. Une autre, interminable, s'arrête et ne s'arrête pas, comme à un bord mal défini, et commence aussi peu, elle nous ennoie, elle nous submerge. Une musique coule comme un fleuve, l'autre est la mer. La musique et le temps.

> [Music runs. It begins, it ends. Or rather one kind of music runs. It runs from silence to silence, it has something like a source and an end-point. Another, interminable, kind of music stops and does not stop, as at an ill-defined edge. Neither does it start; it drowns us, submerges us. One music flows like a river, the other is the sea. Music and time.]
>
> (NP)

One can discern in Mallarmé hints of the two kinds of music Serres suggests. There is that which, like the ocean, can drown one in a sea of emotivity, "La mer dont mieux vaudrait se taire que l'inscrire dans parenthèse si, avec, n'y entre le firmament. [The sea, about which it would be better to say nothing than to inscribe it in a parenthesis, unless it enclosed the firmanent also.]" For the "crise de vers [crisis of verse]," "orage lustrale [lustral storm]" whose "bouleversements [upheavals]" attempt to liberate "la musicalité de tout [the musicality of the whole]," the sea exercises a "vertu autrement attrayante [virtue holding a different attraction]," a "plénitude [plenitude]" which is impossible to describe other than by allusion, suggestion. Mallarmé would appear to prefer to the music-sea the music-river, that which has a source and a terminus, but which nevertheless can impart movement, fluidity, to *le vers*. And yet, like navigation in "Un Coup de dés," river navigation can have its dangers, as the "maraudeur aquatique [aquatic marauder]" of "Le Nénuphar blanc" discovers. As Serres points out:

Tous les mariniers savent bien ... qu'ils ne descendent pas
toujours un fleuve sans efforts. Les contre-courants les immobilis-
ent parfois, parfois les chassent en amont. Le fleuve n'est pas
toujours une route qui les mène où ils veulent aller.

[All mariners know ... that they do not always go down a river
effortlessly. Backwashes sometimes immobilize them and sometimes push them back upstream. The river is not always a road
that takes them where they want to go.]

(NP)

Yet if one tries to go beyond one's limits, one's boundaries, the "borne
à l'infini [limit on infinity]" of "Un Coup de dés," one risks that passage
from local to global that for Serres leads to potential violence, risk, death.
The uncharted river in "Prose pour Des Esseintes" presents in the course of
its navigation what for Serres is one of the greatest threats: "La croissance,
perçue comme menace, danger incontrôlables [Growth perceived as an uncontrollable menace or danger]." One cannot always control one's navigation; the turbulence of the *clinamen* can produce order, reversibility in
irreversibility, but like all "meteors" it occurs unpredictably: it flickers
("clignotant") in the blink of an eye ("clin d'oeil"), causing a shipwreck of
the "yole à clins": "Le sens est formé par le bruit et le dérive vers le bruit:
espace-temps du clignotement et du déclin. Les signaux d'univers font les
clins d'oeil de la profondeur du nuage. [Meaning is formed by noise ... (and
the drift) toward noise; the space-time of blinking and decline. Universe
signals wink from the depths of the cloud.]" In Mallarmé's terms, "Un coup
de dés jamais n'abolira le hasard [A dice-throw never will abolish chance]";
"rien n'aura eu lieu que le lieu."

Derrida in "La Double Séance" alludes to the *clinamen* in the flow of
rhythmos: "un clin d'hymen. Une chute rythmée. Une cadence inclinée. [a
wink of the hymen. A rhythmic fall. A (w)inclined cadence]." The hymen,
itself a kind of angle, a joint ("clin"), a fold, indicates a suspense, an interval, "Car la différence est au moins l'intervalle nécessaire, le suspens entre
deux échéances, le 'laps' entre deux coups, deux chutes, deux chances. [For
difference is the necessary interval, the suspense between two outcomes, the
"lapse of time" between two shots, two rolls, two chances.]" The play
between contingency, necessity and chance becomes the textual spacing of
"différence," "entre-deux," a "crise du *rythmos* ... rythme, cadence
inclinée, déclinaison, décadence, *chute* et retour [crisis of *rythmos* ...

rhythm, decline, inclined cadence, decadence, *fall* and return]." The "crisis" becomes the risks of reversibility in irreversibility, a "coup de dés":

> Hymen selon le vers, blanc encore, de la nécessité et du hasard. . . .
> Si—elle était, la littérature se tiendrait—elle dans le suspens où
> chacune de ses six faces garde la chance. . . . La crise de la
> littérature a lieu quand rien n'a lieu que le lieu, dans l'instance où
> personne n'est là pour savoir. Personne—ne sachant—avant le
> coup—qui le déjoue en son échéance—lequel des six dés—chute.

> [In the hymen depending on the verse, blank once more, com-
> posed of chance and necessity . . . If—it were, literature would
> hang—would it, on the suspense in which each of the six sides
> still has a chance . . . The crisis of literature takes place when
> nothing takes place but the place, in the instance where no one
> is there to know. No one—knowing—before the throw—which
> undoes it (him) in its outcome—which of the six—(die falling).]

"Un Coup de dés" puts into motion the oppositions between chance and necessity, irreversibility and reversibility, the sea and the firmament, music and letters. It exploits metaphors of whirlwinds and turbulences, of navigation and shipwreck, of the "lieu." Mauron maintains that Mallarmé's temporality attempts to reverse the flow of entropy. Jean-Paul Sartre sees Mallarmé as balancing "ce couple de contraires qui perpétuellement s'engendre et se repousse: le hasard . . . la nécessité [this pair of opposites which perpetually engender and repel each other: chance . . . necessity]" in a heroic stance against the inevitability of entropy: "L'homme mourant sur tout le globe d'une désintégration de l'atome ou d'un refroidissement du soleil. [Man dying all over the world from a disintegration of the atom or a cooling of the sun . . .]" ("Mallarmé" in *Situations IX*).

Blanchot transfers the oppositions to problems of textuality. Mallarmé would be "liberated" from linear, temporal succession, from "irreversibility," in favor of ruptures, discontinuities, a new kind of mobility. "Un Coup de dés" "est né d'une entente nouvelle de l'espace littéraire, tel que puissent s'y engendrer, par des rapports nouveaux de mouvement, des relations nouvelles de compréhension [is born of a new understanding of the space of literature which enables new relationships of comprehension to be engendered in it by new relations of movement]." Language is perceived spatially, the "lieu [place]" evoked by Serres, "où, avant d'être paroles déterminées et exprimées, le langage est le mouvement silencieux de rapports [where, before being the expression of determinate words, language is the silent movement of relations . . .]" where "jamais l'instant ne succède à l'instant selon le déroulement horizontal d'un devenir irréversible [instants never succeed one another following the horizontal unfolding of an irreversible becoming]" (*Le Livre à venir.*).

For Cohn, the movement of "Un Coup de dés" is engendered more "epistemologically," by the oscillation of opposites in paradox. But the resonances of some of his readings echo with those of Serres: "In a clustering of words, as in atoms or planets, lies the law." The organizational capacities of atoms, compared to the eternal "revolution" of the firmament, emphasize however form over movement. His reading of "circonstances" is antithetical for this reason to that of Serres: if "circonstances" are that which "stand around," "circonstances éternelles [eternal circumstances]" would not be perpetual motion, but the freezing of time for one event.

Mallarmé evokes in his preface to "Un Coup de dés" music as a resource which textual spacing and movement should exploit. He cautions one in seeing in this work little more than a "spacing of reading": which is engendered by the dispersion of traditional prosody by blank space and typography is not space, but movement. It accelerates the pace of reading; space does not exist in itself, but is "scanned," "intimated" in a "simultaneous vision of the Page" which is not however static: "La fiction affleurera et se dissipera, vite, d'après la mobilité de l'écrit [The fiction will arise and dissipate, quickly, according to the mobility of the writing]." The successiveness of narrative, as well as that of time, by "raccourci [shortcut]," "hypothèse [hypothesis]," multiple meanings. Thought moves through "retraits, prolongements, fuites [withdrawals, prolongations, flights]": the effect of the text is that of a musical score, a "partition" which could be an accompaniment for many of the *motifs* found in Michel Serres.

Cohn suggests in passing that the project of the Master, his "anciens calculs [outworn calculations]," could evoke "the mathematical and physical laws which lead to man's emergence." As in Serres, the circumstances which surround the dice thrown "from the depths of a shipwreck," however "eternal," are unpredictable, and ultimately menacing. The "Abyss" contains both potential, oscillating, virtual movement—the *chora*—and the possibility of a *clinamen*—order out of turbulence: "Soit que l'Abîme . . . étale . . . sous une inclinaison plane désespérément [Whether the Abyss . . . slack . . . under an incline desperately soars]." The movement of the Abyss suggests a downward flight, and its "wing" could point to an effort to reverse the flow of entropy: "par avance retombée d'un mal à dresser le vol [beforehand fallen after trouble taking flight]." The rocking of the boat reinforces abortive movement: "voile alternative," "penché de l'un ou l'autre

bord [alternate sail tossing from side to side]"; open and closed also alternate: "très à l'intérieur résume l'ombre enfuie dans la profondeur ["deep
inside resumes the shadow buried in the depths"]" "couvrant les jaillisse-
ments coupant au ras les bonds ["containing the spurts and cutting the leaps
at the root"]." "L'envergure" alternates with "béante profondeur" to suggest that which is buried, potential, but which could emerge, "chaos-verseau"
or "chaos-nuage."

    The Master navigates by means of the oblique "barre [helm]"; he "se
prépare s'agite et mêle au poing qui l'étreindrait comme on menace un
destin et les vents [prepares itself (himself) is tossed and merges / with the
fist that might embrace it (him) / as one threatens / a destiny and the winds]."
At odds with the elements, his conflict is indeed between them and destiny.
His dilemma: should he throw "l'unique Nombre qui ne peut pas être un
autre [the one Number that can be no other]" the ultimate dice-throw,
"dans la tempête en reployer la division et passer fier [into the storm / to
close its gap and go proudly]" or "jouer . . . la partie au nom des flots [play
. . . the match / in the name of the waves]"? Should he attempt, with the
ultimate Number, to master nature, to rejoin divisions, or should he play the
game in the name of the waves, in the hope that the waves themselves,
through their movement and turbulence, can somehow produce order? His
ancestors—"l'aïeul"—have had a perpetual intercourse with the sea: "né
d'un ébat la mer par l'aïeul tentant ou l'aïeul contre la mer une chance
oiseuse Fiançailles dont le voile d'illusion chancellera s'affalera folie
[born / of a frolic / the sea by the ancestor tempting or the ancestor against
the sea / an idle chance / Betrothal / whose veil of illusion . . . will
waver / plummet / madness]." Such an uncertain union wavers, falters, slides
down to madness, a kind of entropy engendered by decline, emplified by the
large-type N'ABOLIRA immediately following. The root of "chancellera" is
cadencia, suggesting for Cohn the fall of the dice. But it could also indicate
the "cadence rythmée [rhythmic cadence]" of Derrida, the "chute [fall]" of
rythmos, the spacing movement of the *chora,* the equilibrium to which all
must return, but also the ordering of chaos through movement from which
all codes, languages, texts, emerge.

    The next set of double pages confirms this intuition, beginning not only
a section in italics, but forming almost the literal center of the poem: "Une
insinuation simple au silence enroulée avec ironie ou le mystère précipité
hurlé dans quelque proche tourbillon d'hilarité et d'horreur voltige autour
du gouffre sans le joncher ni fuir et en berce le vierge indice. [A simple
insinuation / to silence twined with irony / or / the mystery / hurled / yel-
led / in some nearby eddy of hilarity and horror / hovers over the abyss /

without scattering it / nor fleeing / and lulls its virgin mark.]" Cohn sees the "tourbillon [eddy]" as a spiral surrounded by the words "comme si" ["as if" or "as yes"], indicating an eddy, a momentary stasis, an expansion which figures circles which almost, yet not quite, turn back on themselves. Such a figure resonates with the very word "si": both "if" and "yes," "s" is the analytical, dissolving, disseminating letter; "i" is the letter which "resumes." The essence of the whirlpool is to suck in its surroundings and yet to fling out a circle of itself. But Cohn insists on the circular, enclosed nature of the spiral throughout his interpretation, even though the pattern of words clustered around the whirlpool-center can move out of itself, making a spiral whose outer contour is roughly elliptical.

For Serres, the spiral-whirlpool-turbulence is equally crucial, indicating the inclination of the *clinamen* and the flow of atoms, order from chaos and the flow toward entropy, a configuration that would preclude the circular. Such a configuration also indicates conflict, menace, danger, even physical distress, as the perceiving subject is buffeted by competing signals, a distress one can also find in Mallarmé. Cohn does indeed sense the same combination. "Insinuation" could indicate the tortuous writhing of the Chimera which in Mallarmé's "La Musique et les lettres" creates language itself, but Cohn emphasizes the negative side of "art" rather than a productive movement. "Joncher" indicates for Cohn that neither the "insinuation" nor the "tourbillon" succeed in penetrating the "silence-mystère" from which they arose, nor do they succeed in fleeing it. Cohn would thus undercut the possibilities of dissemination of the "tourbillon." "En berce le vierge indice" would be the first "letter" emerging from turbulence, as Serres might also suggest: the "horror" of disorder, the "hilarity" of creation. But the spiral for Cohn ultimately indicates an eternal return, though continuing to indicate that no circle turns back on itself. He explains however that this is because no concept can exist without its opposite; we have seen that straightforward polarities are displaced by the very movement that engenders them. Serres points out that an inclination plus a circle equals a spiral: "La turbulence de la nature, un poème écrit en tourbillon qui se boucle sans se boucher [Nature's turbulence, a poem written like a vortex that loops back without forming a circle]" (NP). The spiral would thus call into question movements of synthesis of oppositions; eternal return would be always superseded by entropy.

The "comme si" also governs the following section of "Un Coup de dés." "Comme" is the establishment of a relation; "si" an affirmation after negation: this section appropriately enough evokes Hamlet, "prince amer de l'écueil ["bitter prince of the reef"]" (recall the "récif ["reef"]" of "Salut")

whose feathered cap is ludicrously erect in the face of "la foudre ["lightning"]": "plume solitaire éperdue . . . cette blancheur rigide dérisoire en
opposition au ciel trop . . . sa petite raison virile en foudre [solitary bewil-
dered plume . . . this rigid whiteness / derisory / in opposition to the sky / too
much / . . . his little virile mind / in lightning]." But we recall with Serres
that "la foudre" is in a sense the condition of possibility of reason, a rarity
which falls with the cadence of *rythmos* and the *clinamen*. Derrida remarks
that "l'élévation de la plume est toujours l'imminence ou l'événement de sa
chute [the raising of the quill always marks the imminence or the occurrence
of its fall]" and cites the "effets de glotte [glottal effects]" of Mallarmé's *Le
Livre*—"plus je plu me plume jet chute choc [more I—quill—quill I—quill
jet of water]"—which, oddly enough, resonate with many metaphorical
connections found in Serres. Hamlet's crisis, figuring that of the Master, is
echoed in the "crise de vers [crisis of verse]," which, we recall, is meteorological. Derrida recalls that the original title of "Crise de vers" was
"Averses," suggesting an "orage historique . . . pluie . . . Faits d'hiver [his-
torical storm . . . rain . . . winter facts (news items)]." We recall as well that
the navigation of "Salut" was governed by a poetic avant-garde, "l'avant
fastueux [sumptuous prow]" which "cuts"—always obliquely—"le flot de
foudres et d'hivers [tide of thunderbolts and winters]." The "hilarity and
horror" of the whirlwind is echoed by the "rire que SI [laugh which IF
(YES)]" of Hamlet who "scintille de vertige [scintillates with vertigo]," and
by the contorsions of drowning sirens, recalling the "insinuation" of the
Chimera, and also the "Telle loin se noie une troupe / De sirènes [As far
away drowns a troop of sirens]" of "Salut." The "torsion de sirène . . . par
d'impatientes squames ultimes bifurquées [siren's torsion . . . by impatient
ultimate forked scales]" of "Un Coup de dés" remind one, with Serres, that,
in the unlimited topology of the *chora*, it is the bifurcation that produces
"catastrophes" in the fall of "chréodes." But bifurcation also creates meaning, direction; in "Un Coup de dés," the "écueil" of Hamlet becomes a "roc
faux manoir tout de suite évaporé en brumes qui imposa une borne à l'infini
[rock / false manor / suddenly / evaporated into mist / which imposed / a
limit on infinity]": a limit, a sort of order, out of the "chaos-nuage."

The Number would be the ultimate order, "issu stellaire [stellar birth]"
a rare, agonized result of buffeting movement which nevertheless, in the
uncertainty of its apparition, does not abolish chance:

EXISTÂT-IL autrement qu'hallucination ésparse d'agonie COM-
MENCÂT-IL ET CESSÂT-IL sourdant que nié et clos quand
apparu enfin par quelque profusion répandue en rareté SE

CHIFFRÂT-IL évidence de la somme pour peu qu'une IL-LUMINÂT-IL CE SERAIT pire non davantage ni moins indifférent mais autant LE HASARD

[EVEN IF IT EXISTED / other than as a thin hallucination of agony / EVEN IF IT BEGAN AND EVEN IF IT CEASED / welling up but negated and closed after appearing / at last / by some profusion spread in rarity / EVEN IF IT FIGURED ITSELF / evidence of the sum as small as it may be / EVEN IF IT LIT UP / THIS WOULD BE / worse / no / more nor less / indifferently but just as much / CHANCE]

The Number bubbles up when denied, profuse and rare, participating in infinity ("chiffrât [figure]" but also in order ("existât," "commencât," "cessât," "illuminât" [exist, begin, cease, light up]): the music of the sea and that of the river, with a beginning and an end. But it participates no less in the rhythmical cadence which tends, despite archipelagoes of negentropy on the sea of background noise, toward equilibrium, neutrality, entropy: "Choit la plume rythmique suspens du sinistre s'ensevelir aux écumes originelles naguères d'où sursauta son délire jusqu'à une cime flétrie par la neutralité identique au gouffre [Falls / the plume / rhythmic suspense of the sinister / to shroud itself / in the primitive foam / from which lately its delirium surged to a peak / withered / by the identical neutrality of the abyss]." That which subsists is not therefore the Number, but the place, the "lieu [place]," the *chora:*

RIEN de la mémorable crise où se fût l'événement accompli en vue de tout résultat nul humain N'AURA EU LIEU une élévation ordinaire verse l'absence QUE LE LIEU inférieur clapotis quelconque pour disperser l'acte vide abruptement que sinon par son mensonge eût fondé la perdition dans ces parages du vague en quoi toute réalité se dissout

[NOTHING / of the memorable crisis / where / the event / might have been accomplished with a view to all nil result / human / WILL HAVE TAKEN PLACE / an ordinary elevation pours forth absence / BUT THE PLACE / any lower plashing as if to disperse the empty act / abruptly which otherwise / by its lie / would have founded / perdition / in these parts / of the vagueness / in which all reality dissolves]

We find the flow of the "chaos-verseau" ("verse"), the descent of the "point extrémal" of the "crise" toward the "inferior"; the dispersal, dissemination, dissolution, distribution of the "chaos-nuage": the vagueness into which all reality is ultimately dissolved.

But the final pages indicate that far-off hope: the constellation which is not however a static transcendence, but which participates in the same movement of shocks and declines which engenders it:

> EXCEPTÉ à l'altitude PEUT-ÊTRE aussi loin qu'un endroit fusionne avec au-delà hors l'intérêt quant à lui signalé en général selon telle obliquité par telle déclivité de feux vers ce doit être le Septentrion aussi Nord UNE CONSTELLATION froide l'oubli et de désuétude pas tant qu'elle n'énumère sur quelque surface vacante et supérieure le heurt successif sidéralement d'un compte total en formation veillant doutant roulant brillant et méditant avant de s'arrêter à quelque point dernier qui le sacre

> [EXCEPT / at an altitude / PERHAPS / as far away as a place fuses with beyond / outside interest / for its part signaled / in general / by such obliquity and such declivity / of fires / towards (verse) (*vers*) / it must be / the Septentrion also North / A CONSTELLATION / cold from neglect and disuse / not so much / that it does not enumerate / on some empty and higher surface / the successive knock / sidereally / of a total count in formation / watching / doubting / revolving / shining and meditating / before stopping / at some final point which consecrates it]

We encounter again that elevation ("altitude"), that "point extrémal" of crisis. In "La Musique et les lettres" however Mallarmé indicates that pyrotechnical fusion at great height is not a transcendence, but another kind of ephemeral pattern. The constellation belongs perhaps less to the firmament of eternal revolution than to the reflection and refraction on a bias of words on a page, which, in "L'Action restreinte," mirror the stars black on white, white on black: "Tu remarqueras, on n'écrit pas, lumineusement, sur champ obscur, l'alphabet des astres, seul, ainsi s'indique, ébauché ou interrompu; l'homme poursuit noir sur blanc [You will note, one does not write, luminously, against a dark background, the alphabet of the stars, alone, thus is indicated, outlined or interrupted; man pursues black on white]."

In "Un Coup de dés," the "total number" is in formation only, observed only at the moment *before* its supposed consecration, the halting of its movement. The time of "Un Coup de dés" is the *futur antérieur,* of incomplete, deferred action. The Mime of "Mimique," "ici devançant, là remémorant, au futur, au passé, *sous une apparence fausse de présent* . . . installe, ainsi, un milieu, pur, de fiction [here preceding, there remembering, in the future, in the past, *in a false appearance of the present* . . . installs, thus, a pure space, of fiction]": "rien n'aura eu lieu que le lieu, excepté peut-être une constellation [Nothing will have taken place but the place, except perhaps a constellation]." But the constellation does not "take place" any more than does the "place": never formed, always in motion, it participates in entropy while restraining its movement, like music, like language, like the movement of atoms, "turbulences," "tourbillons," in Michel Serres.

Jean Hyppolite links "Un Coup de dés" with information theory, entropy, and Maxwell's Demon. For Hyppolite, "Un Coup de dés," by replacing chance with necessity, confirms by questioning the conditions of possibility of the message itself, that the "content" of the message is its "form." Information is characterized by an almost impossible miracle, which emerges only to almost inevitably disappear. Yet it is opposed to entropy: the general system may tend toward equilibrium, but local singularities (what Serres calls turbulences) produce order out of disorder. The increase of entropy is for an instant avoided; the unpredictable (Serres's "meteorological") replaces the monotony of irreversibility. Maxwell's Demon is the personification of attempts to retard that flow: his calculations, like those of Mallarmé's "aïeul," would extract maximum information from the probable, pure chance, disorder and repetition. Typography would also for Hyppolite confirm those calculations, "modelling" information, affording form in regularity, originality within the unpredictable, distinguishable from background noise, chance, the dissipation of any message. The message would thus for Hyppolite abolish chance, becoming a sort of necessity. The constellation would exhibit this tendency toward the static, the constitution of meaning through the risk of tracing a message which is a message only. Neither triumphant *logos* nor extreme finality, the message revolves like the stars, "révolu aussitôt que jeté [over with as soon as it is thrown]." While Hyppolite senses the movement to which I have pointed at the end of "Un Coup de dés," like Deleuze, like Cohn, he maintains polarities—chance and necessity, information and entropy. The Master, like Maxwell's Demon, sorts disorder to obtain the greatest possible amount of information, producing, through Number, the constellation: "Toute pensée émet un coup de dés [Every thought emits a dice-throw]," but stability is emphasized over movement, an interpretation we have seen opposed by figures as diverse as Blanchot, Derrida and Serres.

Serres sees the attempt to gain greater and greater quantities of information, to make more and more exact measurements, as an indication of potential transcendence in a scientific discourse: the universe that can be measured can be mastered through Number, a constellation. But, as Serres points out, exactitude is paid for—"anciens calculs [outworn calculations]"—in an infinite quantity of negentropy; the "money" of knowledge is obtained only at the expense of an infinite amount of future time in which to acquit one's debt. Thus mastery can produce bankruptcy, and we are "hurled, precipitated" to that future anterior where nothing is accomplished, all is deferred, where entropy is halted but where movement is incessant: the time-space of the "lieu," of the Number, of the "tourbillon," of the Constellation. Maxwell's Demon is the fiction by which the Second Principle of thermodynamics fails; he is the sorter producing the spatial deviation that is the condition of possibility of order, differentiation, information: that which differs is deferred, introducing reversibility in irreversibility. His order is not static necessity, but participates in the kind of movement that characterizes chance itself. As negentropy increases, one discovers that rich, exceptional situation that was capable of producing a constellation: "celle où se trouve le Démon de Maxwell à la fin de son oeuvre de sélection et de tri [when Maxwell's Demon is at the end of his work of selection and sorting out]."

But Maxwell's Demon implies a desire for order: the tendency in science is to master, measure laws of nature. But, Serres suggests, science should view the acquiring of information as a game rather than as a combat. It is a game with adversaries, rules, ordered play; the player must make a choice or decision from a multiplicity of possibilities. But if science were less concerned with absolute mastery, it would have open to it the movement of the aleatory, of risk, but of possible gain. Serres suggests a new displacement of science, which also implies a redefinition of communication, whereby one can nevertheless sort, read, know, form relations.

Mallarmé, in "Un Coup de dés," may well have, rather than failed, simply renounced the kind of mastery that necessity, appropriation, measurement implies. But renunciation or displacement of mastery does not imply the renunciation of the forming of relationships, of information, of communication. In "La Musique et les lettres," and elsewhere, Mallarmé introduces the categories of "game" or "fiction" to displace any potential moment of final unity, of transcendent synthesis. He points to the "supercherie" of an "attirance supérieure comme d'un vide," of "quelque élévation défendue et de foudre! le conscient manque chez nous de ce qui là-haut éclate [some forbidden lightning-struck elevation! Our consciousness lacks what fulminates there]." One can play the game with all seriousness, but the "final move" never takes place, or rather is displaced by "un tour de trop [an excessive, unnecessary turn]," or "de trope [a feat of trope]," by a constant movement of textuality itself. "A quoi sert cela? [What is it good for?]" Mallarmé asks in the same above-cited passage: of what use is the potential for transcendence? "A un jeu [A game]," he answers: the dice-throw that thought emits, "du fond d'un naufrage."

LEO BERSANI

The Man Dies

How does the study of verse lead to the experience of Nothingness? Toward the end of April 1866, Mallarmé writes to his friend Henri Cazalis that he has finished a draft of the "musical opening" of his poem "Hérodiade," and that, after three or four more winters of work, "j'aurai enfin fait ce que je rêve, écrire un Poème digne de Poe et que les siens ne surpasseront pas. . . . Malheureusement, (I will finally have realized my dream: to write a poem worthy of Poe and just as good as his. . . . Unfortunately)," Mallarmé continues, "en creusant le vers à ce point, j'ai rencontré deux abîmes, qui me désespèrent (in delving so far into verse, I have come upon two abysses, which are driving me to despair)." One "abyss" is in Mallarmé's chest: he has trouble taking deep breaths, and, wondering if he has only a few years to live, complains of the time lost to art which he must spend teaching English in order to earn a living. The other "abyss" is Nothingness, a "pensée écrasante"—a crushing or overwhelming thought—which has made Mallarmé stop working and even lose faith in his poetry. In this letter, the discovery of Nothingness appears to be correlative to a sense of the finality of matter:

> Oui, *je le sais,* nous ne sommes que de vaines formes de la matière, mais bien sublimes pour avoir inventé Dieu et notre âme. Si sublimes, mon ami! que je veux me donner ce spectacle de la matière, ayant conscience d'être et, cependant, s'élançant forcenément dans le Rêve qu'elle sait n'être pas, chantant l'Ame et toutes les divines impressions pareilles qui se sont amassées en

---

185

nous depuis les premiers âges et proclamant devant le Rien qui
est la vérité, ces glorieux mensonges!

(Yes, *I know* that we are only empty forms of matter, empty and
yet sublime for we have invented God and our soul. So sublime,
my friend, that I want to offer myself this spectacle of matter
conscious of its own being and yet plunging frantically into the
Dream which it knows does not exist, singing of the Soul and all
such divine impressions stored up in us since the earliest times,
and proclaiming, in the face of the Nothing which is truth, those
glorious lies!)

What status shall we give to this text? It is a solemn, philosophically
sentimental and yet appealingly juvenile document. Its interest is somewhat
tangential to its apparent message; to a certain extent, it even lies in a
tangentiality in Mallarmé himself. The profound exploration of verse has
the peculiar effect of moving the poet to the side of his verse. Far from being
caught up in his own poetic illusion, Mallarmé immediately becomes the
critic of that illusion. The more profound his penetration into poetic language, the more acute his sense of that language's emptiness, of the lack of
correspondence between verbal fictions and being. Poetic composition
heightens the poet's sense of alienation from poetry; he experiences himself
as only a vain form of matter at the very moment he produces the sublime
and glorious lies of poetry.

To write "Hérodiade" is therefore a divisive enterprise: it separates
Mallarmé's work from Mallarmé's being. And the distance between the two
at once becomes the occasion for a further division. We already have matter
conscious of being, and plunging into a Dream which it knows not. Now we
have another split, so to speak, in the other direction, and the poet wills into
existence a consciousness of the first split as a sublime spectacle. To write
poetry is an exercise in ontological analysis: it separates imagination from
being, and then produces a consciousness of the process by which the two
are separated. To put this in another way, we might say that for Mallarmé
the writing of verse is a multiplication of distances; or, in still other terms,
poetry generates an ironic consciousness of poetry.

Mallarmé's "crisis" of the 1860s—the bouts of physical illness, the
creative sterility, the metaphysical anguish—is inseparable from his poetic
ambitions and experimentation. Without trivializing that crisis, one might
note that it is frequently articulated in a context of certain strategic (rather
than philosophical) concerns. The passage on the "two abysses" in the April

1866 letter to Cazalis by no means cancels out Mallarmé's enthusiasm for his recent esthetic achievement. His work on the musical opening of "Hérodiade" is first referred to not as having led to an encounter with Nothingness, but rather as having given rise to an extraordinary self-confidence in Mallarmé. The poem will not be finished for another three or four years, but the poet has already assigned himself an exalted rank in the history of art on the basis of its (as yet unrealized) merits. If the dreams of art are, at best, glorious lies, the historical record of those lies invites both emulation and critical discriminations. An *image d'Épinal* is "common . . . compared to a painting by Leonardo da Vinci," and Mallarmé proudly places himself in the most aristocratic genealogy of art: from the *Mona Lisa* to the *Raven* [sic] to "Hérodiade."

Mallarmé's meeting with Nothingness takes place in the context of a remarkably well-designed poetic career. On the one hand, his absorbed study of verse paralyzes composition. Almost three years after the letter from which I have quoted, Mallarmé, writing once again to Cazalis, asserts: "le simple acte d'écrire installe l'hystérie dans ma tête . . . je ne suis pas encore tout à fait quitte de la crise puisque la dictée à mon bon secrétaire [his wife Marie] et l'impression d'une plume qui marche par ma volonté, même grâce à une autre main, me rend mes palpitations (the mere physical act of writing sets off an attack of hysteria . . . I am still not entirely over my crisis, since giving dictation to my faithful secretary, and the impression of a pen moving as a result of *my* will, even though its movements depend on some-one else's hand bring back my palpitations)." On the other hand, the very terror of writing becomes part of an ambitious literary project. The discovery of Nothingness is followed by the discovery of the Beautiful, and each becomes the subject of a volume in the grand Work outlined in so many of Mallarmé's letters. One version of that outline mentions "quatre poèmes en prose, sur la conception spirituelle du Néant (four prose poems, on the spiritual conception of Nothingness)"; the latter is to provide one section of " 'l'ensemble de travaux littéraires qui composent l'existence poétique d'un Rêveur' et qu'on appelle, enfin, son œuvre ('the totality of literary works which make up the poetic existence of a Dreamer' and which is called, finally, his *œuvre*)." The Work will be the "image" of the poet's "spiritual developments." The very crisis which threatens the writing of poetry sustains poetic composition. The split between Mallarmé's work and Mallarmé's being is not only a sublime spectacle for the poet; it is also an important subject for his poetic fictions. Poetry is simultaneously the experience and the record of psychic division; it incorporates a fundamentally anti-poetic consciousness of its own emptiness. Mallarmé's paralyzing encounter with Nothingness immediately finds its place in an ambitious program of literary productivity.

To speak of the 1860s only in terms which suggest metaphysical melodrama would therefore be to neglect Mallarmé's constant and extreme attentiveness to the creative advantages of a frequently grave creative sterility. Mallarmé's very existence as a writer is endangered by the solitary years in Tournon and Besançon; at the same time, they are years of apprenticeship in which Mallarmé prepares himself—and others—for his future career as a man of letters. In part, Mallarmé's letters are experimental publicity. They are tentative soundings into the poetic *métier*—ways of sounding like a poet and testing an esthetic. The proposed esthetic will, in large measure, be dropped, and the promised masterwork never delivered; but, as we shall see, the experience of poetry as a kind of separation from the self remains the condition for all the "inessential" texts which signal both Mallarmé's failure to produce his Work and his entrance into the activity of writing.

The experience of the poet's absence from his verse is precipitated by an artistic credo which equates poetry with a form of subjectivity. Mallarmé begins by defining his work in terms of an impressionistic esthetic. He writes to Cazalis in the fall of 1864 that he has at last begun his "Hérodiade" "avec terreur, car j'invente une langue qui doit nécessairement jaillir d'une poétique très nouvelle, que je pourrais définir en ces deux mots: *Peindre, non la chose, mais l'effet qu'elle produit* (in fear and trembling, for I am inventing a language which must spring from a completely new poetics that might be briefly defined in the following way: *Describe not the object itself, but the effect which it produces).*" Not content to propose this suppression of the external world in favor of its "effects," Mallarmé goes on to suggest that language itself should disappear for the sake of a pure subjectivity: "le vers ne doit donc pas, là, se composer de mots; mais d'intentions, et toutes les paroles s'effacer devant la sensation (therefore, a line of verse must not be made up of words, but rather of intentions; all the words must retreat and be replaced by sensations)." A few months later, referring once again to "Hérodiade" in another letter to Cazalis, Mallarmé speaks of having found "une façon intime et singulière de peindre et de noter des impressions très fugitives (an intimate and peculiar way of painting and setting down very rapid impressions)," impressions which follow one another as in a symphony. And several years later in the essay "Crise de vers," Mallarmé appears to reaffirm this subjectivist esthetic when he praises the contemporary poet for having abolished the esthetic "error" of filling the pages of his book with anything but, for example, "l'horreur de la forêt, ou le tonnerre muet épars au feuillage; non le bois intrinsèque et dense des arbres (the dread of the forest or the silent thunder scattered through the foliage; not the intrinsic and dense wood of the trees)."

Mallarmé's qualified defense of *le vers libre* is based on his interest in the possibility of an unconstrained allusiveness of language to particular impressions. The *vers libre,* freed of the rhythmical constraints of traditional verse, fashions itself according to the "music" of individual souls ("Toute âme est un nœud rythmique (every soul is a rhythmic knot)." Prose qualifies as poetry, Mallarmé writes in the essay "Étalages," when there remains "quelque secrète poursuite de musique, dans la réserve du Discours (some secret pursuit of music, within the margins of Discourse)." Within the semantic pursuits of language there are certain rhythmical projects, projects which—at least according to one important current in Mallarmé's thought—displace our attention from the sense of words to those "cadences" through which wordless impressions simultaneously structure and erase language.

The impressionist esthetic has served as an important guideline in critical readings of Mallarmé. It provides a reasonable explanation for the difficulty of his writing and implicitly proposes a technique by which that difficulty can be reduced (not merely lessened but even abolished). If the poet neglects things for their effects, the critic will infer the former from the latter. The very success with which Mallarmé erases the world of things would presumably authorize the re-establishment of that world by criticism—which is to say that it would authorize a profoundly anti-Mallarméan bias in Mallarmé criticism. Criticism can attempt to verbalize the subjectivity pursued within (or to the side of, or perhaps even against) poetic verbalizations. I will shortly be arguing against this enterprise. We should, however, first of all recognize how logical it is. A psychologically thematic criticism would be the complement to psychologically impressionistic verse. The words of a poem disappear so that we may hear only the cadences of an individual soul; criticism would be the translation of those cadences into language, their *first* adequate verbal expression. The critic reconstitutes the poet's subjectivity by generalizing the impressions or sensations alluded to in his writing into a structure or "family" of preferred images. Thus, while the pursuit of impressions or sensations by no means implies the wish to portray a coherent personality in literature (Mallarméan impressionism is not designed to construct a self), even a discontinuous subjectivity encourages us to infer a self—that is, a more or less systematic intentionality in which discrete sensations and impressions are grounded. Mallarmé's reader can unify the invisible, nonverbal, fleeting effects of things in stabilized structures of response to the world. Sensations, impressions and intentions form groups, or constellations, which allow the critic to speak of the "universe" of Mallarmé's subjectivity.

But it is precisely while trying to write verses composed not of words but of impressions that Mallarmé discovers the anguishing distance between his work and his being. Even more: his subjectivist esthetic is promoted during a period when Mallarmé's principal experience appears to be that of his own death. "Je suis mort," he writes to Théodore Aubanel in July 1866. And yet in the same paragraph Mallarmé speaks once again of books composed of sensations. What can it mean to transcribe a sensation which no one has had, a sensation without a human subject? It is true that Mallarmé refers in this letter to his resurrection. But "his" has become immensely problematic: it is not Mallarmé who has come back to life but—to judge from the letters of this period—a kind of structuralizing magnet. "Tout est si bien ordonné en moi, qu'à mesure, maintenant, qu'une sensation m'arrive, elle se transfigure et va d'elle-même se caser dans tel livre et tel poème. Quand un poème sera mûr, il se détachera. (Everything is so well ordered in me that each of my sensations is at once transfigured and finds its place, on its own, in a particular book and a particular poem. When a poem is ripe, it will fall away from me.)" The book is first of all internal; Mallarmé, having died, *is* a book in the process of being composed. The written work is merely Mallarmé-as-book having come to fruition, having dropped away—like a fruit from a tree—from a nurturing center. "Tu vois que j'imite la loi naturelle," Mallarmé tells Aubanel, and in another letter to the same friend, about two weeks later, Mallarmé claims that he was recently able to outline his entire work after having found the "key" or "keystone" or "center" of his being—"centre de moi-même, où je me tiens comme une araignée sacrée, sur les principaux fils déjà sortis de mon esprit, et à l'aide desquels je tisserai *aux points de rencontre* de merveilleuses dentelles, que je devine, et qui existent déjà dans le sein de la Beauté. (You see that I am imitating natural law . . . the center of my being, where I am sitting like a sacred spider, on the main threads already spun out from my mind, threads which will help me to weave at the *intersecting points* marvelous lacework, which I can imagine, and which already exist in the heart of Beauty.)"

Having died, Mallarmé displaces the authorship of his poems from his defunct self to the universe. Thus, in what is perhaps his best known letter to Cazalis, Mallarmé proclaims: "je suis maintenant impersonnel et non plus le Stéphane que tu as connu,—mais une aptitude qu'a l'Univers spirituel à se voir et à se développer, à travers ce qui fut moi. Fragile comme est mon apparition terrestre, je ne puis subir que les développements absolument nécessaires pour que l'Univers retrouve, en ce moi, son identité. (I am now impersonal and no longer the Stéphane you once knew, but one of the ways the spiritual Universe has of seeing itself and developing, through what used to be me. Given the fragility of my ghostly presence on earth, I can only develop in ways absolutely necessary for the Universe to recapture, in that self, its identity.)" Such orphic pronouncements may be taken as Mallarmé's effort to *think* the eerie experience of literary expression as the abolition of an identifiable human source of literary expression. The attempt to render the effects of things rather than things themselves has, surprisingly, erased the individual subject necessary, one would think, to register such effects. And it is as if impressions and sensations themselves were then projected onto the external world as a kind of ordering, nonmaterial structure of the very objects which produce them. Mallarmé thus proposes a non-psychological version of phenomena—such as intentions, impressions and sensations—which are ordinarily assumed to be constitutive of psychological subjectivity. "Toute âme est une mélodie," but Beauty is the music without the individual.

By what logic has a project of self-expression (the wish to make poetry transparent to the most particular cadences or rhythms of individual responses to the world) led to Mallarmé's death? Self-concentration destabilizes the self. It is as if the very attempt to hold on to a thought or a sensation produced a kind of snapping movement away from that thought or sensation. The project of making verse transparent to the music of individual souls is realized with a certain ontological violence. At times, Mallarmé describes this violence as a decomposition of being. Three days after announcing to Cazalis that he is now impersonal, "une aptitude qu'a l'Univers spirituel à se voir et à se développer, à travers ce qui fut moi," Mallarmé writes to Eugène Lefébure that he is "véritablement décomposé, et dire qu'il faut cela pour avoir une vue très—une de l'Univers! Autrement, on ne sent d'autre unité que celle de sa vie (truly fragmented, and to think that's necessary for me to have a very—unified view of the Universe! Otherwise, the only unity one feels is that of one's own life)." Mallarmé must destroy a merely historical or biographical unity in order to become the "sacred spider" weaving with the threads of his own mind the "marvelous lacework" of objective Beauty. But he also laments the destructive divisions of his being; the concentrated self seems to be immediately recognized as a partial self. Mallarmé complains to Lefébure of having worked the preceding summer with thoughts coming only from his brain, and he describes an effort he made to stop working only cerebrally: "j'essayai de ne plus penser de la tête et, par un effort désespéré, je roidis tous mes nerfs (en pectus) de façon à produire une vibration en gardant la pensée à laquelle je travaillais alors, qui devient le sujet de cette vibration, ou une impression—et j'ébauchai tout un poème longtemps rêvé, de cette façon. (I tried to stop thinking with my head and, with a desperate effort, I stiffened all the nerves in my chest in order to produce a vibration, still holding onto the thought I was then working on, which becomes the subject of that vibration, or an impression—and in that state I sketched an entire poem which I had been dreaming of for a long time.)" In this curiously abstract analysis of what might be taken as a willful eroticizing of thought, the vibration produced by stiffened nerves "receives" a purely cerebral thought and transforms it into an impression. Mallarmé is now thinking, as he writes, "with his entire body"; thought becomes concrete when it provides the occasion or content for (when it is the "subject" of) a vibrating stiffness of nerves. A "desperate" (and desperately ingenious) effort at self-concentration is meant to forestall the explosive effects of . . . self-concentration.

But the vibrating self-concentration which emerges as a major creative mood of Mallarmé's early years does not immobilize the "thought" which it eroticizes. On the contrary: once a thought begins to vibrate, it also begins to be scattered or disseminated. In his major poetic achievement during the period of the letters to which I have been referring, Mallarmé investigates the possibility of non-disseminating vibrations. "Hérodiade" could be thought of as Mallarmé's attempt to imagine an escape from the consequences of the mode in which the work is composed. Both Mallarmé's heroine and his own poetic procedures move between extreme versions of mobility and immobility. There is a strong pull toward specular immobilizations in "Hérodiade." This is the period in Mallarmé's career when his interest in musical effects in poetry mainly takes the form of verbal repetitions. Certain words—such as *aurore, ombre, or*—keep returning in the first two sections of "Hérodiade." They of course designate thematic centers in the poem, but, perhaps more powerfully, they operate like simplifying and stabilizing reflectors. It is as if lexical mirrors had been placed throughout the poem, mirrors which pick up reflections of earlier verses and, to a certain extent, reduce the verbal heterogeneity of the work through the force of a shimmering sameness.

The variety of the poetic space of "Hérodiade" is almost devoured by this pursuit of the verbal couple, by emphatic replications which create a dizzying structural stability. All these repetitions help to organize the sense of the poem, but their principal function appears to be the very placing of the repetition itself. Mallarmé's ingenious rhymes serve the same function even more clearly: a few startling rhyme-couples (such as *lune* and *l'une*, and the negative *pas* with *pas* as step) encourage our receptiveness to various sorts of linguistic pairing. Far from merely punctuating rhythmic units, such rhymes actually divert our attention from rhythm and make us *stop* at a surprising sameness of sound which, so to speak, wins out over the more obvious but now suppressed semantic diversity. Hérodiade's narcissistic ambitions are most satisfactorily realized in Mallarmé's arresting (astonishing and immobilizing) poetic procedures.

The pairing of *l'une* with *lune* is considerably easier to accomplish than the specularization of Hérodiade herself. The princess seeks to find and to fix her own image. The main obstacle to Hérodiade's narcissistic project is that *she cannot be found;* in order to possess her identity, Hérodiade must first of all be sure of her location. The very first question the nurse asks in the "Scène" is whether she is seeing Hérodiade or "l'ombre d'une princesse (the shadow of a princess)." Hérodiade is referred to several times in the poem as an "ombre," and when she seeks her memories under the frozen water of her mirror's surface, she appears to herself as "une ombre lointaine (a distant shadow)." The sense of self in "Hérodiade" is inseparable from a sense of both distance and anteriority.

But in order to understand the notion of shadow-being, we should first of all note some apparent contradictions. If Hérodiade is a mere shadow, she is also a star. She speaks, for example, in the "Scène" of her "pudeur grelottante d'étoile (shivering star-like modesty)," and she asserts that her mirror "reflète en son calme dormant / Hérodiade au clair regard de diamant (reflects in its slumbering calm / Hérodiade with the clear diamantine look)." What does it mean to be simultaneously darkness and light, a shadow and a bright diamond? Mallarmé, who claimed that he hadn't slept for years, reportedly told L. Dauphin of a month during which his insomnia had been so painful that, in order to work, he had to put his hand in front of his eyes after each sentence he wrote, and keep it there for a long while, in order to breathe in a little darkness. The darkness is necessary not as a relief or rest from work, but in order to make work—writing—possible. Mallarmé's wakefulness is the enemy of his thought. We might say—generalizing the Mallarméan experience—that insomnia impedes the functioning of thought, the suspension (even more: the suppression) of external reality on which thought depends. Thought is a clarifying murder; it illuminates the world by plunging it into darkness. Thus the darkness of night and of sleep is necessary to the light of consciousness. *This light is a night.* And to speak of consciousness as a de-realizing illumination of the world, or as a replicating abolition of its objects, is not even to propose a paradox; no logical category can adequately describe the fundamental operation of mind on which all movements of logic depend.

The illuminations of thought are nocturnal or shadow versions of reality. They repeat reality somewhat as a shadow repeats its object: by simultaneously darkening and defining it. From this perspective, Hérodiade's
perception of herself as both shadow and star or diamond becomes intelligible as a vision of the nature of thought. But I should say at once that, at
this level of abstraction, the notion of vision itself becomes unintelligible,
and in "Hérodiade" Mallarmé brilliantly uses narcissism as a psychological
metaphor for the replicating and annihilating operations of thought. The
attempt to achieve self-possession through specular self-immobilization is,
in the poem, a dramatic figure for the inevitably abortive adherence of
thought to its object. In both cases, separation is at once the condition for
an effort to fix the self (or to immobilize a thought object, or a thought
thought), and the guarantee that such an effort will fail. Hérodiade moves
away from herself *by* seeking herself; she is a shadow-self to the extent that
she has become the *thought of* herself.

Hérodiade's self-contemplation is, by definition, a kind of self-removal:
she has lost herself (existentially, historically, as someone with *souvenirs*
and not only *songes*) by virtue of her ontologically divisive interest in herself. "Je viens de passer une année effrayante (I have just spent a terrifying
year)," as Mallarmé confides to Cazalis: "ma Pensée s'est pensée, et est
arrivée à une Conception pure (my Thought thought itself and reached a
pure conception)." The thinker is lost (appears to die) in the very movement
by which he becomes the object of his own attention. Even more radically,
once the thinker of his thought has become nothing more than a replicating
reflex, thinking can no longer *go on;* and, as Mallarmé writes in the letter
just quoted from, he has to look at himself in a mirror "in order to think"—
that is, in order to certify the existence of a thinking subject whose thinking
can be thought in a reflexive duplication of its own movements.

Now if narcissism illustrates the replicating movement of all thought, it
also enacts the tendency of thought to immobilize its object. Thinking the
world is at once a removal from, and an attempted replication of the world;
but this replication includes the project of resuscitating the abolished world
in the form of stabilized ideas or concepts. Thought seeks to be arrested by
solidified sense, to extract and to possess the "meanings" of its own movements. Narcissism exacerbates and explodes this project of consciousness.
The solidified sense pursued in narcissism is not conceptual but corporeal:
evidence of a self is provided by the image of a body in a mirror. The self,
however, may be nothing more than a derivation of mental mechanics, the
compensatory sign of thought's exhaustion with its own objectless replications, with the ceaseless erasures of its own representations. Hérodiade, the

bright shadow of a princess, wanders through her palace grounds, and stops in front of her mirror in search of her errant self. Her continuous movement away from herself is thus (uselessly) contravened by an attempt to catch a self prior to that movement. Going away is misinterpreted as going towards, and a nostalgia for psychic origins leads to a positing of goals and climaxes to psychic mobility. The movements of consciousness are always productively mistaken replications of its objects; the narcissistic consciousness would substitute for these nonmimetic replications a perfect identity between thought and its objects. But only the illusory being reflected in a mirror realizes that identity. The mirror deceives human consciousness into believing that it can be externalized as pure representation, that the movements of a desiring being can be immobilized in a total form.

And yet, as I have said, Hérodiade significantly does not find such a form in her mirror. The fragility, and ultimately the failure of the narcissistic project in the poem are indicated by the princess's difficulty in producing a reflection of herself, as well as by her fright at what she sees. Either she finds an exact but curiously distant replica of herself, or she sees the "nudity" of her "scattered dream." The first image is nothing more than the reptition of the shadow which dreams of discovering a mineral-like hardness and luster in the mirror; and the second image—if it can be called that—is perhaps a frightening (and unimaginable) "representation" not of a lustrous, stellar self but of the very abstractness by which that dream separates itself from the shadowy movements of consciousness. "Hérodiade" is a poem of distress: distress at the failure of the narcissistic dream, and especially at the consequences of not being able to immobilize consciousness. The anecdotal sign of narcissism's defeat is Hérodiade's confession, after the nurse's departure, that the "naked flower" of her lips has been lying, and that she is waiting for an "unknown thing," an event which may simply be the "thawing" of her adolescent, mineral-like hardness and her consenting initiation into sexuality. But this initiation would merely be one result of the more fundamental failure of a dream of self-possession, a failure which is itself the corollary of certain unavoidable movements of consciousness.

Perhaps the best way to describe these movements is to consider their intrusion into what I have called the works' specularizing procedures. On the one hand, there are all the verbal and structural repetitions which tend to create a kind of monumental stillness in the poem. A system of verbal reflectors throughout the piece works toward the abolishing of intervallic differences. On the other hand, there is an extraordinary amount of what might be called unstable designation in "Hérodiade." The poem's difficulty is largely due to the sliding identities of persons and things, to casual and unexplained shifts in the register of being. This is particularly true of the "Ouverture ancienne." (The nurse, speaking of Hérodiade's room, describes:

> sa tapisserie, au lustre nacré, plis
> Inutiles avec les yeux ensevelis
> De sibylles offrant leur ongle vieil aux Mages.
> Une d'elles, avec un passé de ramages
> Sur ma robe blanchie en l'ivoire fermé
> Au ciel d'oiseaux parmi l'argent noir parsemé,
> Semble, de vols [partis] costumée et fantôme,
> Un arôme qui porte, ô roses! un arôme,
> Loin du lit vide qu'un cierge soufflé cachait,
> Un arôme d'[os] froids rôdant sur le sachet,
> Une touffe de fleurs parjures à la lune
> (A la cire expirée encor s'effeuille l'une),
> De qui le long regret et les tiges de qui
> Trempent en un seul verre à l'éclat alangui.

[its tapestry, with pearly lustre, useless / Folds with the buried eyes / Of sibyls offering their old fingernails to the Magi. / One of them, with floral embroidery / On my bleached dress locked in the ivory chest / With a bird-filled sky amid the black silver, / Seems, in a costume of departed flights and phantom-like, / An aroma which carries, oh roses! an aroma, / Far from the empty bed hidden by a blown-out candle, / An aroma of cold bones prowling on the sachet, / A bunch of flowers unfaithful to the moon / (By the extinguished candle one of them is still shedding its petals), / Whose long regret and whose stems / Stand in a single glass with languid glitter.])

I am thinking, for example, of the metamorphoses of *plis:* from the "useless folds" of the tapestry in Hérodiade's room in stanza two to the "yellow folds of thought" in which the voice of the next stanza "drags," to the "stiffened folds" of the shroud-consciousness evoked by the nurse, and finally to the dream-book folds no longer inscribed on the unwrinkled linen of Hérodiade's unused bed. Or, in the second stanza, there is the curious displacement of one of the sibyls. They are first mentioned as figures woven into the tapestry of Hérodiade's room, but then one of them is described as being part of the design on the nurse's dress in the closed ivory chest. Even more: we could think of this same movable sibyl as not only displaced but also metamorphosed: she "seems" to be an "aroma," which in turn may come from a sachet perhaps in the chest or may be the odor of the wilted flowers near Hérodiade's bed. Hérodiade's room, which the beginning of the stanza encourages us to visualize as a fixed tableau seen through the window's frame from the courtyard below, is actually a scene of fantastic movements: the gesture of the sibyls offering their aged fingernails to the Magi ("offrant leur ongle vieil aux Mages") on the tapestry, the "flight" of the sibyl-aroma, the prowling of the scent of cold bones ("un arôme d'os froids rôdant sur le sachet"), and the ambiguous movement—of an aroma carrying an aroma of cold bones, *or* of an aroma of cold bones bearing the scent of a "touffe de fleurs"—between the ivory chest and Hérodiade's bed (a movement whose point of departure may be either the chest or the bed, or both at once, or neither one).

This is an awkward summary of a few passages of the "Ouverture ancienne," but I think that the poem itself is an awkward mixture of immobilizing strategies and what appears to be the distressing mobility of its images. The balancing factors are excessively obvious, and the unexplained displacements and metamorphoses block the poem's narrative progression. This ambitious work may thus strike us as esthetically pretentious; it is dramatically thin, and yet its structure and texture are overworked, and overwrought. Excessively ingenious rhymes, excessively neat structural repetitions, excessively daring narrative discontinuities: it is not too hard to sympathize with Albert Thibaudet's dismissive description of "Hérodiade" as a cold masterpiece of technical virtuosity, a "morceau de concours (*La Poésie de Stéphane Mallarmé*). But even if the poem strikes us as a brilliant "exercise," as Mallarmé's most "literary," even academic work, its overwrought quality is perhaps the effect of an extremely dramatic play of conflicting pressures in the poem, pressures which will never entirely disappear from Mallarmé's writing.

The sliding identities which I mentioned a moment ago subvert the specular recognitions to which Hérodiade aspires *and* the impressionistic esthetic which presumably governs the composition of Mallarmé's poem. I have spoken of lexical mirrors scattered throughout the work; but, as the metamorphoses of the word *plis* suggest, repetition is not only a structurally immobilizing factor but also works to de-stabilize sense. An echo turns out to be also a displacement. The "yellow folds of thought" and the "stiffened folds" of the shroud do not merely send us back to the folds of tapestry in the preceding stanza. They initiate differences, differences all the more disorienting in that the word "folds" applied to a shroud repeats (unlike the folds of thought) the literal plausibility of folds in a tapestry, at the same time that the shroud itself is a startling metaphor for the vanquished and exhausted consciousness from which the memory-filled voice evoked in stanza 3 painfully rises. A certain narrative logic (according to which the various uses of *plis* both characterize the nurse and provide an apt metaphor for the inert burden of consciousness) is disrupted by the rhetorical wandering of the word *plis:* from its merely denoting the tapestry's visible folds to a metaphorical status in "les plis jaunes de la pensée," and finally back to a denotative function within the elaborate metaphor of the shroud. The specular effects and stabilizing power of recurrence are thus qualified by *a*-symmetrical repetitions in "Hérodiade." In the case of *plis,* there is even something lopsided in the symmetry itself. Sound reptition is almost emphatically divorced from semantic repetition: the reflections of sense which metaphorically describe thought for us in a coherent way are really provided by the adjectives ("useless," "yellow," and "old" and "stiffened"), and the sense is one to which the word *plis* itself rather feebly contributes, to which it merely *lends itself.*

The very beginning of the"Ouverture ancienne" provides us with a condensed version of both the specular and the anti-specular or *a*-symmetrical pressures in "Hérodiade." Here are the first seven verses of the poem:

> Abolie, et son aile affreuse dans les larmes
> Du bassin, aboli, qui mire les alarmes,
> Des ors nus fustigeant l'espace cramoisi,
> Une Aurore a, plumage héraldique, choisi
> Notre tour cinéraire et sacrificatrice,
> Lourde tombe qu'a fuie un bel oiseau, caprice
> Solitaire d'aurore au vain plumage noir.

(Abolished, and its frightful wing in the tears / Of the pool, abolished, that mirrors the alarms, / Thrashing the crimson space of naked gold, / A Dawn has, heraldic plumage, chosen / Our cinerary and sacrificial tower, / Heavy tomb which a beautiful bird has fled, solitary / Caprice of dawn with vain black plumage.)

The claustrophobic effects of what I have been calling Mallarmé's specularizing intentions are immediately evident here. The passage is extravagantly self-reflexive. The sound *a* is repeated 17 times, seven times in the first two verses. *Aboli* in verse 2 sends us back (with the slight asymmetry of a masculine rather than a feminine ending) to the initial, and initiating *abolie,* just as *plumage* in verse 7 reflects *plumage* in verse 4, and the *aurore* of verse 7 repeats (again, in slightly a-symmetrical fashion: the capital A is dropped) the *Aurore* of verse 4. Such repetitions of words and letters, as well as all the internal rhymes, practically bring the poem to a standstill; the first seven verses of "Hérodiade" are almost an immobile verbal block, a mass in which the only movement is one of shimmering internal reflections. The monotony of sameness immediately plunges us into the desolate atmosphere which the nurse will continue to describe. Here, one might argue, is an excellent example of what it means to describe "not the object itself, but the effect which it produces." Impressions of sinister stillness, and of potentially violent negations, are communicated before any attempt is made to establish narrative coherence. Dawn, for example, is identified three verses after the nurse's *sense of* the dawn (as "abolished," as plunging its "frightful wing" into the pool) is given.

But the opening passage of "Hérodiade" undermines the very symmetries which it so carefully establishes. Repetition is accompanied by ontological dislocation. The identity of bird-dawn is no sooner confirmed than the vehicle of that metaphor is repeated as, apparently, a real bird that has fled the tower. However, the words "caprice / Solitaire d'aurore au vain plumage noir" can be read in several ways. They could refer to the bird's flight (it was a solitary caprice which took place at dawn, a caprice having, strangely, a "vain plumage noir"), or they might be in apposition to "oiseau," in which case "vain plumage noir" becomes more plausible while caprice as a synonym for bird obviously becomes less plausible. But we might of course also connect the expression to the Dawn's choice of "notre tour cinéraire et sacrificatrice": that choice is the caprice of a dawn already referred to, in verse 4, as having a "plumage héraldique" (now modified as "vain" and "noir.)" "Aurore" in "caprice solitaire d'aurore" can thus either refer to the subject of the action (dawn's choice of the tower) or merely have an adverbial status (it tells us when the bird's flight took place). Furthermore, we shortly discover that the beautiful bird is also Hérodiade, who has left her rooms and is walking through the palace grounds. Consequently, the first four verses may express the nurse's sense of the princess's having abandoned her rooms. Dawn has entombed itself, has been "abolished," in the equally abolished pool; birds and swans no longer inhabit "l'eau morne"; and the princess's room has been abandoned by Hérodiade, to whom "le cygne / inoubliable," of verses 10 and 11 may refer.

> (L'eau morne se résigne,
> Que ne visite plus la plume ni le cygne
> Inoubliable.

[The gloomy water resigns itself, / No longer touched by a feather or by the unforgettable / Swan.])

The similarities among these instances are clear, and yet the passage which exploits their similarities is extremely obscure. If the reader is disoriented by Mallarmé's writing in "Hérodiade," it is not because the poem has an exceptional metaphorical complexity, but rather because Mallarmé gives us ontological sliding rather than metaphorical resemblances. That is, what interests him is not that Hérodiade is *like* a bird or a swan, but rather that, *in being Hérodiade, she is also a swan*. Somewhat like the movable sibyl who also seems to be an aroma, the princess is not fundamentally more Hérodiade, so to speak, than "she" is the dawn or a bird in flight (or a bird with a "frightful wing").

The kind of shifting that may occur in a metaphorical relationship does not usually affect the priority accorded to one of the terms. Even Proust, who might appear to be destroying this priority when he claims, in *Le Temps retrouvé,* that the interest of a metaphorical joining together of two distinct objects or sensations lies in the emergence of an immaterial, timeless "essence" common to those objects or sensations, always distinguishes between the literal term and the figurative term. Metaphorical terms are, it is true, interchangeable in *A la recherche du temps perdu,* and the density of the novel's texture is due less to its range of reference than to the multiple functions served by a privileged set of references. At Doncières, to take just one example, images drawn from art elucidate military strategy; later on in the work, jealousy will be described partly in terms drawn from the military life. In both cases, what might be called an essence of the Manoeuver disengages itself from the juxtaposed terms of painting, military campaigns and the tactics inspired by jealousy. But in neither case does a supratemporal essence disperse the narrative ordering of terms. The actual episode—life in a garrison or life in a Paris apartment with Albertine—is never lost from sight; it is the ground, or the focus, of every description. As a result, the other term of each extended metaphor simultaneously detemporalizes the narrative and reinforces narrative sequence and coherence. Even in a lyrical poem as exclusively metaphorical as Shakespeare's Sonnet 73 (*That time of year . . .*), the images of autumn, twilight, and a dying fire occupy almost the entire piece, and yet we are of course meant to see them as vehicles for the implicit tenor of age. If, as Proust claims, metaphors disengage a supratemporal essence, they work toward the elimination or at least the insignificance of differences in the world by emphasizing a community of sameness. And to the extent that they maintain differences within the compared qualities themselves, these distinctions are hierarchical in that one term has an historical or perceptual priority over another "imaginary" term evoked in order to elucidate a "real" or concretely experiential point of departure.

In "Hérodiade," on the other hand, the appearance of a strong narrative priority is undermined by the fact that description blocks rather than facilitates narrative progress. Hérodiade is not more satisfactorily described as a result of the various images which appear to refer to her: rather, it is as if the poet's thinking of Hérodiade were problematized by all the *other* thoughts which characterize—precisely, and paradoxically—his thought *of her.* The extraordinarily easy movements in the poem—movements which operate against all the immobilizing factors—are metamorphic rather than metaphoric. The *addition* of identities in "Hérodiade" works against the reduction of all identities to a specular sameness (in which the dawn and the swans would merely reflect the princess). The abolished dawn inaccurately replicates the absent princess; toward the end of the "Ouverture," Hérodiade, "exilée en son cœur précieux (exiled in her precious heart)," is a way of thinking "un cygne cachant en sa plume ses yeux (a swan hiding its eyes in its plumage)"; and the sibyl on the nurse's bleached dress is at once a misplaced tapestry pattern and an aroma from another part of the room.

As these examples suggest, the poem is less successful in proposing likenesses than in recording a sameness among different mental images. The latter is a more fundamental operation of consciousness than the metaphoric process. To metaphorize objects of consciousness is already to be concerned about the legitimacy of transporting one object to another, of rearranging objects in our perceptual and imaginary space. "Hérodiade" gives us something more primitive: a relation legitimized by nothing more than the fact that one term manifests the activity of thinking the other term. Difference is merely a function of the snapping away of consciousness from its object; and identity can be equivalent to absolute difference (sibyl = aroma) because it consists of a replicating movement rather than of perceived resemblances.

I said at the beginning of this discussion of "Hérodiade" that the principal obstacle to self-possession in the poem is the unlocatability of the self. The nurse and the princess are fascinated by infinitely remote or unlocatable realities. In the first stanza, the nurse speaks of the swan (and perhaps, obliquely, also of Hérodiade) plunging into the "pale mausoleum" of its feathers a head "désolée / Par le diamant pur de quelque étoile, mais / Antérieure, qui ne scintilla jamais (desolated / By the pure diamond of a star, but / Long ago, and which never sparkled)." I am thinking also of the voice buried under the folds of the shroud of consciousness, as well as

of those "ors ignorés," invoked by Hérodiade, "gardant leur antique
lumière / Sous le sombre sommeil d'une terre première (unknown golds,
keeping their ancient light / Under the somber sleep of a primeval earth),"
and, finally, of the princess's "distant shadow" which appears to her in the
"deep hole" of her mirror. Anecdotally, all these haunting distances remain
somewhat enigmatic in the poem; they become more intelligible as figures
for the peculiar remoteness of Hérodiade as an object of description for
Mallarmé himself. The nostalgic mood of the princess's narcissism is perhaps best explained by the system of ambiguous designation in the poem, by
what may have been the poet's own agonized discovery that to fix an
impression is to lose its source, to disperse the person whom impressions are
supposed to designate and to characterize.

The death of self announced in Mallarmé's letters can be thought of as
the consequence of the poet's subjectivist esthetic. The transformation of
thought into impressions—a transformation produced by taut, vibrating
nerves—is a function of mobility. To put this in other terms, the eroticizing
of thought destroys the thinking subject as a stable identity. Mallarmé
wished to fix impressions, but the result of his self-concentration appears to
have been an acceleration of the moving away which I have spoken of as
intrinsic to all thought. What Mallarmé called thinking with his body can
also be formulated as a masturbatory attention to certain images, an attention which, inevitably, cannot stop producing other images in its annihilating replication of mental objects of *jouissance*. Sexual fantasy is thinking
with an especially liberal margin of error and *errance*. The compositional
procedures of "Hérodiade" record the moves of a sexualized mental text.
Mallarmé's specularizing strategies are attempts to reduce, even to abolish
all the inexplicable, anguishing distances created by excited thought, just as
Hérodiade's narcissism is the princess's wished-for solution to the unending
self-remoteness which is the price of her secret wish to be shattered by the
desiring look of another.

Perhaps the most important lesson to be drawn from all this is the *sheer
exteriority of subjectivity*. The description of the mind is a description of
dawn and of swans and of stagnant pools; or of yellow folds, or "un confus
amas d'ostensoirs refroidis (a heap of monstrances gone cold)," or the pure
lacework of a finely stitched shroud. The attempt to hold on to an impression multiplies images of the world. What Mallarmé referred to as his own
death was perhaps his experience of wandering among alien images evoked
by his intense concentration on his own sensations, impressions and intentions.

But this last word raises a crucial question: to what extent do all those images express intentionality, outline a unique set of projects toward the world? If subjectivity is exteriority, the latter may nonetheless chart an interiority no less real *and* analyzable for taking the form of a certain picture of the world. If introspection leads to abolished pools, tomblike towers, yellow folds, and incensed stars rather than to sentiments and faculties, there is perhaps no reason to abandon the notion of personality along with the psychologically analytic vocabulary which has usually been used to describe personality. Can the techniques of analysis change without our questioning the most fundamental assumptions about the object of analysis?

Mallarmé appears to provide the most conservative answer to this question. Nothing is easier than to find a family of images in his work which conveniently present themselves as alternatives to dominant feelings or passions, alternatives which alter the atmosphere of psychology without putting its validity into question. One can reasonably claim that Mallarmé's poems of the 1860s establish a comparatively small family of images which will characterize his work until his death, and that on the basis of this familial network one can discover that universe of the imagination which Jean-Pierre Richard has so magisterially delineated in *L'Univers imaginaire de Mallarmé*. From the very beginning, there is a recognizable thematic structure in the poet's work. With elegance and thoroughness, Richard tracks down the recurrences of preferred images: windows, transparent lakes and windows, the blue sky, swans, folds, fountains, winter, wings and feathers, blood-red sunsets, the foam of waves, shipwrecks. But to make such a heterogeneous list of images is to miss the coherence of Mallarmé's "imaginary universe." Richard's study leaves no doubt about the phenomenological unity which sustains the recurrent images of Mallarmé's work. Furthermore, this unity does not merely characterize one period of Mallarmé's life. Certain images are naturally more dominant in some pieces than in others, and these differences indicate affective variations both from one poem to another and from one time to another, but none of this should affect our confidence in the translatability of Mallarmé's thematic imagery into a phenomenological portrait of the Mallarméan imagination.

And yet Mallarmé the person is dead—*as a result of* wandering precisely that world which provides the thematic critic with the material for his portrait of a unified and coherent human subjectivity. How can this be? Richard thematizes Mallarmé's work as an effort to solve "a problem of upward dynamic movement: in a world whose laws are dispersion and entropy, where can the initial impulse towards an ascending movement be found?" This is subtle and, in a sense, right. But it is also a critical version of those immobilizing strategies by which Hérodiade seeks to possess her own image, as well as of those equally immobilizing strategies by which Mallarmé seeks to control intervals which would otherwise function as radically differentiating spaces within his poem. Richard allows for temporal movement and change within the system of Mallarméan imagery, but the movement which he ignores is precisely that replicating-abolishing movement which has no other intention than to repeat a phenomenon of excited consciousness. And that mobility makes for ontological discontinuity among thematically related images. The latter should perhaps be thought of as one of the superstructures of consciousness. Far from expressing that immediate contact with the world of what Gaston Bachelard called our material imagination, the system of preferential images investigated by thematic or phenomenological criticism is already a *structuralizing strategy*. It is the result of reflective movements of mind, although the reflection is of course not of the same order—and not at the same level of consciousness—as in, say, a system of philosophical thought.

The type of criticism practised by Bachelard, Richard and Georges Poulet is at once persuasive and repressive. It would be impossible to imagine a more perceptive study of thematic imagery in Mallarmé's work than *L'Univers imaginaire de Mallarmé*, but Richard never looks suspiciously at the very activity (in the poet and in the critic) which creates such networks. The images catalogued by both thematic criticism and most psychoanalytic criticism appear to be obsessive modes of contact with the world; we should also remember that they are highly visible modes of contact. That is, they are obsessive without being secretive; indeed, they are the writer's preferred version of his own intelligibility. A criticism of deep intentionality (whether it be phenomenological or psychoanalytic) invites us to locate such intentionality in specific themes or images; but it neglects (because it shares) the *intention to create intentionality* as a means of disguising the discontinuity between the act of thinking and the object of thought. Thus thematic criticism is in complicity with the repressive activity in the literary work itself by which the moves of consciousness are concealed by a stabilizing intelligibility of consciousness.

It is precisely that intelligibility which Mallarmé will come to treat as negligible. This is not to say that he rids himself of it, or even that he repudiates it: his thematic system—his "imaginary universe"—is evident from the childhood verse to "Un Coup de dés" of 1897. But "Hérodiade"—to re-phrase my main point about that poem—can be read as an ambivalent rejection of the very consistencies which justify and nourish thematic and psychoanalytic criticism. The distressful failure of Hérodiade's narcissistic project is the poetic form taken by Mallarmé's willingness to renounce the

specular securities of an historically coherent "person." And what he refers
to as his death, far from being another theme in his writing, is the move
which ruins the possibility of thematic understanding. For it is a continuous
moving away from stabilizing (and obsessive) images. Mallarméan death is
a state of radically unsettled being, a state in which the poet is always
different from whatever may be said about him. What can be said, however,
will not be erased; rather, it will remain in order to create the points between which Mallarmé will be, merely, different from them. The themes of
a self do not disappear when Mallarmé "dies," but they do become psychologically inert; they memorialize the personality to which they posthumously refer.

The difference between Mallarmé as an intelligible historical person
and Mallarmé as depersonalizing movements of consciousness can be traced
in the two versions of "Le Pitre châtié."

> Pour ses yeux,—pour nager dans ces lacs, dont les quais
> Sont plantés de beaux cils qu'un matin bleu pénètre,
> J'ai, Muse,—moi, ton pitre,—enjambé la fenêtre
> Et fui notre baraque où fument tes quinquets.
>
> Et d'herbes enivré, j'ai plongé comme un traître
> Dans ces lacs défendus, et, quand tu m'appelais,
> Baigné mes membres nus dans l'onde aux blancs galets,
> Oubliant mon habit de pitre au tronc d'un hêtre.
>
> Le soleil du matin séchait mon corps nouveau
> Et je sentais fraîchir loin de ta tyrannie
> La neige des glaciers dans ma chair assainie,
>
> Ne sachant pas, hélas! quant s'en allait sur l'eau
> Le suif de mes cheveux et le fard de ma peau,
> Muse, que cette crasse était tout le génie!

(For her eyes,—to swim in those lakes, on whose embankments
/ Are planted beautiful eyelashes which a blue morning penetrates,
/ I have, Muse,—I, your clown,—climbed through the
window / And fled our tents where your oil lamps are smoking.

And drunk from grasses, I dove like a traitor / Into those forbidden lakes, and, when you called me, / I bathed my naked
limbs in the water filled with white pebbles, / Forgetting my
clown's costume on the trunk of a beech tree.

The morning sun was drying my new body / And, far from your tyranny, I felt / The snow from the glaciers cooling in my purified flesh,

Unaware, alas, when the soot from my hair and the paint from my body were carried away by the water, / Muse, that all my genius was in that dirt!)

(Version of 1864)

Yeux, lacs avec ma simple ivresse de renaître
Autre que l'histrion qui du geste évoquais
Comme plume la suie ignoble des quinquets,
J'ai troué dans le mur de toile une fenêtre.

De ma jambe et des bras limpide nageur traître,
A bonds multipliés, reniant le mauvais
Hamlet! c'est comme si dans l'onde j'innovais
Mille sépulcres pour y vierge disparaître.

Hilare or de cymbale à des poings irrité,
Tout à coup le soleil frappe la nudité
Qui pure s'exhala de ma fraîcheur de nacre,

Rance nuit de la peau quand sur moi vous passiez,
Ne sachant pas, ingrat! que c'était tout mon sacre,
Ce fard noyé dans l'eau perfide des glaciers.

(Eyes, lakes [nets] with, simply, my drunken wish to be reborn / Different from the clownish actor who through his gestures called forth / As feather the ignoble soot of the oil lamps, / I have ripped through the canvas wall a window.

A limpid traitorous swimmer with my arms and legs, / With numerous leaps, repudiating the bad / Hamlet! it is as if I were creating in the water / A thousand tombs in which—a virgin—to disappear.

Laughing cymbal-gold with fists irritated, / All at once the sun strikes the nudity / Which, pure, emanated from my pearly cool freshness,

Rancid night of the skin when you passed over me, / Not knowing ungrateful one! that my entire consecration lay in / That paint now drowned in the treacherous water of the glaciers.)

(Version of 1887)

If we consider the poem thematically, we may be able to account for the poet's revisions only through a rather conventional distinction between manner and substance. In both versions, Mallarmé appears to be using the image of a clown who jumps through the canvas wall of a circus tent into the lakes, and/or the nets, or a woman's eyes as a dramatic metaphor for the artist who either betrays his Muse for sensual pleasure, or mistakenly believes that he can still be an artist if he renounces the given materials of his craft (the clown's make-up; perhaps the imagery which "disguises" simple statement, or the inherited language from which individual poems are forged). From this perspective, we might say that Mallarmé does away with the narrative continuities of the first version in order, principally, to bring us closer to the clown's subjectivity—to his sensations and intentions. The poem naturally becomes more obscure, but the gain in dramatic immediacy is considerable. Thus, the perception of the woman's eyes as lakes is no longer spelled out ("Pour ses yeux,—pour nager dans ces lacs"), but is rather given as an unexplained verbal equivalence in the first two words of the poem: "Yeux, lacs avec ma simple ivresse de renaître." And, in the most striking example of this apparent effort to make words transparent to sensation, the effect of the sun striking the swimming clown's naked body is rendered in verse 9 by "Hilare or de cymbale à des poings irrité." The image is explained in verse 10 ("Tout à coup le soleil frappe la nudité"), whereas the earlier version of the first tercet had been all explanation. The reader's task in the later version consists less in establishing a correct narrative line (which remains comparatively clear) than in translating verbal analogues of sensations back into sensations. "Hilare or de cymbale" becomes transparent to sensations (of joyously bathing in the "loud," reverberating golden sunlight) thanks to a critical exercise which erases language by (verbally . . .) elucidating the rightness of certain words as a translation of sensations experienced, originally, without language.

There is, however, a way of considering Mallarmé's revisions not as strategies designed to increase the dramatic immediacy of his theme, but rather as a means of changing the status of meaning itself in the poem. To begin with, the first condensation ("Yeux, lacs") makes the love theme problematic; we really have no grounds for asserting that the clown leaps, as he says in the first version, in order to swim in the woman's eyes. Instead of a rather clichéd tension between love and art, the final version asks the simpler, and yet more puzzling, question of whether or not a certain kind of leap is consistent with the "consecration" of a performing artist. But what is this leap? It is no longer a move toward a specific object of desire; rather, it has become a perhaps objectless breaking away from what the clown has been until now. He is motivated by nothing more definite than "ma simple ivresse de renaître / Autre." *Re,* the reiterative prefix, occurs three times in these two words. In the final version of "Le Pitre châtié," Mallarmé also increases both the structural visibility and the frequency of *re* as a terminal rhyme: the first and last verses of both quatrains end in *re* ("pénètre / fenêtre" had ended the second and third verses of the first quatrain in the earlier version, while "traître" and "hêtre" rhymed the first and fourth verses of the second quatrain), and a new rhyme in *re* is added in the tercets ("nacre" and "sacre"). Reiterative and yet displaceable: except for "renaître," Mallarmé uses *re* not as a prefix but as an ending, thus modifying the sign of repetition with the suggestion (provided by the feminine ending) of indefinite extension. In *re,* we have, as it were, a floating reiterative: capable of being attached to almost any word, and of occupying different positions in different words. This lexical availability is analogous to what the clown seeks: an indeterminate repetition of his birth. Finally, such a rebirth is equivalent to death: to leap into a perpetually virginal being is to disappear into the thousand watery sepulchers which the clown "innovates." His incessant dying is his constant moving away from himself, his "simple ivresse de renaître autre."

This movement also describes the relation of the later version of "Le Pitre châtié" to the earlier version. The latter is the poetic sepulcher in which the former's thematic contrasts disappear. It is our first example of what I will presently describe as Mallarmé's burial of poetry. The originality of "Le Pitre châtié" is not that it replicates an already written poem, but it is nonetheless *by thinking the earlier version* that the poet produces a new version. The process of revising does not oppose a new work to the old work; so as long as the former does not exist, the latter will be abolished *as* it is being read—that is, as it is received into, in a sense replicated by, a receptive consciousness.

Revision could be taken as a model of criticism: in both cases, the work of art is annihilated by being embraced. Intimacy abolishes its object. It is perhaps this violent passivity which Henry James has in mind when, referring in his preface to *The Golden Bowl* to his revisions for the New York edition of his novels, he claims that the later versions are merely the "only possible" vision he has of the earlier versions, and that revision is nothing more than "re-perusal, registered." The later text is the recording of an experience of the earlier text. The later version of "Le Pitre châtié" could be read as a statement about what it was like to read the earlier version. It is as if Mallarmé's recording of his "re-perusal" of the latter resulted in a record of the poet-reader's "simple ivresse" to have his poem be born again, no longer the same, as another. The later version would therefore be a self-reflexive movement which has as its object of reflection the exhilarating violation of the first poem. To "re-peruse" the clown's jump from love to art is to leap away from that jump; and, rather than merely substitute another thematic contrast for the one between the Muse and the woman, Mallarmé, in his new poem, "replicates" the thematic leap with a poem about a leap from any definable being into mere, and radical otherness.

However, it is as if Mallarmé also repudiated his poetic leap in the very act of accomplishing it. Both versions of "Le Pitre châtié" end on the sombre assertion that the clown's genius has been washed away with his make-up. He has fled from "la suie ignoble des quinquets" (or, in the first version, "notre baraque où fument [les] quinquets [de la Muse]"); he has lost "le suif de mes cheveux et le fard de ma peau" in the lake; and his clown's costume has been left by the trunk of the beech tree. The exhilarating nudity evoked in the first tercet of both versions of the poem is bitterly equated with sterility in the two conclusions of "Le Pitre châtié." The argument made in the poem seems to be that artistic genius depends on certain conventional accessories or accompaniments to artistic performance. Outside the circus tent, without his costume and his make-up, the clown in the first version is deprived of his genius; in the final version, a sun-drenched rebirth becomes a "rance nuit de la peau" when the clown's make-up—which he equates with his artistic consecration—is drowned in the glacier's treacherous waters. The disgust with performance (with "le mauvais Hamlet," "l'histrion qui du geste évoquais / Comme plume la suie ignoble des quinquets") is accompanied by an apparent inability to formulate the performative innovations realized in the final version. The peculiarity of this position is that it persists into Mallarmé's demonstration that art can be created without a good deal of the "make-up" of the first version. The poet has not, it is true, leapt into a pure availability to language; but in dropping the principal narrative ornamentation of the early version—the reference to the woman, the address to the Muse—he has effectively put into question the clown's simple equation of his genius with the given conditions of his art.

The fable about art in "Le Pitre châtié" is inadequate to the innovative performance given in the later version of the poem. To put this in another way, we might say that Mallarmé's betrayal of the earlier version is itself betrayed by an anecdotal fidelity of the revised poem to its model. The abolishing movement away from the first "Pitre châtié" is compensated for by a specular movement at the end of the second version, a movement in which revision is conservatively mythologized as replicative reflection. Dislocation is qualified by relocation, and the latter bizarrely implies a nostalgia for the conventional procedures of the first version. Mallarmé sentimentally implies that the alternative to the esthetic choices of his earlier poem is silence, whereas he has in fact begun to show that he can leap through the "canvas wall" of narrative, thematic and psychological props, and continue to perform poetically. The disruptive play of such lines as "Hilare or de cymbale à des poings irrité" is not simply a disguise of the explicit statements of the first "Pitre châtié." That play *is* the meaning of the later version; far from giving greater dramatic immediacy to the clown's story, it makes the story itself an obsolete reminder of a dead person and a dead art.

BARBARA JOHNSON

Les Fleurs du mal armé:
Some Reflections on Intertexuality

*Oui, le suspens de la Danse, crainte contradictoire ou souhait de voir
trop et pas assez, exige un prolongement transparent.*

[*Yes, the suspense of the Dance, contradictory fear or wish to see too
much or not enough, demands a transparent prolongation.*]

—MALLARMÉ

The title, "Les Fleurs du mal armé," is designed to be read as a paradigm
for the questions of intertextuality under discussion here. On the one hand,
it appears to posit a linear, developmental, slightly overlapping relation
between a precursor text (*Les Fleurs du mal*) and a disciple (Mallarmé)
engendered out of it. On the other hand, the double function of the word
"mal" renders Baudelaire's title and Mallarmé's name both inseparable
from each other and different from themselves, creating new dividing lines
not *between* the two oeuvres but *within* each of them. The proper names
thereby lose their properness, and their free-floating parts can combine into
new signifying possibilities.]

Contemporary discussions of intertextuality can be distinguished from
"source" studies in that the latter speak in terms of a transfer of property
("borrowing") while the former tend to speak in terms of misreading or
infiltration, that is, of violations of property. Whether such violations occur
in the oedipal rivalry between a specific text and its precursor (Bloom's

From *Lyric Poetry: Beyond New Criticism,* edited by Chaviva Hosek and Patricia
Parker. © 1985 by Cornell University Press.

in the history of its language and literature (Kristeva's paragrams, Riffaterre's hypograms), "intertextuality" designates the multitude of ways a text has of not being self-contained, of being traversed by otherness. Such a conception of textuality arises out of two main theoretical currents: (a) Freud's discovery of the unconscious as an "other scene" that intrudes on conscious life in the form of dreams, slips of the tongue, parapraxes, etc., and (b) Saussure's discovery of the haunting presence of proper names anagrammatically dispersed in the writings of certain late Latin poets. These two discoveries have been combined by Jacques Lacan into a conception of the "signifying chain" that "insists" in the human subject in such a way that "the unconscious is structured like a language." One might say by analogy that for modern theorists of intertexuality, the language of poetry is structured like an unconscious. The integrity and intentional self-identity of the individual text are put in question in ways that have nothing to do with the concepts of originality and derivativeness, since the very notion of a self-contained literary "property" is shown to be an illusion. When read in its dynamic intertextuality, the text becomes differently energized, traversed by forces and desires that are invisible or unreadable to those who see it as an independent, homogeneous message unit, a totalizable collection of signifieds.

What happens, though, when a poet decides to transform the seemingly unconscious "anxiety of influence" into an explicit theme in his writing? Can the seepage and rivalry between texts somehow thereby be mastered and reappropriated? In an early piece of poetic prose entitled "Symphonie littéraire," Mallarmé prefaces his homage to his three "masters" (Gautier, Baudelaire, and Banville) with the following invocation:

> Muse moderne de l'Impuissance, qui m'interdis depuis longtemps le trésor familier des Rythmes, et me condamnes (aimable supplice) à ne faire plus que relire,—jusqu'au jour où tu m'auras enveloppé dans ton irrémédiable filet, l'ennui, et tout sera fini alors,—les maîtres inaccessibles dont la beauté me désespère; mon ennemie, et cependant mon enchanteresse aux breuvages perfides et aux melancoliques ivresses, je te dédie, comme une raillerie ou,—le sais-je?—comme un gage d'amour, ces quelques lignes de ma vie où tu ne m'inspiras pas la haine de la création et le stérile amour du néant. Tu y découvriras les jouissances d'une âme purement passive qui n'est que femme encore, et qui demain peut-être sera bête.

(O modern Muse of Impotence, you who have long forbidden me the familiar treasury of Rhythms, and who condemn me [pleasurable torture] to do nothing but reread—until the day you will envelop me in your irremediable net, ennui, and all will then be over—those inaccessible masters whose beauty drives me to despair; my enemy, yet my enchantress, with your perfidious potions and your melancholy intoxications, I dedicate to you, in jest or—can I know?—as a token of love, these few lines of my life written in the clement hours when you did not inspire in me a hatred of creation and a sterile love of nothingness. You will discover in them the pleasures of a purely passive soul who is yet but a woman and who tomorrow perhaps will be a dumb animal.)

It would seem that this text is quite explicitly describing the castrating effect of poetic fathers upon poetic sons. The precursors' beauty drives the ephebe to despair: he is impotent, passive, feminized, *mal armé.* Yet this state of castration is being invoked as a Muse: the lack of inspiration has become the source of inspiration. Mallarmé, as has often been noted, has transformed the incapacity to write into the very subject of his writing. In the act of thematizing an oedipal defeat, Mallarmé's writing thus maps out the terms of an escape from simple oedipal polarities: it is no longer possible to distinguish easily between defeat and success, impotence and potency, reading and writing, passivity and activity.

Before pursuing further the Mallarméan relation between impotence and writing, let us glance for a moment at the father's side of the story. At a time when Baudelaire would have had ample occasion to read Mallarmé's "Literary Symphony" along with the prose poems Mallarmé had dedicated to him, the older poet wrote the following remarks in a letter to his mother in which he had enclosed an article about himself written by Verlaine:

Il y a du talent chez ces jeunes gens; mais que de folies! quelles exagérations et quelle infatuation de jeunesse! Depuis quelques années je surprenais, ça et là, des imitations et des tendances qui m'alarmaient. Je ne connais rien de plus compromettant que les imitateurs et je n'aime rien tant que d'être seul. Mais ce n'est pas possible; et il paraît que l'*école Baudelaire* existe.

(These young people do have talent, but there is such madness! such exaggeration and such youthful infatuation! For several years now I have here and there come across imitations and tendencies that alarm me. I know of nothing more compromising than imitators and I like nothing so well as being alone. But it is not possible; and it seems that the *Baudelaire school* exists.)

The "father" here is "alarmed" not by the hostility but by the imitative devotion of his "sons," whose writing lacks the measure and maturity that he, Baudelaire, by implication attributes to his own. To be imitated is to be repeated, multiplied, distorted, "compromised." To be alone is at least to be unique, to be secure in the boundaries of one's self. And to have the luxury of rejecting one's imitators is both to profit from the compliment and to remain uncontaminated by the distortions. Yet even in Baudelaire's expression of alarm and self-containment, otherness surreptitiously intrudes. For while Baudelaire is ambivalently but emphatically imprinting his own name on the writing of his admirers, another proper name is manifesting itself in the very writing of his letter: in speaking of "des tendances qui M'ALARMAIENT," Baudelaire has unwittingly inscribed the name of one of the sources of his alarm. The almost perfect homophony between "m'alarmaient" and "Mallarmé" reveals a play of intertextuality in which the text, while seeming to decry the dangers of imitation, is actually *acting out,* against the express purposes of its author, the far graver dangers of usurpation. And what is usurped is not only Baudelaire's claims to authority over the work of his disciples, but also and more significantly the claims of his conscious intentions to authority over the workings of his own writing. The suppressed name of Mallarmé shows through.

Both of these thematizations of the oedipal dynamics of intertextuality are thus more complex than they at first appear. In both cases, the ongoingness of literary history is acted out by the text despite an apparent attempt to arrest it. Mallarmé carves new territory for poetry out of what looks like a writing block; Baudelaire's writing, in the act of blocking out the successors, inscribes the inevitability of their usurpation.

But what are the effects of this Muse of Impotence not on Mallarmé's critical prose but on his poetry itself? In a poem entitled "L'Azur," written the same year as the "Symphonie littéraire," Mallarmé dramatizes the predicament of the poet who seeks *forgetfulness* as a cure for impotence (thus implying that what the impotent poet is suffering from is too much memory). The poem begins:

> De l'éternel azur la sereine ironie
> Accable, belle indolemment comme les fleurs,
> Le poëte impuissant qui maudit son génie
> A travers un désert stérile de Douleurs

(The eternal azure's serene irony
Staggers, with the indolent grace of flowers,
The impotent poet who damns his genius
Across a sterile desert of sorrows.)

The poet tries to flee this oppressive azure, throwing night, smoke, and fog across it, until he reaches a moment of illusory victory, followed by a recognition of defeat:

—Le Ciel est mort.—Vers toi, j'accours! donne, ô matière,
L'oubli de l'Idéal cruel et du Péché
A ce martyr qui vient partager la litière
Où le bétail heureux des hommes est couché,

Car j'y veux, puisque enfin ma cervelle, vidée
Comme de pot de fard gisant au pied du mur,
N'a plus l'art d'attifer la sanglotante idée,
Lugubrement bâiller vers un trépas obscur . . .

En vain! l'Azur triomphe, et je l'entends qui chante
Dans les cloches. Mon âme, il se fait voix pour plus
Nous faire peur avec sa victoire méchante,
Et du métal vivant sort en bleus angélus!

Il roule par la brume, ancien et traverse
Ta native agonie ainsi qu'un glaive sûr;
Où fuir dans la révolte inutile et perverse?
Je suis hanté. L'Azur! l'Azur! l'Azur! l'Azur!

(—The sky is dead.—To you I run! give, o matter,
Forgetfulness of the cruel Ideal and Sin
To this martyr who comes to share the straw
Where the happy herd of men is stabled,

For I wish—since my brain no longer, emptied
Like the grease paint pot that lies against the wall,
Has the art to prettify the sobbing idea—
To yawn lugubriously toward an obscure death . . .

In vain! The Azure triumphs, I can hear it sing
In the bells. My soul, it becomes voice,

The better to scare us with its mean success,
And from the living metal bluely rings the angelus.

It rolls through the mist of old and pierces
Like a skillful sword your native agony;
Where is there to flee, in useless and perverse revolt?
I am haunted. Azure! Azure! Azure! Azure!)

This text has always been read—even by Mallarmé himself—as a description of the struggle between the desire to reach a poetic or metaphysical ideal and the attempt to escape that desire for fear of failing. As Guy Michaud puts it, "Even if the poet is freed neither of his dream nor his impotence, he has at least affirmed the originality of his poetry. He has achieved the *general effect* he was seeking: the obsessive concern with the eternal, which the azure symbolizes" (*Mallarmé*). But should this "azure" be understood only in a *symbolic* sense? The fact that the word is repeated four times at the end of the poem would seem to indicate that what haunts Mallarmé is not simply some ideal symbolized by azure but the very word "azure" itself. Even a casual glance at nineteenth-century French poetry reveals that the word "azure" is par excellence a "poetic" word—a sign that what one is reading is a poem. The repetition of this word can thus be read as the return of stereotyped poetic language as a *reflex,* a moment when initiative is being taken by the words *of others,* which is one of the things Mallarmé will later call "chance." Azure, says Mallarmé, "becomes voice." The text ends: "I am haunted: cliché! cliché! cliché! cliché!"

Impotence is thus not a simple inability to write, but an inability to write *differently.* The agony experienced before the blank page arises out of the fact that the page is in fact never quite blank enough.

To write thus becomes for Mallarmé a constant effort to silence the automatisms of poetry, to "conquer chance word by word," to perceive words "independent of their ordinary sequence." But if the blankness of the page is in a sense the place from which literary history speaks, Mallarmé ends up writing *not* by covering the white page with the blackness of his originality but rather by including *within* his writing the very *spaces* where poetic echoes and reflexes have been suppressed. "Leaving the initiative to words" is a complex operation in which the linguistic work of poetic calculation must substitute for the banalities of poetic inspiration. And the blanks figure as a major ingredient in that calculation. As Mallarmé puts it in a note on the "Coup de dés," his symphony in white: "The 'blanks' indeed take on importance. . . . The paper intervenes each time an image, of its own accord, ceases or dies back, accepting the succession of others." And as for prose, Mallarmé explains that his blanks take the place of empty transitions: "The reason for these intervals, or blanks . . . —why not confine the subject to those fragments in which it shines and then replace, by the ingenuousness of the paper, those ordinary, nondescript transitions?" The act of reading Mallarmé, of sounding that "transparency of allusions," becomes—in his own words—a "desperate practice" precisely because "to read" means "to rely, depending on the page, on the blank," to take cognizance of the text as a "stilled poem, in the blanks." Through the breaks and the blanks in his texts, Mallarmé internalizes intertextual heterogeneity and puts it to work not as a relation *between* texts but as a play of intervals and interruptions *within* texts. Mallarmé's intertextuality then becomes an explicit version of the ways in which a text is never its own contemporary, cannot constitute a self-contained whole, conveys only its non-coincidence with itself. While the desire to escape banality seemed to situate the challenge of poetry in the impossibility of saying something *different,* Mallarmé here reveals through the text's own self-difference an equal impossibility inherent in the attempt to say something *same.* Indeed, his notion of the Book ("the world is made to end up as a Book") is a correlative to this: if for Mallarmé all poets have unwittingly yet unsuccessfully attempted to write THE Book, and if at the same time "all books contain the fusion of a small number of repeated sayings," then difference can only arise out of the process of repetition, and the "defect of languages" that verse is supposed to make up for resides in the fact that it is just as impossible to say the *same* thing as to say something different.

It is perhaps this paradox of intertextual relations, this "unanimous blank conflict between one garland and the same," that is staged by the famous "Swan" sonnet:

> Le vierge, le vivace et le bel aujourd'hui
> Va-t-il nous déchirer avec un coup d'aile ivre
> Ce lac dur oublié que hante sous le givre
> Le transparent glacier des vols qui n'ont pas fui!
>
> Un cygne d'autrefois se souvient que c'est lui
> Magnifique mais qui sans espoir se délivre
> Pour n'avoir pas chanté la région où vivre
> Quand du stérile hiver a resplendi l'ennui.
>
> Tout son col secouera cette blanche agonie
> Par l'espace infligé à l'oiseau qui le nie,
> Mais non l'horreur du sol où le plumage est pris.

Fantôme qu'à ce lieu son pur éclat assigne,
Il s'immobilise au songe froid de mépris
Que vêt parmi l'exil inutile le Cygne.

(The virgin, vivacious, and lovely today—
Will it rend with a blow of its dizzying wing
This hard lake forgotten yet haunted beneath
By the transparent glacier of unreleased flights!

A bygone day's swan now remembers it's he
Who, magnificent yet in despair struggles free
For not having sung of the regions of life
When the ennui of winter's sterility gleamed.

All his neck will shake off this white agony
space
Has inflicted upon the white bird who denied it,
But not the ground's horror, his plumage inside
it.

A phantom assigned by his gloss to this place,
Immobile he stands, in the cold dream of scorn
That surrounds, in his profitless exile, the Swan.)

The poetry of "today" would thus constitute the rendering of something that is both forgotten and haunted—haunted by the way in which a "bygone day's swan" *did not sing*. The choice of a swan as a figure for the precursor is both appropriate and paradoxical. On the one hand, if the swan sings only at the moment of death, then the poet who says he is haunted by the precursor-swan's song would in reality be marking the *death* of the father. But on the other hand, to seek to silence the father, to speak of his *not* having sung, is to run the risk of bringing the father back to life, since if he does not sing, there is no proof that he is dead. In other words, the survival of the father is in a sense guaranteed by the way in which the son does *not* hear him.

It is interesting to note that this sonnet about a bygone day's swan actually itself refers to the swan of a bygone day—a poem entitled "The Swan," written by Baudelaire and dedicated to *his* poetic precursor, Victor Hugo. It would seem that the swan comes to designate the precursor as such, and it is doubtless no accident that the predecessor-figure in Proust's *Remembrance of Things Past* should also be called by the name of Swann.

But in each of these cases, what is striking about the precursor figure, what in a sense seals his paternity, is the way in which he himself is already divided, rent, different from himself. In Proust's novel, Swann is the model of a man who is never the contemporary of his own desires. Baudelaire's "Swan" poem tells of being divided between the loss of what can never be recovered and the memory of what can never be forgotten, so that irreparable loss becomes the incapacity to let anything go. To return to Mallarmé's sonnet, we can see that the very division between "aujourd'hui" (today) and "autrefois" (bygone day) names the temporality of intertextuality as such. And this division in itself constitutes a textual allusion—to the division of Hugo's *Contemplations* into two volumes entitled precisely "Autrefois" and "Aujourd'hui." "They are separated by an abyss," writes Hugo: "the tomb."

In his preface to *Contemplations,* Hugo suggests that his book should be read "as one reads the work of the dead." In reflecting on this quotation, one can begin to see a supplementary twist to the traditional oedipal situation. For if the father survives precisely through his way of affirming himself dead, then the son will always arrive too late to kill him. What the son suffers from, then, is not the simple desire to kill the father, but the impotence to kill him whose potency resides in his ability to recount his own death.

It is perhaps for this reason that the so-called "fathers of modern thought"—Mallarmé, Freud, Marx, Nietzsche—maintain such a tremendous authority for contemporary theory. In writing of the subversion of the author, the father, God, privilege, knowledge, property, and consciousness, these thinkers have subverted in advance any grounds on which one might undertake to kill off an authority that theorizes the death of all authority. This is perhaps the way in which contemporary theory in its turn has *lived* the problematics of intertextuality.

From the foregoing it would appear that intertextuality is a struggle between fathers and sons, and that literary history is exclusively a male affair. This has certainly been the presumption of literary historians in the past, for whom gender becomes an issue only when the writer is female. In the remainder of this essay, I would like to glance briefly at the ways in which questions of gender might enrich, complicate, and even subvert the underlying paradigms of intertextual theory. What, for example, does one make of Mallarmé's experience of the "pleasures of a purely passive soul who is yet but a woman"? Is Mallarmé's femininity a mere figure for castration? Or is the Muse of Impotence also a means of access to the experience of femininity? Or, to approach it another way, how might we factor into these intertextual relations the fact that Baudelaire's protestations of solitude and paternity are written to his *mother,* and that the tomb that

separates "autrefois" and "aujourd'hui" for Hugo is that of his *daughter?*
What, in other words, are the poetic uses to which women—both inside and
outside the text—have been put by these male poets?

It is interesting that the only text by Mallarmé on which Baudelaire is
known to have commented is a prose poem in which a beautiful, naked
woman stands as a figure for the poetry of the past. Mallarmé's poem, "Le
Phénomène futur," describes a degenerating world in which a "Displayer of
Things Past" is touting the beauties of a "woman of Bygone Days." Droop-
ing poets-to-be are suddenly revived, "haunted by rhythm and forgetting
that theirs is an era that has outlived beauty." Baudelaire, in his notes on
Belgium, has this to say about Mallarmé's vision of the future: "A young
writer has recently come up with an ingenious but not entirely accurate
conception. The world is about to end. Humanity is decrepit. A future
Barnam is showing the degraded men of his day a beautiful woman artificially preserved from ancient times. 'What?' they exclaim, 'could humanity
once have been as beautiful as that?' I say that this is not true. Degenerate
man would admire himself and call beauty ugliness." This encounter between the two poets is a perfect figuration of the progress of literary history
from one generation to another. But the disagreement on which Baudelaire
insists is less profound than it appears. While the elder poet fears that people
will admire something he no longer recognizes as beautiful and the younger
poet fears that beauty may no longer be recognizable in his work, Baudelaire
and Mallarmé actually agree on two things: beauty is a function of the past,
and beauty is a woman.

Nothing could be more traditional than this conception of Beauty as a
female body: naked, immobile, and mute. Indeed, the beauty of female
muteness and reification reaches its highest pitch when the woman in question is dead (cf. Poe's statement that the most poetic subject is the death of
a beautiful woman) or at least—as here—artificially preserved and statufied.
The flawless whiteness of the female body is the very image of the blank
page, to be shaped and appropriated by the male creative pen. As Susan
Gubar remarks in a recent article entitled " 'The Blank Page' and Female
Creativity":

> When the metaphors of literary creativity are filtered through a
> sexual lens, female sexuality is often identified with textuality. . . .
> This model of the pen-penis writing on the virgin page partici-
> pates in a long tradition identifying the author as a male who is
> primary and the female as his passive creation—a secondary

object lacking autonomy, endowed with often contradictory meaning but denied intentionality.

In Mallarmé's work, the correlation between Poetry and Femininity is pervasive from the very beginning. The great unfinished poem, "Hérodiade," begun in 1864 and still lying uncompleted on Mallarmé's desk at the time of his death in 1898, provides a telling record of the shifting importance and complexity of his attempt to make poetry speak as a female Narcissus, self-reflexive and self-contained. The failure of Mallarmé's attempt to *dramatize* his poetics under the guise of female psychology is certainly as instructive as the centrality of that project, and deserves more extensive treatment than is possible here. But in Mallarmé's later writing, the identification of femininity with textuality, which becomes both more explicit and more complex, becomes as well completely de-psychologized:

A déduire le point philosophique auquel est située l'impersonnalité de la danseuse, entre sa féminine apparence et un objet mimé, pour quel hymen: elle le pique d'une sûre pointe, le pose; puis déroule notre conviction en le chiffre de pirouettes prolongé vers un autre motif, attendu que tout, dans l'évolution par où elle illustre le sens de nos extases et triomphes entonnés à l'orchestre, est, comme le veut l'art même, au théatre, *fictif ou momentané.*

(To deduce the philosophical point at which the dancer's impersonality is located, between her feminine appearance and a mimed object, for what Hymen: she pricks it with a confident point and poses it; then unrolls our conviction in the cipher of pirouettes prolonged toward another motif, presuming that everything, in the evolution through which she illustrates the sense of our ecstasies and triumphs intoned in the orchestra, is, as art itself requires it, in theatre, *fictive or momentary.*)

A savoir que la danseuse *n'est pas une femme qui danse,* pour ces motifs juxtaposés qu'elle *n'est pas une femme,* mais une métaphore résumant un des aspects élémentaires de notre forme, glaive, coupe, fleur, etc., et *qu'elle ne danse pas,* suggérant, par le prodige de raccourcis ou d'élans, avec une écriture corporelle ce qu'il faudrait des paragraphes en prose dialoguée autant que descriptive, pour exprimer, dans la rédaction: poëme dégagé de tout appareil du scribe.

(That is, that the dancer *is not a woman dancing,* for the juxtaposed motives that she *is not a woman,* but a metaphor epito-
mizing one of the elementary aspects of our form, sword, goblet,
flower, etc., and that *she is not dancing,* suggesting, through the
prodigy of short cuts and leaps, with a corporal writing what it
would take paragraphs of dialogue and descriptive prose to express, if written out: a poem freed from all scribal apparatus.)

This would certainly seem to be an example of the denial of female interiority and subjectivity and the transformation of the woman's body into an
art object. Textuality becomes woman, but woman becomes poet only unconsciously and corporally. But is it different for a man? The question of
autonomy and intentionality becomes sticky indeed when one recalls that
for Mallarmé it is precisely the intentionality of the poet as such that must
disappear in order for initiative to be left to words: "L'oeuvre pure implique
la disparition élocutoire du poëte, qui cède l'initiative aux mots." Therefore,
the fact that the dancer here is objectified and denied interiority is not in
itself a function of her gender. That state of "scribelessness," of "impersonality," is, rather, the ideal Mallarmé sets up for poetry. But the fact
remains that the poet is consistently male and the poem female:

L'Unique entraînement imaginatif consiste, aux heures ordinaires
de fréquentation dans les lieux de Danse sans visée quelconque
préalable, patiemment et passivement à se demander devant tout
pas, chaque attitude si étranges, ces pointes et taquetés, allongés
ou ballons, "Que peut signifier ceci" ou mieux, d'inspiration, le
lire. A coup sûr on opérera en pleine rêverie, mais adéquate:
vaporeuse, nette et ample, ou restreinte, telle seulement que
l'enferme en ses circuits ou la transporte par une fugue la ballerine
illettrée se livrant aux jeux de sa profession. Oui, celle-là (serais-
tu perdu en une salle, spectator très étranger, Ami) pour peu que
tu déposes avec soumission à ses pieds d'inconsciente révélatrice
ainsi que les roses qu'enlève et jette en la visibilité de régions
supérieures un jeu de ses chaussons de satin pâle veretigineux, la
Fleur d'abord *de ton poétique instinct,* n'attendant de rien autre
la mise en évidence et sous le vrai jour des mille imaginations
latentes: alors, par un commerce dont paraît son sourire verser le
secret, sans tarder elle te livre à travers le voile dernier qui toujours
reste, la nudité de tes concepts et silencieusement écrira ta vision
à façon d'un Signe, qu'elle est.

(The sole imaginative training consists, in the ordinary hours of frequenting Dance with no preconceived aim, patiently and passively, of wondering at every step, each attitude, so strange, those points and *taquetés, allongés* or *ballons*, "What can this signify?" or, better, by inspiration, of reading it. One will definitely operate in full reverie, but adquate: vaporous, crisp, and ample, or restrained, such only as it is enclosed in circlings or transported in a figure by the illiterate ballerina engaging in the play of her profession. Yes, that one [be you lost in the hall, most foreign spectator, Friend] if you but set at the feet of this unconscious revealer, submissively—like the roses lifted and tossed into the visibility of the upper regions by a flounce of her dizzying pale satin slippers—the Flower at first *of your poetic instinct,* expecting nothing but the evidencing and in the true light of a thousand latent imaginations: then, through a commerce whose secret her smile appears to pour out, without delay she delivers up to you, through the ultimate veil that always remains, the nudity of your concepts, and silently begins to write your vision in the manner of a Sign, which she is.)

What the woman is a sign of, what she *unconsciously* reveals, is the nudity of "your" concepts and the flower of "your" poetic instinct. The woman, dancing, is the necessary but unintentional medium through which something fundamental to the male poetic self can be manifested. But this state of unconsciousness, which would seemingly establish the possibility of a female poet, turns out to be valuable only when reappropriated by the male poet. This becomes clear in Mallarmé's discussion of women and jewels.

Precious stones figure often in Mallarmé's descriptions of poetry:

L'oeuvre pure implique la disparition élocutoire du poëte, qui cède l'initiative aux mots, par le heurt de leur inégalité mobilisés; *ils s'allument de reflets réciproques comme une virtuelle traînée de feux sur des pierreries,* remplaçant la respiration perceptible en l'ancien souffle lyrique ou la direction personnelle enthousiaste de la phrase.

(The pure work implies the elocutionary disappearance of the poet, who leaves the initiative to words, through the shock of their mobilized inequality; *they light up with reciprocal reflections like a virtual trail of fire over precious stones,* replacing the

breath perceptible in the old lyric inspiration or the passionate
personal direction of the sentence.) (Italics mine.)

In an interview with Jules Huret, Mallarmé expands upon the image of
jewelry in the following terms:

> —*Que pensez-vous de la fin du naturalisme?*
> —L'enfantillage de la littérature jusqu'ici a été de croire, par
> exemple, que de choisir un certain nombre de pierres précieuses
> et en mettre les noms sur le papier, même très bien, c'était *faire*
> des pierres précieuses. Eh bien! non! La poésie consistant à *créer,*
> il faut prendre dans l'âme humaine des états, des lueurs d'une
> pureté si absolue que, bien chantés et bien mis en lumière, cela
> constitue en effet les joyaux de l'homme: là, il y a symbole, il y
> a création, et le mot poésie a ici son sens: c'est, en somme, la
> seule création humaine possible. Et si, véritablement, les pierres
> précieuses dont on se pare ne manifestent pas un état d'âme, c'est
> indûment qu'on s'en pare. . . . La femme, par exemple, cette
> éternelle voleuse . . .
>
> Et tenez, *ajoute mon interlocuteur en riant à moitié,* ce qu'il y
> a d'admirable dans les magasins de nouveautés, c'est, quelquefois,
> de nous avoir révélé, par le commissaire de police, que la femme
> se parait indûment de ce dont elle ne savait pas le sens caché, et
> qui ne lui appartient par conséquent pas.

> (—*What do you think of the end of naturalism?*
> —The childishness of literature up to now has been to think,
> for example, that to choose a certain number of precious stones
> and to put their names down on paper, even superbly well, was
> to *make* precious stones. Not at all! Since poetry consists of
> creating, one must take from the human soul certain states, cer-
> tain glimmerings of such absolute purity that, skillfully sung and
> brought to light, they constitute indeed the jewels of man: there,
> there is symbol, there is creation, and the word poetry takes on
> its meaning: that, in sum, is the only human creation possible.
> And if, truly, the precious stones one dresses in do not manifest
> a state of mind or mood, then one has no right to wear them. . . .
> Woman, for example, that eternal thief . . .
>
> And think, *adds my interlocutor half laughing:* what is admi-
> rable about those high fashion stores is that they have sometimes
> revealed to us, through the chief of police, that women have been

illegitimately wearing what they didn't know the hidden meaning of, and which consequently does not belong to them.)

Women's unconsciousness of meaning—that which makes them capable of
standing for the male poetic instinct—is what denies the legitimacy of their
ever occupying the role of poetic subject. Men know what they are doing
when they leave initiative to words or jewels; women don't. It is interesting
to recall that Mallarmé almost single-handedly produced a fashion journal,
La Dernière Mode, which dealt in great detail with jewelry, clothing, and
other items of female decoration, and which he often signed with a feminine
pseudonym. It is as though Mallarmé's interest in writing like a woman
about fashion was to steal back for consciousness that women had stolen by
unconsciousness, to write *consciously* from out of the female unconscious,
which is somehow more intimately but illegitimately connected to the stuff
of poetry. Intertextuality here becomes intersexuality.

   Mallarmé's instatement of the impersonal or unconscious poetic subject thus somehow exposes rather than conceals a question that haunts him
from the very beginning: is writing a gendered act? It is this question that
informs a poem entitled "Don du poème," which serves as a dedicatory
poem to "Hérodiade." The fact that Hérodiade and Mallarmé's daughter
Genevieve were "born" at the same time serves as the background for
Mallarmé's reflection on gender differences:

> Je t'apporte l'enfant d'une nuit d'Idumée!
> Noire, à l'aile saignante et pâle, déplumée,
> Par le verre brûlé d'aromates et d'or,
> Par les carreaux glacés, hélas! mornes encor,
> L'aurore se jeta sur la lampe angélique.
> Palmes! et quand elle a montré cette relique
> A ce père essayant un sourire ennemi,
> La solitude bleue et stérile a frémi.
> O la berceuse, avec ta fille et l'innocence
> De vos pieds froids, accueille une horrible
>   naissance:
> Et ta voix rappelant viole et clavecin,
> Avec le doigt fané presseras-tu le sein
> Par qui coule en blancheur sibylline la femme
> Pour les lèvres que l'air du vierge azur affame?

> (I bring you the child of a night spent in Edom!
> Black, with pale and bleeding wing, quilless,

Through the glass burned with spices and gold,
Through the icy panes, alas! mournful still,
The dawn flew down on the angelic lamp.
Palms! and when it had shown this relic
To this father attempting an enemy smile,
The blue and sterile solitude was stirred.
O cradler, with your daughter and the innocence
Of your cold feet, welcome a horrible birth:
And your voice recalling viol and harpsichord,
With faded finger will you press the breast
Through which in sibylline whiteness woman flows
For lips half starved by virgin azure air?)

The question of gender is raised immediately in two very different ways in the first line. The word "enfant" is one of the few words in French that can be either masculine or feminine without modification. And the name "Idumée" refers to ancient Edom, the land of the outcast Esau, or, according to the Kabbalah, the land of pre-Adamic man, where sexless beings reproduced without women, or where sexual difference did not exist. The poem thus begins on a note of denial of sexual difference, only to end with a plea that the woman agree to nurture the fruit of such a denial. The means of such nourishment is "blancheur sibylline": white textuality, the blankness that challenges interpretation. The woman, then, is to provide the nourishing blanks without which the newborn poem might die of "azure," which, as we have seen, represents the weight of poetic history. "Idumée" and "Palmes" can be found in Boileau's Satire IX in a passage in which he lists a string of Malherbian poetic commonplaces. (It is curious to note that the word with which "Idumée" rhymes in Boileau is "alarmée," and that "alarmes" is the first rhyme in the overture to "Hérodiade," which follows and imagistically grows out of "Don du Poème." Mallarmé's anagrammatical signature seems to lurk just behind these citations of poetic history.)

It would seem at first sight that Mallarmé in this poem draws a contrast between the fecundity of natural reproduction and the sterility of poetic creation, and that this poem stands as a typical example of the male pen expressing its womb envy. Yet the masculine here is equated with sexlessness, while the woman functions not as a womb but as a source of music and sibylline whiteness. The opposition between male and female is an opposition between half-dead language and nourishing non-language. But while many writers have valued the woman as something extratextual, such non-language is valued in Mallarmé's system not because it is outside, but because it is *within,* the poetic text. Both music and whiteness are extraordinarily privileged in Mallarmé's poetics precisely because they function as articulations *without* content. Mallarmé's insistence that what the word "flower" evokes is what is *absent* from any bouquet, that the text is a structure of relations and not a collection of signifieds, that there is no given commensurability between language and reality, functions polemically in the late nineteenth century debates over realism and naturalism. His emphasis on music as a "system of relations" and on blankness as a structured but "stilled" poem functions precisely as a *critique* of the pretensions to representationalism and realism in the literary text. By thus opposing naive referentiality and privileging blankness and silence, Mallarmé also, however, implicitly shifts the gender values traditionally assigned to such questions. If the figure of woman has been repressed and objectified by being equated with the blank page, then Mallarmé, by *activating* those blanks, comes close to writing from the place of the silenced female voice. In his ways of throwing his voice as a woman, of figuring textuality as a dancing ballerina, and of questioning simplistic pretensions to expressivity, potency, and (masculine) authority, Mallarmé's critique of logocentrism opens up a space for a critique of phallocentrism as well. Intertextuality can no longer be seen simply as a relation between fathers and sons. But although Mallarmé's many feminine incarnations make it impossible to read him as "simply" masculine, the reevaluation of the *figure* of the woman by a male author cannot substitute for the actual participation of women in the critical conversation. Mallarmé may be able to speak from the place of the silenced woman, but as long as *he* is occupying it, the silence that is broken in theory is maintained in reality. And while there is no guarantee that when a "real" woman speaks, she is truly breaking that silence, at least she makes it difficult to avoid facing the fact that literal "women" and figurative "women" do not meet on the same rhetorical level of discourse. Indeed, in this essay we have barely begun to explore the true intertextualities of intersexuality.

Chronology

1842   Étienne (Stéphane) Mallarmé is born on March 18 in Paris to Numa-Florence-Joseph Mallarmé, Deputy Chief Clerk in the Registry and Public Property Office, and Elizabeth-Félicie Demolins.

1847–48   Mother dies and father marries Anne-Hubertine Mathieu.

1857   Younger sister, Maria, age 13, dies.

1860   Mallarmé receives baccalaureate in November, after having failed it in August.

1861   Develops a friendship with the young teacher Emmanuel des Essarts; reads *Les Fleurs du Mal,* and begins writing early "Baudelairean" verse.

1862   First poems and an article published. Travels to England with Maria-Christina Gerhard, later his wife, to learn English.

1863   Father dies and it becomes necessary for Mallarmé to choose a profession. To delay his decision, he travels to Brussels, Antwerp, and London, and begins translating Poe into French. Marries Maria on August 10, takes a teaching exam a month later, and is appointed Deputy Teacher of English at Tournon.

1864   Publishes first prose poems and begins working on "Hérodiade." Daughter Geneviève is born on November 19.

1866   Publishes ten poems in *Le Parnasse contemporain* and is appointed Professor of English at Besançon.

1867   Professor at the lycée in Avignon.

1869   Sends the first part of "Hérodiade" to the second *Le Parnasse contemporain* but because of the Franco-Prussian war it is not published until 1871.

1871   Son Anatole born on July 16. Receives a teaching appointment in Paris at the Lycée Fontanes.

1872   "Tuesday evening" poetry sessions with other young poets begin. Prose poems and translations of Poe appear in a number of journals.

1874   Eight issues of *La Dernière Mode*, Mallarmé's fashion magazine, appear.

1875   Translation of Poe's "The Raven" published with illustrations by Manet.

1876–77   "L'Après-midi d'un faune" and other Poe translations published.

1878   *Petite Philologie à l'usage de Classes et du Monde: Les Mots anglais*, a textbook, published.

1879   Son Anatole dies on October 6.

1880   *Les Dieux antiques*, also a textbook, published.

1883   Named an officer of the Academy on July 14.

1884   Named Professor of English at the Lycée Janson-de-Sailly.

1885   Named Professor at the Collège Rollin. Writes "Autobiographie" in response to a query by Verlaine.

1886   Begins to publish "Notes sur le théâtre" regularly in *La Revue Indépendante*.

1887   *Les Poésies de Stéphane Mallarmé*, a volume of *La Revue Indépéndante*, and *Album de Vers et de Prose* (Brussels) published.

1894   First performance of Debussy's "Prélude à l'après-midi d'un faune." Mallarmé reads "La Musique et les lettres," announcing a "crisis in verse" at Oxford and Cambridge.

1896   Elected Prince of Poets.

1897   "Un Coup de dés" and "Divigations" published.

1898   Dies on September 9 at Valvins, his vacation home.

Contributors

HAROLD BLOOM, Sterling Professor of the Humanities at Yale University, is the author of *The Anxiety of Influence, Poetry and Repression,* and many other volumes of literary criticism. His forthcoming study, *Freud: Transference and Authority,* attempts a full-scale reading of all of Freud's major writings. A MacArthur Prize Fellow, he is general editor of five series of literary criticism published by Chelsea House. During 1987–88, he was appointed Charles Eliot Norton Professor of Poetry at Harvard University.

MAURICE BLANCHOT is a French writer. In more than fifty years of writing he has published hundreds of essays and two dozen books. Those available in English range from novels and shorter fiction (*Thomas the Obscure, Death Sentence, The Madness of the Day,* and *When the Time Comes*) to works in literary criticism and theory, political theory and analysis, and philosophy (*The Sirens' Song, The Space of Literature, The Writing of the Disaster,* and *The Gaze of Orpheus*).

GEORGES POULET was a member of the Institute de France in Nice and formerly Chairman of the Department of Romance Languages at Johns Hopkins University. His books which have appeared in English include *The Interior Distance, Metamorphoses of the Circle, Studies in Human Time,* and *Exploding Poetry: Baudelaire/Rimbaud.*

ROBERT GREER COHN is Professor of French at Stanford University. The founding editor of Yale French Studies, he is the author of a number of books on Mallarmé, as well as *The Poetry of Rimbaud.*

PHILIPPE SOLLERS, former editor of *Tel Quel,* now edits *L'Infini* in Paris. He is the author of novels and philosophical works including *Nombres, Les cinq sens, Logiques,* and a collection of essays: *Writing and the Experience of Limits.*

PAUL DE MAN was, until his death in 1983, Sterling Professor of Comparative Literature at Yale University. He is the author of *Blindness and Insight: Essays in Contemporary Criticism, Allegories of Reading, Figural Language in Rousseau, Nietzsche, Rilke, and Proust,* and *The Rhetoric of Romanticism,* and posthumously of the forthcoming collections *The Resistance to Theory, Aesthetic Ideology,* and *Fugitive Essays.*

JACQUES DERRIDA is Directeur d'Etudes at the Ecole des Hautes Etudes en Sciences Sociales in Paris, Visiting Professor in the Humanities at Yale University, and Andrew D. White Professor-at-large at Cornell University. He has written two books on Nietzsche, *Otobiographies* and *Spurs/Éperons,* and is the author of many articles and books including *La voix et le phénomene (Speech and Phenomena), La Dissemination* (Disseminations), *Marges—de la philosophie (Margins—of Philosophy), Glas,* and *La carte postale.*

E. S. BURT is Assistant Professor of French at Yale University. She has written on Montaigne and Mallarmé, and is the author of the forthcoming *Rousseau's Autobiographics.*

ROGER DRAGONETTI is Professor of Medieval French Literature at the University of Geneva. He is the author of *La vie de la lettre au moyen age* and *Aux Frontières du langage poétique.*

HANS-JOST FREY is Professor of Comparative Literature at the University of Zurich. In the United States, he has taught at Cornell and Yale Universities. He is co-author of *Kritik des freien Verses.*

BARBARA JOHNSON is Professor of Romance Languages and Literatures at Harvard University. She is the author of *Défigurations du language poétique, The Critical Difference,* and *A World of Difference.*

BONNIE J. ISAAC is Assistant Professor of French at the University of California at Berkeley. She has written on Baudelaire and Mallarmé.

LEO BERSANI is the Chairman of the French Department at the University of California at Berkeley. His books include *Balzac to Beckett, A Future for Astyanax, The Death of Stéphane Mallarmé,* and *The Freudian Body.*

Bibliography

Austin, Lloyd James. "The Mystery of a Name." *L'Esprit créateur* 1 no. 3 (1961): 130–38.

Bersani, Leo. *The Death of Stéphane Mallarmé.* Cambridge: Cambridge University Press, 1982.

Blanchot, Maurice. "The Absence of the Book." In *The Gaze of Orpheus,* translated by Lydia Davis, 149–60. Barrytown, N.Y.: Station Hill Press, 1981.

———. "Mallarmé and Literary Space" and "The Book to Come." In *The Sirens' Song,* edited by Gabriel Josipovici and translated by Sacha Rabinovitch, 110–20 and 227–48. Bloomington: Indiana University Press, 1982.

Bowie, Malcolm. *Mallarmé and the Art of Being Difficult.* Cambridge: Cambridge University Press, 1978.

Caws, Mary Ann. "Mallarmé and Duchamp: Mirror, Stair, and Gaming Table." *L'Esprit créateur* 20, no. 2 (1980): 51–64.

Chiari, Joseph. *Symbolisme from Poe to Mallarmé: The Growth of a Myth.* New York: Macmillan, 1956.

Chisholm, A. R. "Mallarmé and the Act of Creation." *L'Esprit créateur* 1 (1961): 111–16.

———. "Three Difficult Sonnets by Mallarmé." *French Studies* 9 (1955): 212–17.

Cohn, Robert Greer. *Mallarmé, Igitur.* Berkeley: University of California Press, 1981.

———. *Mallarmé's "Un Coup de dés": An Exegesis.* New Haven: Yale French Studies, 1949.

———. *Mallarmé's Masterwork.* The Hague: Mouton, 1966.

———. "New Approaches to 'Hérodiade.' " *Romanic Review* 72 (1981): 472–81.

———. *Toward the Poems of Mallarmé.* Berkeley: University of California Press, 1965.

———. "Urban Mallarmé." *Stanford French Review* 9 (1985): 61–70.

Davies, Gardner. "The Demon of Analogy." *French Studies* 9 (1955): 197–211 and 326–47.

———. *Mallarmé et le drame solaire.* Paris: José Corti, 1959.

———. *Les Noces d'Herodiade.* Paris: Gallimand, 1959

de Man, Paul. "Criticism and Crisis." In *Blindness and Insight,* 2d ed, 3–19. Minneapolis: University of Minnesota Press, 1983.

L'Esprit créateur 1, no. 3 (1961).

Fischler, Alexander. "The Ghost-Making Process in Mallarmé's 'Le Vièrge, le vivace,' 'Toast Funèbre,' and 'Quand l'ombre menaça.'" *Symposium* 20 (1966): 306–20.

Fowlie, Wallace. *Mallarmé*. Chicago: University of Chicago Press, 1953.

Franklin, Ursula. *Anatomy of Poeisis: The Prose Poems of Stéphane Mallarmé.* Chapel Hill: University of North Carolina Press, 1976.

———. "Segregation and Disintegration of an Image: Mallarmé's Struggle with the Angel." *Nineteenth Century French Studies* 12 (Fall/Winter 1983–1984): 145–67.

Gill, Austin. *The Early Mallarmé*. Oxford: Clarendon, 1979.

———. "Mallarmé's Use of Christian Imagery for Post-Christian Concepts." In *Order and Adventure in Post-Romantic French Poetry: Presented to C. A. Hackett,* edited by E. M. Beaumont, J. M. Cocking, and J. Cruikshank, 72–88. Oxford: Blackwell, 1973.

Grubbs, Henry A. "Mallarmé's 'Ptyx' Sonnet: An Analytical and Critical Study." *PMLA* 65 (1950): 75–89.

Hampton, Timothy. "Virgil, Baudelaire and Mallarmé at the Sign of the Swan: Poetic Translation and Historical Allegory." *Romanic Review* 73 (1982): 438–51.

Hyppolite, Jean. "Le Coup de dés de Stéphane Mallarmé et le message." *Les Études Philosophiques* n.s. 13 (1958): 463–68.

Johnson, Barbara. "Allegory's Trip-Tease: *The White Waterlily*" and "Poetry and Syntax: What the Gypsy Knew." In *The Critical Difference,* 13–20 and 67–76. Baltimore: Johns Hopkins University Press, 1980.

Kravis, Judy. *The Prose of Mallarmé: The Evolution of a Literary Language.* Cambridge: Cambridge University Press, 1976.

Kristeva, Julia. *Revolution in Poetic Language.* Translated by Margaret Waller. New York: Columbia University Press, 1984.

Kromer, Gretchen. "The Redoubtable PTYX." *MLN* 86 (1971): 563–72.

La Charité, Virginia. "Mallarmé's *Livre:* The Graphomatics of the Text." *Symposium* 34 (1980): 249–59.

McLuhan, Marshall. "Joyce, Mallarmé, and the Press." In *The Interior Landscape,* edited by Eugene Maxwell, 5–21. New York: McGraw-Hill, 1969.

Mauron, Charles. *Mallarmé l'obscur.* Paris: José Corti, 1968.

Mehlman, Jeffrey. "Mallarmé/Maxwell: Elements." *Romanic Review* 71 (1980): 374–80.

Nelson, Robert J. "Mallarmé's Mirror of Art." *Modern Language Quarterly* 20 (1959): 49–56.

Parker, Patricia A. "'Inescapable Romance'—Mallarmé, Valéry, Stevens." In *Inescapable Romance: Studies in the Poetics of a Mode,* 219–44. Princeton: Princeton University Press, 1979.

Paxton, Norman. *The Development of Mallarmé's Prose Style.* Geneva: Librarie Droz, 1968.

Poulet, Georges. "Mallarmé." In *The Interior Distance,* translated by Elliott Coleman, 235–83. Baltimore: Johns Hopkins University Press, 1959.

Richard, Jean-Pierre. *L'Univers imaginaire de Mallarmé.* Paris: Éditions du Seuil, 1961.

St. Aubyn, Frederic Chase. *Stéphane Mallarmé*. New York: Twayne, 1969.

Saldivar, Ramon. "Metaphors of Consciousness in Mallarmé." *Comparative Literature* 36 (1984): 54–72.

Scott, David H. T. "Mallarmé of the Octosyllabic Sonnet." *French Studies* 31 (1977): 149–63.

Sonnenfeld, Albert. "Eros and Poetry: Mallarmé's Disappearing Visions." In *Order and Adventure in Post-Romantic French Poetry; Presented to C. A. Hackett*, edited by E. M. Beaumont, J. M. Cocking, and J. Cruikshank, 89–98. Oxford: Blackwell, 1973.

Terdiman, Richard. *Discourse/Counter-Discourse: The Theory and Practice of Symbolic Resistance in 19th Century France*. Ithaca, N.Y.: Cornell University Press, 1985.

Thibaudet, Albert. *La Poésie de Stéphane Mallarmé*. Paris: Gallimard, 1926.

Villami, Sergio. "Mallarmé's Missing Narrative." *L'Esprit créateur* 17, no. 3 (Fall 1977): 228–34.

Weinberg, Bernard. *The Limits of Symbolism: Studies of Five Modern French Poets*. Chicago: University of Chicago Press, 1966.

Weisberg, Richard. " 'Hamlet' and 'Un Coup de dés': Mallarmé's Emerging Constellation." *MLN* 92 (1977): 779–96.

Welch, Cyril and Liliane Welch. *Emergence: Baudelaire, Mallarmé, Rimbaud*. State College, Pa.: Bald Eagle Press, 1973.

Williams, Thomas A. *Mallarmé and the Language of Mysticism*. Athens: University of Georgia Press, 1970.

Yale French Studies 54 (1977). Special Mallarmé issue.

Acknowledgments

"The *Igitur* Experience" by Maurice Blanchot from *The Space of Literature,* translated by Ann Smock, ©1955 by Editions Gallimard, © 1982 by the University of Nebraska Press. Reprinted by permission of the University of Nebraska Press.

"Mallarmé's 'Prose pour Des Esseintes' " by Georges Poulet from *The Metamorphoses of the Circle* translated by Carley Dawson and Elliott Coleman in collaboration with the author, © 1966 by the Johns Hopkins University Press, Baltimore/London. Reprinted by permission of the Johns Hopkins University Press.

"Hommage (à Richard Wagner)" by Robert Greer Cohn from *Toward the Poems of Mallarmé* by Robert Greer Cohn, © 1965 by the Regents of the University of California Press. Reprinted by permission of the University of California Press.

"Literature and Totality" by Philippe Sollers from *Writing and the Experience of Limits,* edited by David Hayman and translated by Philip Barnard with David Hayman, © 1983 by Columbia University Press. Reprinted by permission of Columbia University Press.

"Lyric and Modernity" by Paul de Man from *Blindness and Insight: Essays in the Rhetoric of Contemporary Criticism* by Paul de Man, ©1971, 1983 by Paul de Man. Reprinted by permission of Oxford University Press.

"The Double Session" by Jacques Derrida from *Dissemination,* translated by Barbara Johnson, © 1972 by Editions du Seuil, © 1981 by the University of Chicago. Reprinted by permission of the University of Chicago Press, and the Athlone Press Ltd., and Editions du Seuil.

"Mallarmé's 'Sonnet en *yx* ' " (originally entitled "Mallarmé's 'Sonnet en *yx*' :The Ambiguities of Speculation") by E. S. Burt from *Yale French Studies* 54 (1977) by *Yale French Studies.* Reprinted by permission.

" 'Le Nénuphar blanc': A Poetic Dream with Two Unknowns" by Roger Dragonetti from *Yale French Studies* 54 (1977), © 1977 by *Yale French Studies.* Reprinted by permission.

"The Tree of Doubt" by Hans-Jost Frey from *Yale French Studies* 54 (1977), © 1977 by *Yale French Studies.* Reprinted by permission.

"Poetry and Performative Language: Mallarmé and Austin " by Barbara Johnson from *The Critical Difference: Essays in the Contemporary Rhetoric of Reading* by Barbara Johnson, © 1980 by the Johns Hopkins University Press, Baltimore/London. Reprinted by permission of the Johns Hopkins University Press.

" 'Du fond d'un naufrage': Notes on Michel Serres and Mallarmé's 'Un Coup de dés' " by Bonnie J. Isaac from *Modern Language Notes* 96, no. 4 (1981), ©1981 by The Johns Hopkins University Press, Baltimore/London. Reprinted by permission of The Johns Hopkins University Press.

"The Man Dies" by Leo Bersani from *The Death of Stephane Mallarmé* by Leo Bersani, © 1982 by Cambridge University Press. Reprinted by permission of the author and Cambridge University Press.

"*Les Fleurs du mal armé*: Some Reflections of Intertextuality" by Barbara Johnson from *Lyric Poetry: Beyond New Criticism,* edited by Chaviva Hosek and Patricia Parker, © 1985 by Cornell University Press. Reprinted by permission of Cornell University Press. A shorter version of this essay entitled "Discours et Pouvoir" first appeared in *Michigan Romance Studies* 2 (1982). Reprinted by permission.

Index

Abrams, M. H., 64–65, 66, 73
Adam, Villiers de l'Isle, 25
"Apparition," 40
"Après-midi d'un faune, L' ": Faun as
   narrator, 146–47; Faun as object,
   148–49; function of meaning,
   142–44; meaning of nymphs,
   144–48; relationship to nymphs,
   142; traditional reading of,
   141–42, 143; tree as image, 143,
   148
Aubanel, Théodore, 190
Auerbach, Erich, 65
Austin, J. L., 151, 154–60, 165–66
"Azur, L'," 214–15

Bachelard, Gaston, 204
Barthes, Roland, 42
Baudelaire, Charles: allegory in poetry
   of, 69, 75–76; article on Wagner,
   39; and beginning of modern
   poetry, 65, 66, 67, 75, 76, 77;
   comments on Mallarmé, 220;
   compared with Mallarmé, 3, 37;
   concept of literature, 41; continua-
   tion of Diderot, 74; experience of
   nothingness, 28; first-person narrator in, 168; German critics of,
   67; letter to mother, 219;
   Mallarmé's relation to, 43, 75–77,
   211, 212–13; Mallarmé's sonnet
   on, 75–77; reactions to imitators,

213–14; "Spleen," 103; "Swan"
   poem, 218, 219
Benjamin, Walter, 67
Benveniste, Emile, 156
Blake, William, 3
Blanchot, Maurice, 42, 174, 182
Boileau-Despréaux, Nicolas, 226
"Brise marine," 167–68
Browning, Robert, 3
Burke, Kenneth, 112

Cazalis, Henri: letter on disappearance
   of author, 190–91; letter on
   "Hérodiade," 185, 188; letter on
   Igitur, 5; letter on nature of
   thought, 194; letter on "Sonnet en
   yx," 100–101, 109–10, 117;
   Mallarmé's crisis, 187–88
Celan, Paul, 76–77
Cézanne, Paul, 42
Chisholm, A. R., 111
Citron, Pierre, 111
Cohn, R. G., 95, 98, 104, 108, 141,
   152, 168, 175–77, 181
"Coup de dés, Un": the blank and the
   fold, 216–17; cloud symbolism in,
   70; compared with Igitur, 13–15;
   death as theme, 73; entropy and,
   181–82; equilibrium in, 176;
   evocation of Hamlet in, 177–78;
   images in, 174; the Master in,
   175–76, 181; mastery as theme,

241

Modern Critical Views